Faith in the Fight

Faith in the Fight

RELIGION AND THE AMERICAN SOLDIER IN THE GREAT WAR

Jonathan H. Ebel

PRINCETON UNIVERSITY PRESS

PRINCETON AND OXFORD

Library of Congress Cataloging-in-Publication Data

Ebel, Jonathan H., 1970–
    Faith in the fight : religion and the American solider in the great war /
Jonathan H. Ebel.
        p.   cm.
    Includes bibliographical references and index.
    ISBN 978-0-691-13992-0 (hardcover : alk. paper)
1. Soldiers—Religious life. 2. World War I. I. Title.
    BV4588.E24 2010
    940.4′78—dc22   2009025681

British Library Cataloging-in-Publication Data is available

This book has been composed in Sabon

Printed on acid-free paper. ∞

press.princeton.edu

Printed in the United States of America

10   9   8   7   6   5   4   3   2   1

TO MEREDITH

Thank you

Contents

Acknowledgments

I COULD NEVER HAVE WRITTEN this book without the support of the people who have enriched my life and the institutions in which I have been privileged to study and work over the past ten years. The process of recognizing and thanking them is both joyous and humbling.

Students and teachers and writers all stand on the shoulders of others. I have been blessed beyond imagining to have had such generous supportive friends and mentors from the very beginning of my graduate studies. First among them is Catherine Brekus, who challenged and encouraged me at every stage of this project. Catherine has always provided the perfect balance of critique and encouragement. I can never thank her adequately. I would also like to express my gratitude to Jean Bethke Elsthain, W. Clark Gilpin, Martin Marty, Edith Blumhofer, John Corrigan, Andrew Fort, David Hackett, Melani McAlister, Jon Pahl, Skip Stout, and Grant Wacker for advice and encouragement along the way. I am especially fortunate to count as colleagues and friends Robert McKim, Alexander Meyer, Rajeshwari Pandharipande, Wayne Pitard, Gary Porton, David Price, Valerie Hoffman, Rick Layton, Bruce Rosenstock, Brian Ruppert, James Treat, and Mohammad Khalil. I could not have hoped for a better community in which to work and live. I regret that Jerald Brauer and Darryl Schmidt are not here to read the work in which they encouraged me. Professor Brauer provided a forum, many helpful leads, and a model of scholarship and humanity as I learned the ropes of graduate work in the field of American religion; Darryl Schmidt gave me my first job, helped me with two moves, and celebrated many joys with me and my family. I hope that something of the spirit of both men is reflected in this book.

My friends from the University of Illinois, Texas Christian University, and graduate school have been sources of inspiration, support, and much-needed levity. Thank you to Elizabeth Hayes Alvarez, Amy Artman, John Carlson, Jed Esty, Betsy Flowers, Kathleen Garces-Foley, Andrea Goulet, Rochelle Gutierrez, Jim Hansen, Robin and Liz Hsiao-Wecksler, Brandon Johnson, Pam Jones, Kathryn Lofton, Rajeev Malik, Darren Middleton, Jonathan Moore, William Munro, Kathy Oberdeck, Paul and Karen Ogden, Ned O'Gorman, Erik Owens, Ben Penglase, Brent Plate, Chris and Justin Roberts, Michael Rothberg, Paula Shakelton, Anna Stenport, Renee Trilling, Julius Tsai, and Yasemin Yildiz. In addition to their other assistance and support, John Carlson, Jed Esty, Ned O'Gorman, and Kathryn Lofton read and commented on significant portions of this manuscript, helping me immeasurably in its revision. And thank you also to Sarah Jackman, research assistant *par excellence*, who provided absolutely invaluable help in the late stages of compiling and editing this manuscript.

For their generous financial support I am grateful to the Office of the Vice Chancellor for Research at the University of Illinois, the Illinois Program for Research in the Humanities, the Louisville Institute, the Center for Religion and American Life at Yale, the Martin Marty Center at the University of Chicago, the Gilder Lehrman Institute of American History, and the University of Chicago Office of Graduate Affairs. Seminars led by Matti Bunzl and Christine Catanzarite at the Illinois Program for Research in the Humanities, Jim Lewis and Bill Brosend at the Louisville Institute, Harry Stout and Jon Butler at Yale, and W. Clark Gilpin and William Schweiker at the University of Chicago provided both conversation partners with whom to share ideas and the chance to get to know a wide range of impressive fellow humanists.

I would like to thank Fred Appel of Princeton University Press. When I was still in the very early stages of researching and writing my dissertation, Fred expressed his interest in and support for the project. Since then he has offered valuable advice and has patiently and insightfully helped me navigate the terrain that lies between a dissertation and a book. I am also grateful to Claire Tillman-McTigue whose good humor in the midst of the revision process reminded me to relax and to laugh from time to time, and to Dimitri Karetnikov, Sara Lerner, and Michael McGee for their invaluable help in editing and production.

I am thankful to the librarians and staffs of the New York Public Library and the Regenstein Library at the University of Chicago, to Joe Hovish and his staff at the National Headquarters of the American Legion, to Mary Stuart and the staff of the History, Philosophy and Newspaper Library at the University of Illinois, and to the staff of the base library at the Headquarters of the United States European Command in Stuttgart, Germany. Their bound copy of the entire run of *The Stars and Stripes* from the Great War kept me busy and therefore sane during an otherwise difficult stretch.

I am extremely fortunate to be surrounded by a family that understands and supports both this frequently hard-to-understand career and the long process by which books get written. Susanna Hecht offered a sympathetic ear, encouraging words, and many helpful comments. Marnie Albers actually read and commented on my dissertation. Tom Hecht and Jane Burwell welcomed me to Chicago twelve years ago and since then have been a constant source of support and encouragement, not to mention much-needed doses of laughter and love. Bonnie Forman and Norman Barshai encouraged and nourished the Urbana Ebels during trips to Washington,

D.C., and never complained about the piles of paper on the couch, the dining room table, the floor, and so on. Greg and Jen, and Kip and Sarah, the best brothers and sisters-in-law in the history of Western civilization provided shelter both actual and metaphorical during trips to Manhattan, Chicago, and Albuquerque and during innumerable conversations over food, wine, and bumpage. I hope that I haven't been too much of a bore. The absolute and unconditional love of my parents, David and Holly, expressed in innumerable ways, has been a source of strength and inspiration for longer than I can remember. No words are adequate to express my gratitude.

This project represents the culmination of almost ten years of work that began at the University of Chicago Divinity School. I have been able to reach this point because, twelve years ago, while working on the Divinity School's Wednesday Lunch Crew, I met a woman named Meredith. Through our courtship, engagement, and pursuant ten years of marriage, along with the addition of three beautiful children, Sophia Rose, Charlotte Anais, and Beatrice Helene, she has challenged, tolerated, encouraged, and inspired me. Meredith reminds me daily of the richness and beauty of life, and of all that truly matters.

It is to her that I dedicate this book.

Faith in the Fight

Introduction

BETWEEN AUGUST 2, 1914 and November 11, 1918, European powers waged a war of then unprecedented scale and lethality. Soldiers from the warring nations and their proxies battled each other on three continents, across vast expanses of ocean, and, thanks to technological advances of the preceding decade, in the skies as well. An assassination in Sarajevo started the war. The failure of a tightly choreographed German plan to disable the French military and the subsequent entrenchment of hostile armies along a jagged line stretching from the North Sea south to the Swiss Alps produced the war's Western Front. The involvement of modernizing societies and their stunning capacities to produce and destroy combined with military leaders' equally stunning unwillingness or inability to adjust antiquated tactics to the industrialized violence gave the war its body count: an appalling 8 million dead among the combatants. This was the Great War.

The United States came late to the war, though U.S. citizens were involved in the fighting from the beginning. President Woodrow Wilson waited two years and eight months to ask Congress for a declaration of war against Germany, and he did so with scant capacity to back up the declaration. In 1917, the United States military could claim approximately 200,000 professional soldiers in the regular army and the National Guard combined, and a shipping capacity insufficient to transport a substantial fighting force to France.[1] These facts struck little fear in the hearts of German leaders and inspired little more confidence in America's erstwhile allies. But between April 6, 1917 and November 11, 1918, the United States mobilized four million young men for war service. Two million of these newly minted citizen soldiers and tens of thousands of male and female support service volunteers crossed the Atlantic to fight alongside the French and English. They fought and died in places whose names they believed would be etched forever in American memory: Chateau-Thierry, Belleau Wood, Cantigny, St. Mihiel, Fismes, the Argonne Forest.

This is a study of the faith of these American soldiers and war workers as they prepared for and fought the Great War. It is an attempt to describe a moment in America's religious history when cultural and religious currents, fueled by concerns about the nation's future, gave rise to a military impulse suffused with, and framed by, Christianity. Following this impulse, Americans served and fought and died. This book argues that as they did all three, they believed—believed in the righteousness of the cause, believed in the communal and personal value of their errand, believed that in answering the call to arms they were answering the call of their faith. Experiences of the Great War altered but did not undermine these beliefs. After the war, American soldiers and war workers responded to the peculiar mix of suffering, death, triumph, and disappointment by struggling at home, sometimes violently, for their visions of America. Having vanquished the "Hun" in Europe, they brought the struggle against a hydra-headed "evil" to American soil. The title of this book, *Faith in the Fight*, thus reflects its subject—the religious beliefs and reflections of American soldiers and war workers in the Great War—and an important aspect of those beliefs and reflections, namely the connection between war and redemption.

The men and women who helped fight the Great War were products of a society whose cultural and religious landscape was shaped by a particular understanding of faith, citizenship, and manhood in which all three converged in the realm of strenuous action. Struggle, strain, and sacrifice demonstrated and enhanced physical and spiritual vigor, vitalized American culture, and gave life to the American nation. Calls for, and praise of, action and initiative issued forth from the pages of the *Catholic World* and the mouth and pen of Theodore Roosevelt; liberal theologians and divines touted "progress"; American editorial and sports pages valorized "effort." Billy Sunday seldom held a revival without encouraging Christians to put up their fists and fight for God. "Initiative is the spirit of the explorer and the pioneer, especially in spreading God's faith and His Church," wrote Walter Elliott, C.S.P. in the June 1912 issue of the *Catholic World*. His article, "The Might of the Inward Man," called men of initiative to "covet and ask the place of toil and danger in dealing with God's enemies."

> Initiative is that spirit which makes little of one's own deficiencies when duty or opportunity calls for action; and constantly [strives] to make opportunity stand for duty. To have an adventurous spirit in religious undertakings. To be the first to advance when authority says, "Go!" and the first (however sadly) to stop when authority says "Halt!"[2]

The properly religious man was a man of action, willing to welcome danger and sacrifice, and happy to deal harshly with "God's enemies." Such language could and did encourage *spiritual* warfare. "Religious undertakings" could be understood as evangelism or catechesis. Yet when the authority calling "Go" and "Halt" wore olive drab rather than vestments, the words stayed the same, the connection among duty, faith, and action remained intact, but the effect became deadly. The religious culture of pre-war America gave Americans ideas, images, and beliefs perfectly tailored to war.

I began research for this book hoping to find an unequivocal soldierly critique of the mythic religious framing of war, hoping to find that soldiers were troubled by the coming together of faith and violence, perhaps deepened in their resolve to be less violent, and more and differently faithful. After reading the deeply ambivalent letters of Vinton Dearing, the son of Baptist missionaries and a first lieutenant in the Twenty-eighth Division, I thought that this project would describe a more widespread sense among American soldiers of the Great War that the wheels had come off of "Christian" civilization; that, as Dearing poignantly wrote, things had gone so horribly wrong on earth that heaven itself was confused. But in most cases, realizations of war's horrors occurred within a widely held, compelling, eventually blood-soaked framework of meaning. Where soldiers' experiences challenged the framework, those experiences had to contend with a powerful religio-cultural impulse to see in war and the warrior's experiences the affirmation and strengthening of pre-war faiths. American soldiers of the Great War were more frequently soldiers of those pre-war faiths than they were revolutionaries against them.

THE GREAT WAR AND RELIGION IN AMERICAN HISTORY

Studies of America's wars tend to ignore religion. Studies of American religion tend to ignore war. In the former historiography, one finds the occasional mention of a chaplain or the obligatory reference to atheists and foxholes; in the latter—with a few notable exceptions—wars stand less as events formative of American religion and more as historical markers. When historians of religion in the United States have discussed the Great War—William Hutchison, George Marsden, Grant Wacker, and Diane Winston are the most prominent—they have written mainly about clerical rhetoric, denominational responses, and theological aftermaths.[3] This book is an attempt to integrate these historiographies and to demonstrate that by studying "faith in the fight" we gain a deeper appreciation of the relationship between religion, violence, and citizenship as experienced by ordinary men and women. I proceed in the belief that there is something to be learned by working through the religiousness of war from the inside out, as it were—that by studying the religious thoughts and lives of soldiers and war workers, we can make more intelligible both general phenomena, such as the appeal of war and memories of war, and more specific religious and political events and movements in twentieth-century America.

The last three decades have seen the publication of a rich, if not volumi-
nous, historiography of the Great War as an American experience, with
little discussion of the religious dimensions of that experience.[4] Religion
lives at the outer edges of work on the Great War even as major works
on the culture of the early twentieth century describe religion as central.
Henry May, T. J. Jackson Lears, E. Anthony Rotundo, Gail Bederman,
Clifford Putney, Milton Sernett, and Wallace Best have described eloquently the roles churches, religious leaders, and religious ideas played in
shaping cultural currents and perceptions of race, gender, politics, and
economy. Religion and religious institutions were at work both on the
"official surface"—described by Henry May as "almost intolerable" for
its "placidity and complacency"—and beneath it. Men and women of
faith defended social norms and fueled their transgression, justified economic gains and framed protests against economic exploitation, cultivated notions of American exceptionalism and challenged Americans to
think differently about history, race, gender, and meaning.[5] Religion was
also the source of resistance to, and support for, violence and war.
    Mainstream American Protestantism in the early years of the twentieth
century was dominated by, but not coterminous with, an optimistic liberalism.[6] Some versions of the "massive and varied movement" known as
liberal or social Christianity allowed for a coziness with the instruments
of perceived progress that bordered on unequivocal support of the
wealthy and powerful. Other versions, particularly that articulated by
Social Gospel activist and theologian Walter Rauschenbusch, bordered
on revolutionary. Across this range of understandings regarding the paths
to and mechanisms of progress, America's leading Protestants shared the
belief in the possibility of earthly progress toward the kingdom of God.
Historians of the period have, however, detected a gap between the optimistic, "evasive banality" of "flaccid" Protestantism and the religious and
psychological needs of men and women facing the realities of industrial
urban America. They have noted a widespread desire for more "authentic" modes of religious and literary expression than those that suffused
late-Victorian America.[7] T. J. Lears has argued that late-nineteenth- and
early-twentieth-century existence, uncoupled from profound demanding
structures of meaning, led young men and women of the urban upper and
upper-middle classes to feel "weightless"—adrift in a mediated meaningless world—and to seek answers more profound and experiences more
immediate. Few in America's Protestant mainstream could speak to these
concerns, so men and women turned toward practices and institutions
less "tainted" by modernity and accommodation. This discontent with
self-described "modern" Christianity, often associated with cosmopolitan
elites, was also evident in the Protestant Fundamentalist and Pentecostal
movements. Both movements gathered momentum in the decade prior to

the Great War by offering religious answers that denied the progressive nature of history and rejected attempts to mold Christian teaching to the knowledge and concerns of "the age."[8]

During the first decades of the twentieth century, American Catholicism was also grappling with a shifting identity brought on by a massive influx of Catholic immigrants, the miserable conditions in which many of its urban faithful worked, and by its 1908 designation as a "national" church despite a lack of national unity.[9] Catholic leaders worked to find their social and political voices while simultaneously trying to unify a church that was divided internally by barriers of language and culture. During the Catholic modernist/Americanist controversy of 1890–1907, liberal Catholic bishops and clergy in America found themselves accused by more conservative American Catholics and, in turn, by the Vatican of adapting Catholic teaching and polity to American democratic norms and ecumenical impulses. Concern led to action in 1899 when the Pope condemned "Americanist" teachings in *Testem Benevolentiae*, and again in 1907 when *Pascendi Domenici Gregis* mandated an end to ecumenical exchanges among seminaries and pulled the plug on the liberal *New York Review*, a theological journal to which Francis P. Duffy, chaplain of the Fighting Sixty-ninth, New York's famous National Guard unit, was a frequent contributor.[10] Pushed to assimilate by a frequently hostile culture and pulled by a hierarchy troubled by the theological implications of assimilation and ecumenism, Catholic Americans found few easy answers as to how to live their faith in the United States.

The two major African American thinkers of the early twentieth century, Booker T. Washington and W.E.B. Du Bois were not centrally concerned with religion, but recognized its vital importance to the African American communities they studied. When they and their disciples pondered the African American situation, they invoked religious themes and acknowledged the role religious institutions would play in the up-lift of the race. Historian Milton Sernett recently demonstrated how powerfully religious ideas and images shaped black perceptions of the Great Migration, which began in 1915 partially in response to war-time labor shortages. As Sernett and Wallace Best note, black churches, continuing to serve as "undifferentiated" institutions in African American communities, both acted and were acted upon in this massive movement toward "the Promised Land."[11]

Religion was, without question, a powerful force in many corners of early-twentieth-century America. It was at the heart of Pentecostal critiques of nations and wars and African American resistance to racism and Jim Crow; religion drove acrimonious debates between theological liberals and conservative proto-Fundamentalists, and was a marker of cultural otherness between recent immigrants, many of whom were Catholic or Jewish, and a deeply entrenched Protestant establishment. Religion also shaped, and was shaped by, understandings of and concerns about gender, race, and the future of the nation.

"AMERICAN MANHOOD" AND RELIGION IN CRISIS

The religious turmoil that marked the Progressive Era frequently intersected with a "crisis" in understandings of gender ideals, particularly a reconsideration of "ideal" manhood. An increasingly industrial, urban, and prosperous America often required young men and women to live lives largely devoid of physical exertion. The work of a clerk or mid-level manager called for different skills and different bodies from the work of the farmer, fisher, or tradesman.[12] Rather than treat this perceived change in levels of fitness and vigor as an inevitable consequence of social and economic changes, politicians, physicians, scholars, and clergymen repeatedly voiced concerns about the effeminacy and over-civilization of America's middle- and upper-class men and saw the trend away from physical vigor as a threat to American (white) manhood and culture.

America's late-nineteenth- and early-twentieth-century cultural custodians believed that the Anglo-Saxon race and its manhood were superior among European peoples, and that the American experience had improved the race. They told stories of Anglo-Saxon emergence from Germanic roots and the rise of Anglo-Saxon power in Europe and, finally, in England. The story continued with the colonization and "settlement" of America—a test that American Anglo-Saxon men passed by using "superior" intellect and a storied capacity for violence. Theodore Roosevelt argued that with a new American nation, a new American race had emerged—refined and developed through trial and conquest on the frontiers of America—and now stood apart from and above its English progenitor.[13] But the fact that a race could emerge, progress, and grow stronger, left open the possibility that it could also regress, weaken, and be surpassed. Roosevelt and others gave urgent voice to this concern as the lives of American men became less physically demanding. The impressive physicality and muscle-building manual labor of the "inferior races," among them immigrants from South and Central Europe and African Americans migrating north, lent greater immediacy to the problem of racial decline.

Psychologist G. Stanley Hall was influential in formulating an antidote to American male degeneracy. Hall presupposed the intellectual and cultural superiority—indeed the civilizational adulthood—of American men. (The corollary was that "inferior" cultures and intellects were child-like or "adolescent" by comparison.) From this point, Hall argued that the fully realized, fully masculine man progressed through the stages of civilization as he grew to adulthood, and that children ought to play, run, and fight with abandon in order to move to more advanced stages of intellectual development with physical capabilities in full flower. Those who skipped stages—who were discouraged from exercising their "savage" physicality—would pay later as attenuated, ineffectual, perhaps neurasthenic men. Societies that did not encourage boys to act out their primitive natures risked paying a much steeper price.[14] Influenced by Hall's theories, educators, physicians, politicians, and ministers encouraged boys and young men to seek physical and spiritual betterment through exercise, strenuous outdoor experiences, and physical confrontation.[15]

In this masculinization effort, churches were both tools and targets. A startling shortage of men in American Protestant churches led many Protestant leaders to ask where the men had gone, why they had left, and how they might be brought back to active Christian practice. The answers, the churchmen concluded, were that effeminate sentimental religion had driven younger men away, and that drawing them back was a matter of re-establishing the masculinity of Christ and of the Christian life.[16] Accomplished theologians and clergymen such as Harry Emerson Fosdick, Henry Churchill King, Charles MacFarland, John R. Mott, William Adams Brown, Episcopal Bishop Charles Brent (who would become Chief of Chaplains in the American Expeditionary Force), and James I. Vance frequently exalted the masculine qualities of Christianity. Vance rallied masculine Christians—true Christians—against the embarrassingly effeminate clergyman with a scathing attack. "Where in all the sweep of freaks and failures, of mawkish sentiments and senseless blathery, can there be found an object of deeper disgust than one of these thin, vapid, affected, driveling little doodles dressed up in men's clothes, but without a thimbleful of brains in his pate or an ounce of manhood in his anatomy? He is worse than weak—he is a weaklet."[17]

Just as contemporary notions of manhood emphasized aggressive, physical "masculinity," the "masculinization" of Christianity tended to involve emphases on strenuous action, both social and physical.[18] Moreover, Progressive-Era reconsiderations of who Christ had been, what his message was, and what both meant to American men emphasized, to use the title of R. Warren Conant's 1915 treatise, *The Virility of Christ*. Taking Christ to have been a man of action, actively engaged in the issues of his world, Christian leaders and laity launched numerous movements that challenged American men to reclaim Christianity from sentimentalists and feminizers, and to live lives of Christian action. In some cases, this meant missionary work; in others, it meant aggressive engagement in social action; in still others, "Christian action" was understood as attention to the health and vitality of the male body.[19] Conant provided a passionate example of this convergence when writing of Christ's virility.

The men of a strenuous age demand a strenuous Christ. If they fail to find him the Church is to blame. For Christ himself was strenuous enough to satisfy the most exacting; he was stalwart and fearless, aggressive and progressive; never flinching from a challenge, overwhelming in quickness and sharpness of attack; yet withal wary and wise, never "rattled," always holding himself well in hand.[20]

This view of Christ as an active, often militant man, fed the early-twentieth-century growth of intra- and extra-ecclesial Christian organizations designed to attract and retain young men with a strenuous Christian faith.

By uniting faith and physical exertion and promising a stronger, more vital Christian manhood, muscular Christianity addressed the problem of "over-civilization" among urban, usually Anglo-Saxon, men and helped answer fears that "lower-class workers and muscular immigrants" might topple "middle- and upper-class managerial types."[21] In his study of muscular Christianity, Clifford Putney argues that no group of organizations was "more important than the mainline Protestant churches" when it came to the physical and spiritual development of boys. "These were instrumental in the formation of boys' boarding schools, out-door camping, and the Boys' Brigade. In 1915 they also sponsored 80 percent of all Boy Scout troops, 90 percent of whose members claimed in 1921 to be attending Sunday school."[22] The Boys' Brigade, the Boy Scouts, the Knights of St. Andrew, the Knights of King Arthur, and the YMCA, each of which fused in some way religious institutions and physical activity, were all thriving in the decades prior to the Great War.

The exaltation of the warrior ideal and assent to its correlation between masculine aggressive action and purer, more profound living was woven tightly into the muscular Christianity movement and was a key dimension of the anti-modern antidote to a hyper-mediated weightless existence. It should then be no surprise that solutions to the churches' "man problem," and to perceived Christian effeminacy, often fused the masculine and the military.[23] For example, the Chicago-based Brotherhood of Saint Andrew, aimed at young men, defined itself by an almost seamless union of faith and military idiom. Putney writes that when a young man "arrived at St. James [Church in Chicago]" he was "greeted by a leader of the Brotherhood and directed to one of two aisles where the organization held pews. Each aisle had a 'lieutenant,' who in turn had under him several 'privates,' one or more to a pew. In addition, there was a 'quartermaster,' who kept Brotherhood pews supplied with hymn-books and invitation cards."[24] The uniforms and activities of church-based and church-sponsored boys' organizations accustomed a generation of boys to the mixture of religious and military culture.

The spread of muscular Christian organizations was wide, but the movement's cultural influence was wider. Though often described as an exclusively Protestant phenomenon, concerns for the masculinity of Christian faith were also present in American Catholicism. In pre-war and wartime writings, many Catholic soldiers and clergy went out of their way to note the compatibility of masculinity and Christian practice, and to foreground the qualities of service, duty, struggle, initiative, and toughness in depictions of the ideal Catholic man. Not all parishes sponsored the special hours and "express lanes" for "male only" confession and communion described by Gail Bederman, but it is clear that concerns for the gender of Christian practice and the virility of Christian men extended well beyond neurasthenic Northeasterners and the elite male boarding school crowd.[25] Similarly, though a lofty sense of the war's religious meaningfulness was robust and widespread among wealthy northeastern elites, there was no yawning chasm separating official, elite, and soldierly understandings of the war.[26] "[E]ven a modest sampling of the personal documents left behind reveals common responses to the shared enterprise, and common conventions of perception and language to which these men resorted in the effort to comprehend their experience and relate it to others."[27] In training and in war, young men of all faiths described desires for unmediated experience, the need to express their manhood violently, and tensions between "masculine" and "feminine" Christianities.[28]

Historians have forwarded related explanations for the ubiquity of this worldview and idiom, focusing primarily on wartime forces.[29] Some men and women were certainly brought their views of the war by the propaganda and "advertising" work of George A. Creel's Committee on Public Information and his Four-Minute Men. (Creel was charged by the Wilson administration with stimulating support for the war and encouraging the "accelerated Americanization" of immigrants. To accomplish this end, Creel employed 75,000 men to give four-minute patriotic speeches to any audience they could find.[30]) But a longer view shows the presence of a firm cultural and religious foundation upon which all kinds of voices—governmental, religious, literary, and personal—could build hopes for a romantic, redemptive war experience. Soldiers accepted and repeated official and elite pronouncements on the war—including the official but far from univocal *Stars and Stripes*—not because those pronouncements were forced upon them, but because they corresponded well to soldiers' pre-war worldviews, mythic imaginations, and religiously informed understandings of their task. When the call went forth for the young products of this culture to fight, many responded with enthusiasm. The Wilson administration was concerned that the nation's sons and daughters would struggle with the notion of a draft and might even resist, but beginning on June 5, 1917, roughly ten million men registered for service.[31]

AMERICAN RELIGION AND THE GREAT WAR

The study of the Great War as a religious experience began during the war. As the nation mobilized in the spring of 1917, the leaders of the General War-Time Commission of the Churches—an off-shoot of the Federal Council of Churches of Christ—formed the Committee on the War and the Religious Outlook, whose task it was to survey the religious practices and beliefs of men entering the Army, study the effects of army life and the war on those attitudes and beliefs, and extract lessons for the Church.[32] Their report, *Religion Among American Men: As Revealed by a Study of Conditions in the Army*, published in 1919, is a rich primary source for reasons other than intended (it captures post-war concerns among Protestant leaders better than it captures soldiers' religious lives and thoughts) and a secondary source in need of revision. In the ninety years since the publication of *Religion Among American Men*, three additional works have focused on religious aspects of the Great War. Ray Abrams' *Preachers Present Arms: The Role of the American Churches and Clergy in the World War*, John F. Piper's *The American Churches in World War I*, and Richard M. Gamble's *The War for Righteousness: Progressive Christianity, the Great War, and the Rise of the Messianic Nation*. All three focus their attentions on the home front and the words and actions of religious leaders, but do not consider the thoughts of soldiers or home-front laity. Abrams' book, first published in 1933, is a polemic against the nationalistic faith that he believes consumed America's religious leaders during the war. John Piper, revising Abrams, emphasizes the cautious acceptance of war and the unified diligence with which Protestant and Catholic leadership alike pursued the establishment of a ministry to the men fighting and dying in France. Richard Gamble works the space between Abrams and Piper, explaining but sharply critiquing Progressive Christian worldviews. Though his book is roughly similar to this one in its narrative arc and its desire to situate the Great War in American religious history, our two studies differ in focus. Gamble is concerned with the thoughts and words of religious and political leaders.[33] This book describes the thoughts and beliefs of soldiers and war workers.

RECORDS OF FAITH IN THE FIGHT: LETTERS, DIARIES, MEMOIRS

Wartime, for all of its enduring tragedies and travesties, presents historians of religion in America with amazing opportunities. Wars are times of separation and precariousness; they are times when the normally reticent find their voices and use them to reflect on God's place in their lives and in history, on death and its meaning, and on the contours of the afterlife.[34] There are indeed atheists in foxholes as there are in manholes and mineshafts and tractors and cubicles, but the foxhole (or trench) dweller seems to take more time to reflect on atheism—or the many theisms he or she might claim—and on the relationship between belief and action. Those who survive war and those who live on having lost one or more loved ones also seem to do more than others to preserve memories and records. War's macabre gift to the historian of religion is this combination of existential anxiety, an impulse to write, and a commonly felt desire to preserve.[35]

This study is based on the personal and public writings of American soldiers and war workers who served in the Great War. I am using the term "American soldier" more loosely than will be comfortable for some. I have examined materials written not only by the young men who fought in the American Expeditionary Force, but also by those who, as early as August of 1914, boarded ships bound for France and volunteered their services. I have considered the words of American airmen alongside those of artillerymen and infantry. "American" thus indicates individual nationality rather than the national identity of the army in which a man fought, while "soldier" indicates involvement in the war in a military capacity. The benefits and costs of such a loose definition will become apparent throughout the course of the study. Chief among the benefits is the recovery of experiences of young American men, such as Pennsylvania native Edwin Abbey and South Carolinian Kiffin Rockwell, who understood that their religiously framed duty required them to step outside of the national collective and fight on behalf of the world, and Kenneth MacLeish and Hamilton Coolidge, aviators who reflected on the relationship between faith and violence, the meaning of death, and the shape of the afterlife. Central among the hazards is the diminution of divisions that were, to some, very important. American aviators, for instance, often drew the ire of American infantrymen for the relative comfort of the conditions in which they lived and for an over-developed sense of self-importance. Had I found among the various groups a wider range of understandings of the issues I take up, I would have done more to maintain these distinctions.

By "war workers" I mean the tens of thousands of men and women who served in the many non-military support agencies in France and England. In places, the phrase "war worker" may appear to be synonymous with "woman." That this is not the case is important to keep in mind, especially when considering the relationship between experiences of violence, gender, and authority that were expressed and negotiated in the war's midst.[36] The fact that women and men both served in the YMCA cast a shadow over the claims of "Y-men" to war-verified masculinity. As one solider put it in a letter about veterans organizations, " . . . [war workers] are not soldiers, and there is no more reason why they should belong [to the American Legion] than there is why the women who drove automobiles around in the States and wore fancy uniforms should be included in a veteran corps."[37] I have also included among "war workers" the American men and women who served in the war service corps of Britain and France.

The "personal literature" of American soldiers and war workers includes letters, diaries, and memoirs. I drew the vast majority of these from the New York Public Library's collection of American Great War narratives. Because most of these were preserved through publication—vanity and commercial—my sources include the voices of many young men and women who came from wealthy families, were themselves wealthy enough to fund a private printing, or were otherwise inclined to seek and secure publication and preservation of their war-time thoughts.[38] This impulse to publish and preserve was not, however, the monopoly of the wealthy, and when exercised by them did not catch only "elite" voices. One collection, *Dear Folks at Home: The Glorious Story of the United States Marines in France as Told by Their Letters from the Battlefield*, compiled by Kemper F. Cowing, edited by Courtney Riley Cooper, and published in 1919 contains excerpts from the correspondence of U.S. Marines of all ranks and regions."[39] Another collection, *Echoes from Over There: By the Men of the Army and Marine Corps Who Fought in France*, edited by Craig Hamilton and Louise Corbin and published in 1919, contains thirty-seven separate narratives written by a variety of men, including a corporal who was a chauffeur in Chicago, a sergeant who was a boxing instructor in New York City, a private from Ohio, and a corporal born in Italy. These collections bring a socio-economic and regional diversity that begins to balance the Coolidges and Blodgetts, Roosevelts and Kilmers. I am not the first to examine this literature. Something of it is present in the work of David Kennedy, Jennifer Keene, and Mark Meigs. Charles Genthe compiled a catalog, *American War Narratives, 1914–1918*, that provides brief descriptions of many collections and narratives but gives little in the way of analysis or context. I am, as far as I can discern, the first to examine as many narratives as I do (219 distinct volumes, well over 300 voices) and to do so with an eye toward religion.[40]

The voices of African American soldiers in this book come primarily from a post-war survey of veterans conducted by the Commonwealth of Virginia. The survey was conducted between 1919 and 1921 and collected responses from over 14,000 former soldiers, 2,400 of whom were African American. Though this source is potentially problematic for reasons I discuss in chapter 4, it is also amazingly rich and, unlike the survey of Great War veterans conducted by the United States Army fifty years later, contains a question about the effects of war experiences on religious beliefs. Survey responses are, of course, a limited genre. It was hard if not impossible for a soldier to weave a textured narrative of war experiences in the few lines provided. But the soldiers who responded to the survey were still able to convey their thoughts and emotions quite effectively, and wrote powerfully and poignantly of faith in the fight.[41]

American soldiers and war workers, while religiously concerned and to varying degrees traditionally religiously engaged, did not write with anything like systematic clarity and precision. Their theologies are at times difficult to ascertain. Their narratives are by turns compelling and frustrating, funny and tragic. Religion emerges in surprising places. Thomas Barber, an infantry officer in the A.E.F. (American Expeditionary Force) recalled seeing "two buddies walking abreast in a column," both of whom had conspired to bring together Protestant hymnody and the equipment of war. "One had painted on his [gas mask],–'Abide in me from morn till eve, for without thee I cannot live.' And his friend had,–'I need thee, Oh! I need thee, every hour I need thee.' "[42] In the intermittent chaos of war, these men—tongues firmly in cheeks—turned to a "savior" other than Jesus and offered wry commentary of the kind of salvation most meaningful to them: salvation of their hides. Authors also treat religion in unpredictable ways. Elmer Haslett's memoir, based on his letters and diary and published in 1920, begins with a detailed description of his understanding of prayer.

> I began to think about my first trip over the lines that was soon to come. I was mentally lower than a snake. I hadn't prayed for some time and I was just wondering whether or not I would pray that night. My solemn idea of prayer was that it was an emergency measure. I was always reverently thankful to the Maker for His blessings, but He knew that for He must have known my mind. I believed that God helped him who helped himself, but when the question was too big for man to control, then it was the time to invoke the help of the Supreme Being.

Haslett then revealed that in spite of the dangers involved in his upcoming mission, he had "decided that I would go ahead and handle it as a man to man proposition, reserving invocation for a more serious situation." He changed his mind, however, as he walked back to his room and heard a noise: "a big cat jumped out of a box and ran directly in front of me. It was too dark, of course, to tell the color of the cat, but the condition of my mind convinced me that it could be no other color than black and that it was an omen that bad luck was sure to come my way." It was at that moment, Haslett wrote, that he decided he would pray. The very next paragraph, though, offers no description of the content of his prayers, no evidence that he even carried his decision through to action. Rather, Haslett tells of lying awake for three hours thinking about all of the things that could go wrong with the machine gun he was to operate.[43] What one can discern from this passage—understandings of when a man should and should not pray, the interaction between superstition and the impulse to pray—is a bit removed from the more obvious question: For what did he and other soldiers pray?

I have tried in the course of this study to preserve the rough edges of individual voices while also working from points of near consensus in the sources (of which there are many) to generalizations about the faith of American soldiers and war workers and the interaction of that faith with wartime and post-war realities. I do not wish to write all particularities into insignificance, but to the extent that this project succeeds in the task of generalizing, it will also fail to be entirely true to the unique men and women on whose lives and words it is built. In my use and analysis of soldiers' personal writings I have been mindful of a warning issued by Great War veteran and eminent New Testament scholar Amos Wilder. "It is all too easy to oversimplify the motives of the combatants in the Great War, as in any war. . . . One should recognize the great differences of maturity, perspective, and commitment of those involved. The anonymous soldiery, moreover, are commonly inarticulate, but their collaboration may often be animated by deeper fealties than those generally invoked." To assume that the three hundred voices consulted in reconstructing those moments exhaust all possible religious reactions would be foolish. To assume that language and memory were fully adequate to the task of capturing every religious thought or emotion would betray the words of the soldiers themselves. Still, I believe the conclusions I have reached apply widely, if not uniformly, among the Americans who fought the Great War.[44]

Soldiers' and war workers' writings do not allow the honest historian to write a polemical history or a predictable ideological critique. As much as one may love or hate the idea of war, love or hate the men and women who plan wars and send others to die, love or hate those who profit financially or politically from war, the voices of soldiers and war workers will provide, at most, equivocal support. The voices in this study and this study itself will disappoint those looking either for a story of disillusionment and disgust with the Great War or for a triumphalist paean to the nation, its war dead, and their motives.

LANGUAGE, POETICS, MEMORY, AND RELIGION

Many soldiers and war workers left behind words of caution as they attempted to share their thoughts. What we are experiencing, they wrote, is impossible for the uninitiated to understand. Language, they wrote, is inadequate to describe war.[45] Writing of the moments immediately following a deadly shelling, Leo Jacks observed that the descriptive tools at the disposal of his comrades were simply inadequate to the task. "Curiously enough, one or two of our hardened battalion cried bitterly when they saw . . . friends knocked down, quivering, and dead beside them; passing quickly from tears to outbursts of helpless rage and hoarse vows that they would kill impossible numbers of the enemy in retaliation, angry threats solemnized by a meaningless flood of curses. Language seemed to have lost, finally, all significance, and there were no words left to express men's ideas."[46] Language cannot and did not lose *all* significance. Not, at least, for those who recorded or memorialized their experiences and ideas in writing. At the same time that the Great War unmade language and worlds through pain, it evoked language, analogies, and theologies.[47] Men and women did their best to describe their thoughts and their beliefs, even when language seemed inadequate; and even in inadequate attempts to describe those "dreadful" and "paralyzing" moments, the historian of American religion has much to learn. War belittled soldiers, making them feel insignificant and powerless. War emboldened soldiers, making them glimpse the apparent grandeur of martyrdom and immortality. War made a soldier feel alone and, alone with his faith, led him to draw on the elements of faith that were of the greatest importance to him, and in which he found the greatest comfort.

Religious experiences and war experiences, when distinct from one another, share an indescribability that is as common among those who experience either as it is vexing to those who study either. Yet, at the points in the Great War where experiences of religion and war overlapped, these two "indescribable" experiences helped clarify each other. Infantry officer Vinton Dearing wrote to his mother of one such point in his encounter with war. Struggling to explain his reactions to encounters with wonder and danger, things mystical and things military, he turned to the language of religion.

> This life does give you a love of nature, a love of that which is just beyond the human grasp. You go out into the moonlight and feel the place "holy and enchanted," a new world, half mystical, a different moon, more wondrous lights;–then some tremendous 155 goes off and shatters your dream. . . . Life is great and the aims of the war are great. It is when you see into the aims with your inner eyes that you see the bigness of it all. Just like religion, those moments are few and far between, yet it is like the Mount of Transfiguration when you go up and receive inspiration anew.[48]

Religion provided a vocabulary to help render war experiences meaningful and war provided an arena in which faith could be lived out, tested, and animated. As we will see, religion also did a great deal of the work needed to romanticize war, and allowed many soldiers to ignore or glorify war's horrors.

Soldiers' widespread use of poetry as a means of expression may seem out of character in a self-consciously masculine crowd. The editors of *The Stars and Stripes*, the soldiers themselves, and historians of the Great War have noted, sometimes with amusement, how frequently soldiers lapsed into verse. Three points on soldierly poetry are worth noting briefly. First, poetry was not a "feminine" mode of expression in 1918. The generation of Americans that went to war was reared on the masculine poetry of, among others, Rudyard Kipling and Robert W. Service. Second, soldiers appear to have been quite taken with the war poems of Service, Alan Seeger, Rupert Brooke, and dozens of lesser lights, and to have been moved toward poetics by their work. Third and perhaps most importantly, poetry, as Amos Wilder wrote late in his life, was sometimes the only mode of expression adequate to the task of describing war experiences. Reflecting on his poem "Armageddon," Wilder noted, "Human experience is not one-dimensional, and the deeper import of even less dramatic actions calls across time and space for answering voices. For me, this episode really happened in a way which imposed itself on my later visionary transcription. The toiling line of the whole brigade likewise had its inklings of that transposed reality which the poetic version alone could seek to articulate."[49] Poetry, as literature scholar James Anderson Winn has argued, has long been used to capture, express, and sometimes to obscure experiences of war and the associated emotions.[50] It is often in American soldiers' poems that their most profound religious insights emerge.

I have struggled with the question of what to make of soldiers' poems, letters, and diaries and the strong notes of wartime romanticism they contain.[51] Did soldiers and war workers *really* imagine the war in such strongly religious terms? How much of their minds, hearts, and souls can one actually find in their words, and how much is better treated as a performance staged for friends and family? What are we to make, for example, of the words of Americans Victor Chapman and Richard Blodgett who, having seen the dangers of aerial combat, each wrote letters to friends expressing the belief that they would not survive the war, while also writing to a parent that they were confident of survival?[52] I have chosen in this book to treat the literal meaning of the texts I read as meaningful moments of communication representative of the truth as soldiers saw it in the moment. One must, of course, remain aware of and attentive to the interwoven complexities of human emotion and of language, but I have found that analyzing the words soldiers chose allows one to do just that while avoiding the worst kinds of reductionism. To return briefly to Chapman and Blodgett, while we may wish to treat one voice (the pessimist) as authentic and the other (the optimist) as inauthentic, things are not as simple as that. For Chapman, Blodgett, and others were certainly capable of feeling doomed one day and bulletproof the next, and in their writings we can well imagine that they were addressing (and comforting, and leveling with) themselves as much as they were addressing an external "audience." Poetic invocations of the militant Christ and lyrical appeals to God can be—and were—prayerful and expressive of deep religious emotions; they were, at times, also the product of a moment in which a soldier or war worker, seized by the adventure, chose to indulge in some self-conscious religious romanticism for his or her own benefit and for the edification of a home-front audience.

THE STARS AND STRIPES: AN OFFICIAL RECORD OF FAITH IN THE FIGHT

The "public literature" considered in this study consists mainly of *The Stars and Stripes*, the official newspaper of the American Expeditionary Force, published between February 8, 1918 and June 13, 1919. At its wartime peak on November 8, 1918, the paper's circulation reached 344,000; circulation did not peak, however, until February 7, 1919, when it climbed to a stunning 522,000 copies. Given that approximately ten percent of the copies were designated for stateside consumption and—at its height—the A.E.F. presence in France consisted of roughly two million soldiers, there was one copy of the paper in circulation for every six to seven soldiers while the war was still on, and one for every four to five soldiers after the Armistice.[53]

Caution toward *The Stars and Stripes* as a source is healthy. The paper's relationship to the A.E.F. hierarchy—specifically the morale department of the intelligence branch—should raise concerns about the paper's claim to be "by and for the American soldier," despite the literal truth of this statement.[54] What the masthead meant, and what the mostly enlisted staff cultivated, was the "half-truth" that *The Stars and Stripes* was a completely open forum for the American soldier to express his views and to read those of others, apart from the shaping hand of officialdom. This it was not. The bulk of the writing was indeed done by enlisted men—most of whom had prior experience in journalism, many of whom would go on to dazzling careers in the field. The editorial board was also made up of enlisted men. The paper's editor-in-chief was, as one would expect, an officer—first Guy Visknisski, then future Pulitzer Prize winner Mark

Watson—and the content was sent to headquarters each week to be vetted. The result of this oversight was not, however, a well-combed propaganda sheet. Letters that complained of privations, editorials that railed against home-front Christian moralists, cartoons both solemn and funny, poems militant and mournful, and article-length attempts to make sense of the chaos of war came together in this widely available meaning-making forum. The censorial hand of hierarchs and of the French *Bureau de la Presse* was waiting at the boundaries—as it was for all papers, but those boundaries were both wide and roughly coincident with soldierly opinion as present in the personal literature.[55] Although often without the flair of *The Stars and Stripes* staff writers Grantland Rice, Harold Ross, Hudson Hawley, or Alexander Woollcott, soldiers wrestled in many of the same ways with the same issues raised by war.

As a window onto the religious mind of the American soldier, *The Stars and Stripes* is quite valuable. The meaning-making in which *The Stars and Stripes* editors and contributors engaged was communal and controlled, and at times incorporated imagery and prose that may have been beyond most soldiers. Yet the correlation is strong between the paper's editorial voice and soldiers' writings on clergy, Christian duty, and the aims of war. Soldiers' poems and letters published by the paper echo sentiments contained in soldiers' personal writings as to the fiendishness of the enemy, the religiously transformative nature of combat experience, and the soldier as imitator of Christ. On these points of agreement, I have used *The Stars and Stripes* frequently, treating it as a communal voice. On points of difference—usually differences of degree and not kind—I have noted the differences.

CHAPTERS

This book as a whole focuses on continuity in the midst of rupture. It charts and describes and contextualizes small changes, to be sure, but it is not about the death of an old order and the birth of a new. It is about the reassertion of religious ideas and ideals in the face of war and in war's aftermath. It is, in short, a story of reillusionment.

The narrative begins, as war experiences begin, with ideas about war and speculation as to war's effects on individuals and communities. Chapter 1, "Redemption through War," focuses on soldiers' and war workers' understandings of the religious meaning of the Great War. In it, I examine the religiously framed hopes that Americans waging the war had for the world, the nation, and for themselves. Though different in many ways with regard to theology and practice, men and women, black and white, Protestant and Catholic saw the war in remarkably similar religious terms. Chapter 2, "Chance the Man-Angel and the Combat Numinous," examines soldiers' theologies of the design of combat. Central to this chapter is the connection between encountering overwhelming industrial violence and the invigoration that soldiers and war workers associated with experiences of combat. As the chapter title indicates, I have made reference to the work of Rudolf Otto, whose *The Idea of the Holy* was published first during the war, to help explicate this connection. Chapter 3, "Suffering, Death, and Salvation" looks closely at the religious concepts and symbols soldiers used to make sense of death in war. The suffering and bleeding, writhing and dying they wrote, time and again, were modern forms of martyrdom and *imitatio Christi*, which brought salvation to the fallen.

Chapter 4, "Christ's Cause, Pharaoh's Army," examines continuities and discontinuities between religious dimensions of black soldiers' war experiences and those of their white counterparts. Black soldiers' encounters with war were shaped by the institutionalized racism of the United States, but also by the hope that war service would dissolve that racism. The religious reflections of black soldiers and veterans give a great deal of space to hopes for redemption and to claims of authority derived from war, themes that figured prominently among black soldiers in the Civil War and white soldiers in the Great War, but do not discuss Christ and Christ's relationship to violence in the same militant tone. Chapter 5, "Ideal Women in an Ideal War," examines women's accounts of their war experiences and the gender roles present in them. This chapter describes and discusses the religious dimensions of three overlapping but distinct visions of womanhood in the Great War: War Wives and Mothers, Sisters in Arms, and New Woman Warriors. This formulation helps account for the depth and breadth of women's commitments to the war, to warriors, and to Western Front domesticity, while also drawing attention to women's creative engagement with, and critical reflections on, the culture war. (Though voices of African Americans and women are present in the first four chapters, more focused treatments have enabled me to draw out some distinctive religious dimensions of their war experiences.) Chapter 6, "There Are No Dead," continues to examine the religious implications of life in a world where death was so powerful a presence. This chapter takes cues from the work of Ann Douglas, Colleen McDannell, and Drew Gilpin Faust and reads soldiers' visions of the afterlife, including the porous nature of the boundary between this life and the next, both as projections of soldiers' ideals and as assertions of religious and cultural authority to which a range of individuals and organizations would lay claim after the war. The seventh and final chapter discusses the post-war period, the rise of the American Legion, and the religiousness of the Legion's ongoing war to shape and sanctify the United States.

The events set in motion by the Great War and its resolution shaped profoundly the twentieth century—its ideologies, political actors, tragedies, and cultural voices. Because it became, in relatively short order, a tragic "prequel" to a truly global war, the Great War is often treated as of little ultimate consequence for America. I hope that among the other contributions this work makes, it will aid in bringing back into focus a moment in American history rife with lessons and challenges for our own day. The crowning lesson of the Great War is that war is always and everywhere more powerful than those who wage it. When well-meaning men and women decide to enter a war they are—more than they do on a daily basis—entering into an agreement with history governed only by the laws of unintended consequences. Purity of motive, loftiness of aspiration, and depth of conviction are security blankets rather than insurance policies. They offer comfort but no protection from history's bogeymen. That truth seems to hang just beyond the grasp of every generation. It remained so elusive in the twentieth century due in no small part to America's experience of the Great War and to the post-war actions of America's Great War veterans.

CHAPTER ONE

Redemption through War

EDWIN AUSTIN ABBEY II was an American soldier who never fought under the American flag. War broke out in Europe in August of Abbey's twenty-sixth year. Some American men and women joined European armies and their auxiliaries as quickly as they could, but Abbey did not rush to the fight. Through the spring and summer of 1915, he was busy, far from his parents' home in Philadelphia, "superintending the construction of the bridge at Shaw's Creek" in Ontario, Canada.[1] Abbey often took time, sitting at his desk in the "engineers' shack" to ponder the world situation, America's relationship to it, and what the proper course of action was for him. In May of 1915, he wrote to his parents describing his affection for America, "No country or flag could ever be mine except the United States," but also hinting at a growing sense of responsibility to a larger collective. Abbey thought of himself as "a citizen of the world" and could hear that community calling him to war.

The war occupied Abbey's thoughts more and more as the summer of 1915 passed, and by August he was less tolerant of Wilsonian neutrality. "I am beginning to feel, as you do," he wrote home, "that the flag is disgraced; the honor of the nation being fumbled away." Wilson's policies may have once had their place. They did not any longer. "The time of neutrality," Abbey proclaimed, "has passed."[2] His work on the bridge in Shaw's Creek "providentially" completed, he traveled to Toronto in October of 1915, where he gained acceptance to the Canadian Army. Five months later, the ship carrying Edwin Austin Abbey II and the rest of "B" Company, Second Canadian Pioneer Battalion arrived in France. It was March 8, 1916—Ash Wednesday morning.[3]

Edwin Abbey was raised in the Episcopal Church and worked mightily while at war to practice and develop his faith. He expressed his faith publicly, through regular attendance at his unit's worship services, and privately by marking with a cross in his diary the days on which he had been "brought safe through special dangers." He wrote to his mother of these "cross days"—not the particulars, only the dates: March 27, April 10, April 14—so that she could "make special thanksgiving."[4] On April 23, 1916, Abbey again encountered "special dangers." This time, though, he was not brought safely through. Shortly after midnight on that Easter Sunday, a German shell exploded in Abbey's vicinity, sending shrapnel into his shoulder. Writing to "Father Ward" from his bed in King George Hospital, London, Abbey called it "a Lent that I shall never forget."[5]

When he returned to the trenches, this time as a lieutenant in the Fourth Canadian Mounted Rifles, Abbey kept up his correspondence and his faith. His mother sent him a prayer book, *Manual of Prayers for Workers*, which he read and found edifying, particularly on the topics of "manliness" and duty. He liked that the volume "takes for granted that man is called to a continual struggle with difficulties, and makes it a point of honor not to be dismayed by them."[6] If Abbey was dismayed by his struggles, he wrote nothing of it. He wrote instead that if God allowed him to return, he would fulfill his mother's "long-cherished hopes and prayers" that her son become a priest, and "Perhaps . . . go into the Church."[7] December 20, 1916 was another "cross day."

To mark the beginning of his second Lenten season at war, Abbey's mother sent a package containing a replacement for the small bronze crucifix that he wore pinned inside of his breast pocket. The original had fallen off "somehow." Abbey wrote letters to his mother and father on Ash Wednesday, Palm Sunday, Good Friday, and Easter, noting in his Good Friday letter that the United States had finally entered the war. Also on Good Friday—April 6, 1917—Abbey set aside a few moments to write an additional letter to his parents. His unit was preparing to go forward to press an attack. Abbey wanted the letter delivered in the event that he did not return.

> I have made my Communion, and go with a light heart and a determination to do all that I possibly can to help in this fight against evil, for God and humanity. I do not think of death or expect it, but I am not afraid, and will give my life gladly if it is asked. It is my greatest comfort that I know you too will gladly give all that is asked, and live on happily doing all that can be done, grateful to God for his acceptance of our sacrifice. . . . Now, dearest mother, and dearest father, I will say goodbye for a time. You have given me my faith, which makes this so easy for me, and a wonderful example and inspiration of courage and unselfishness. All my love, and God bless you both. Your son.[8]

On the Tuesday after Easter, April 10, 1917, the men of the Fourth Canadian Mounted Rifles were in the vicinity of Vimy Ridge. A German sniper caught sight of one who had apparently lost his bearings attempting to occupy a forward post. The sniper took aim, squeezed the trigger, and watched for a moment as his enemy "pitched forward and dropped."[9] The war was over for Edwin Austin Abbey. For the United States, the war had barely begun.

The day Edwin Abbey died was an exciting day in New York City. The country was in its fourth day of declared war. Billy Sunday's much-anticipated New York City revival, just two days old, was drawing saints and sinners into a massive tent where God and nation were woven so tightly together that service to one was indistinguishable from service to the other. Father Francis P. Duffy, chastened Catholic modernist and battle-hardened chaplain of the largely Irish-American "Fighting Sixty-ninth," was contacting parish athletic clubs throughout the city, seeking the best and fittest Catholic men to fill the ranks of his infantry regiment. So sure and proud were the members of the Sixty-ninth that they would be nationalized and sent to war that they sent a machine-gun truck through the streets of the city bearing a banner that read, "Don't Join the 69th Unless You Want to Be Among the First to Go to France."[10] African American leaders were also preparing their community for the demands of war. James Weldon Johnson, writing in the *New York Age*, proclaimed—in terms nearly identical to those used by Frederick Douglass to rally free blacks to the Union cause during the American Civil War—that if "the Negro will take up and perform the duty that now falls to him," he will "thereby [strengthen] his protest for his right and [fling] a challenge to the white people of this country."[11] It had been nearly a year since the *New York Times* published an interview with Lady Randolph Churchill, the American-born mother of Winston Churchill, describing war's transformative, redemptive effects on women and womanhood in which she proclaimed, "women have gained from [the war] the mighty prize of earnestness and the fine sense of ability to accomplish firm realities ... the sense which made life splendid for the pioneer women of America." Now the women of New York City and the United States would be able to test her assertions under the American flag.[12]

While Sunday, Duffy, and Johnson worked in their own ways to bring young men to war and Lady Churchill's assurances hung in the air, Quincy Sharpe Mills worked to gather and express his thoughts on the nation's course. In the offices of the *New York Evening Sun*, Mills could not resist writing an "I told you so" into his April 10, 1917 editorial. He had been an advocate of preparedness in the *Evening Sun*'s pages since March of 1915, but his voice and others like his had, in his opinion, not been adequately heeded. Referring to German dismissals of the United States' military, he wrote, "Had we adopted universal military training on the Swiss plan a year ago, there would have been no contemptuous sneering at 'America's wooden sword.' "[13] Mills was not one to talk the talk without walking the walk. He joined other preparedness advocates in training for military service at the Plattsburgh camp in the summers of 1915 and 1916, and hoped that with America now in the war he would be able to follow in the footsteps of his grandfathers and one great-great-great-grandfather, officers in the Confederate and Continental armies.[14] Like the men on the Scotch-Irish Sharpe side of the family, Quincy was not much for churches and ministers, hymns and sermons. "While devotion to their church was the rule," his mother wrote, "the number of men of our stock who could never tie themselves down narrowly to a creed was and is remarkably large. They could not love their Lord by 'rule and line,' though their lives bore testimony to their belief in Him."[15]

During the fateful spring of 1917, with New York City as an audience, the thirty-three-year-old southerner-turned-New-Yorker "bore testimony to [his] belief" by calling his fellow men to war, excoriating obstructionist congressmen slow to commit to raising an army, and arguing in language shot through with myths of righteous American violence for the sanctity and immediacy of the cause.[16] Mills deftly used American myth-history and stark polarizing language to remind his readers of their duties as defenders of freedom and slayers of evil. In his April 19 editorial, "Wake Up America Day," Mills stated, "The people of the United States have been formally at war for fourteen days with the most ruthless enemy that has assailed civilization since the dawn of history." In the face of such a threat and having declared war, he continued, American dawdling was unconscionable. "It is time for them to comprehend that they must play men's parts as did their predecessors at the summons of Paul Revere. What would have happened," Mills invited his readers to imagine, "had the patriots who fired at Lexington 142 years ago to-day 'the shot heard round the world' decided to discuss for a fortnight the advisability of lining up on the field of battle?"[17] A battle of even greater import and meaning for America and the world now faced American men. And lest any doubt linger as to the nature of the foe, on May 5 Mills turned to the evangelist who made a colorful career of seeing only black and white. Though he shared little of Billy Sunday's public faith, Mills did not dispute Sunday's view of Germany and the war. "There can be no two minds as to the right of William Hohenzollern [Kaiser Wilhelm] to head the list of Rev. Billy Sunday's 'Who's Who in Hell.'"[18] Five days later, on May 10, 1917, Quincy Sharpe Mills "laid down his pen," picked up his gun, and marched off to war.[19]

The words and photographs left behind by American soldiers and war workers who, like Edwin Abbey and Quincy Mills, went to France to fight the Great War remind even the casual observer of how different their warring world was from ours. We see young men and women bound for and in the midst of war clad in heavy woolen pants and jackets and leather Sam Browne belts, in long skirts and blouses and bonnets. They write of crisscrossing the French landscape in freight cars, primitive automobiles, and horse-drawn carts. Male and female volunteers describe driving donated trucks laden with the wounded down rutted dirt roads to candlelit hospitals. A young man is captured on film admiring some caged pigeons, his most reliable means of wireless communication. There is much about the material world of the Americans involved in the Great War that strikes the twenty-first-century observer as antique.

Those same letters and pictures depict a warring world similar, if sometimes only vaguely, to our own. Men and women, overseas for the first time, pose proudly with the people they have come to liberate and the monuments of their culture. Some of the weapons that soldiers describe are identifiable ancestors of more modern, more lethal varieties: the tank, the machine gun, long-range artillery, mortars, hand grenades, aircraft. Soldiers and war workers read from *The Stars and Stripes*, first published in Paris on February 8, 1918, and widely available on U.S. military installations today. They hunch over pads of paper, dashing off letters to families and friends, as eager to receive news as they are to convey it. The world inhabited by these men and women—smiling, eager, weary, grim-faced—is a world between eras. It is a world populated by vestiges of the old order but learning to live and die with the technologies and attitudes of the new.

The words and actions of Edwin Abbey and Quincy Mills and their fellow soldiers show the religious culture of the Great War era to be also at once historically distant and strangely familiar. That culture is strongly, publicly Christian in a way since tempered. Evidence of this Christian culture appears in prose and poetry, the elegance of which is also of another era. Not far beneath the surface of this culture is a seemingly perennial concern for how the nation will accommodate ethnic, cultural, and religious differences while staying meaningfully united. Clergy, politicians, editors, fathers, mothers, and soldiers deploy religious texts and images, sometimes artfully, sometimes clumsily, to bolster shared hopes and to temper conflicting ideas as to what the war might accomplish for the United States and its diverse populations. Similar texts and images also serve to sanctify the war and individual involvement in it in a way that is familiar in its lack of subtlety and in its effectiveness. A poem written by Father Thomas Coakley, an A.E.F. chaplain and a Pittsburgh-area Catholic priest, is but one example. On November 1, 1918, soldiers opened *The Stars and Stripes* and read:

> Not all Saints lived in the distant past
> Not all God's heroes died in bygone age
> Each day these deeds of old are far surpassed
> By valorous feats inscribed on history's page.[20]

Literature scholars would surely note that as a piece of poetry, Coakley's composition is flat and predictable. He states that the ranks of the saints and martyrs remain open, and then casts his lot with the "valorous" A.E.F. soldiers whose "feats" far surpass the "deeds" of the ancient dead. The war is so present that he doesn't mention it, let alone engage it in a nuanced way. But flat as this poem may be, it is not far removed from the thoughts of the soldiers who read it ninety years ago; nor does it diverge much from modern recruiting commercials entreating young people—a "few good men," as it were—to "live the adventure."

This chapter aims to describe and analyze the religious culture of American participants in the war, focusing on the ways that soldiers, war workers, and their official public voice, *The Stars and Stripes,* used religious imagery to frame the Great War as redemptive. The American women and men who joined the war effort in France had significant, religiously charged expectations for their war experiences. These expectations were, to be sure, encouraged by official organs of the American Expeditionary Force. They were also, just as clearly, crafted and adapted by the men and women who aspired to be heroes and heroines of God and nation.

It is one thing to note that soldiers and war workers wrote of and hoped for redemption through war. It is another thing to know what "redemption" meant to them and why they saw war's violence as capable of achieving cosmic, national, and individual good. Any single answer to these questions is limited by the size and diversity of the American soldiery, but we can approach the roots of the logic of war as redemptive by considering the progressive mentality and its application to the discontents of the pre-war era, especially the discontents of two very different groups: Anglo-American elites and African Americans. As life became more urban and careers more corporate, upper- and upper-middle-class Anglo-Americans in the early twentieth century felt increasingly constrained physically and professionally. As Gail Bederman has noted, G. Stanley Hall and Theodore Roosevelt reflected on this "problem" and concluded it was serious enough to threaten the status of the supposed standard bearers of American civilization. The seriousness lay not simply in the intra-class crises of purpose and bouts of neurasthenia—the nervous disease of over-civilization—but in the inter-class, inter-ethnic, inter-racial crisis brought on by a growing population of fit and, perhaps, ambitious non-Anglo men. How could the nation survive, let alone prosper if such people surpassed "true" American men? Hall and Roosevelt agreed further that the problem was curable and that strenuous action was an important part of the treatment plan. When an upper-middle-class Anglo-American man wrote of war as redemption then, he might have been referring simultaneously to personal redemption (i.e., release from a constraining life, exposure to the leavening hardships of war), and to national redemption (i.e. the subsequent shoring up of Anglo-American claims to national leadership). He may also have seen these two as necessary preconditions to the redemption of the world from a marauding tyranny.

Though the concerns of African Americans in the 1910s were quite different and in many places put them directly at odds with Anglo-American elites, the internal logic of their approach to war was similar if not identical. African Americans were still struggling to gain recognition as full citizens of the United States sixty years after the Civil War "redeemed" enslaved Africans and saw tens of thousands of African Americans validate their citizenship through war service. Using much the same logic that Frederick Douglass had used to call African Americans to arms against the Confederacy, African American leaders looked to service in the Great War as a means to gaining recognition of their manhood and their fitness for citizenship.[21] When an African American man wrote of the redemptive effects of his war experiences then, he likely meant that war service would elevate him and the African American community to their proper place in American society and, simultaneously, redeem America from its centuries-old captivity to racism.

The word "redemption" carries with it several levels of meaning—from the deeply religious (i.e., salvation of a fallen, sinful individual, community, or world) to the more secular (i.e., restoration of a person or idea fallen somehow into disrepair or disuse). I use "redemption," "redeem," and "redeemer" in this chapter and throughout this book in a sense that is more closely related to the religious than to the secular meaning. Though my subjects did not all share a Christian understanding of redemption or even use the word consistently, the "secular" process of repairing a world or a life seems to have been closely connected in their minds to the belief—the hope—that repair would bring restoration to a more metaphysically "correct" state. They believed that by involving themselves in the war, assenting to its demands, and achieving victory, they would attain at least this more general redemption of the world and of America. By exposing themselves to the mysterious and powerful forces of combat, many believed they would achieve a personal redemption of great metaphysical consequence.

Though this chapter focuses on significant points of convergence among voices, it also includes the testimony of those who focused less on war as redemption and more on war as tragedy, less on the possibility of transformation and more on the certainty of destruction. These voices are important not simply as a chronicle of ideological and religious diversity, but as evidence of the existence of options for soldiers and war workers when it came to reflecting on the religiousness of the war. That many viewed the war as religiously significant and chose to develop that view in the midst of war should not lead us to treat such views as the product of reflex, or a mere parroting of propaganda. The editors of *The Stars and Stripes*, as will quickly become clear, contributed greatly to a robust and violently inclined religious culture. It is my contention that they reflected the opinions of a large swath of their readership, even as they sought to shape those opinions.

A War to Redeem the World

American soldiers and war workers wrote frequently of the Great War as a struggle between forces larger than the nations and the men involved— a struggle between metaphysical forces of good and evil. Three Americans who articulated this view with particular clarity were soldiers Edwin Abbey and Amos Wilder, and war worker Katherine Blake. All three saw "their" war as different from other wars; it was not a war of conquest, but an action taken in defense of ultimate good. Abbey, Wilder, and Blake saw grander forces at work in the struggle to rid the world of tyranny.

Before Edwin Abbey volunteered his services to the British Army in 1915, he described the Great War in language that placed the war's primary significance elsewhere than in the realm of politics and economics. "I can see very little patriotism or flags or countries; it is more a struggle of mankind to defend the principles of humanity and chivalry which the Creator has handed down." To struggle for the divinely ordained principles and ideals at issue in the Great War was to reach beyond the patriotic emotion and the national symbols that drove other wars. Abbey was not convinced that the nations fighting for these principles were uniquely virtuous ("the defenders themselves have abused and sinned against the very principles they now defend") but they were, at least, willing to stand for good. "It is as though the world had sinned to a point where it divided," Abbey wrote, "the one half going over the bounds of human possibility, the other stopping and reaching back to a former good and true tradition, to resist the impulse of the lost half to swallow it up as well."[22] The fate of civilized Christian humanity hung in the balance. Lest they be consumed by those who would turn the world toward sin and sinning, the righteous had to fight.[23]

Experiences of combat also led American artilleryman Amos Wilder to reflect on war's metaphysical dimensions. Wilder, who was born in Madison, Wisconsin in 1895, was studying at Oberlin College in 1915 when he decided to join the war effort.[24] He served as a volunteer ambulance driver in France and the Balkans until the United States entered the war, at which point he enlisted as a private in the A.E.F. Wilder survived the war and went on to a successful career as a Congregationalist pastor and, eventually, a New Testament scholar and pioneer in the study of religion and literature. (His more famous bother, Thornton, became one of the United States' most beloved playwrights.) In a diary entry penned on October 20, 1918, Wilder wrote, "We are 10 kilometers from the front lines here, but the barrages we get here in the dawn, and sometimes (as now) in the afternoon, are formidable. It gives one a sense of the perverse endurance in the enemy." The enemy's endurance was remarkable; so too was the evil that stood behind him and, presumably, urged him to fight on and on. "If I could only explain the strong sense that comes over one of the personality of the evil we are fighting. The Personal Devil: the Unseen Powers of the Air–a superhuman deviltry of conception, a never failing truth-to-type in action. We men are the tools with which greater beings fight each other."[25]

Katherine Blake agreed with Wilder's assessment of the nature of the German enemy. Writing in July of 1918 after fleeing Paris with her children, she allowed no doubt as to the force with which Germany was aligned. "Oh, to kill this power of evil, this brute beast of Germany, to drive this thing forever off the earth and out of our children's future."[26] Though their talents for expression were extraordinary, the views articulated by Blake, Wilder, and Abbey were not. The war was to them and others far more than a struggle between armies representing governments at odds with one another. It was an earthly staging of a cosmic struggle between good and evil. Redemption would come with the triumph of good, however many human "tools" the "greater beings" destroyed along the way.

An anonymous soldier-poet (most likely Private Hudson Hawley[27]) made this case publicly with a poem, "The Stars–From France," that appeared on February 15, 1918 in the second issue of *The Stars and Stripes*. The poet took the perspective of a soldier looking deep into the night sky, reflecting on earth's place in an imagined cosmic community. Do other worlds, he wondered, "have now a share / Of all the horrors this world knows, / Of all the wartime wails and woes?"

> Or is this little world of ours
> the sole one knowing wretched hours
> Of dreary vigils in the sleet
> Of waiting for returning feet
> Of home-bound warriors? Have we, reft
> In war the only bad star left?[28]

Perhaps, the poet reflected, all other worlds had progressed beyond the "age-old war 'twixt Folk and Throne," but there was no way to know. The only right thing to do, in any case, was to attempt to claim earth forever for the forces of good and right.

We do not know now if we are
Upon the only backward star;
Nor do we know that only we
Do spite the planets' harmony.
We only know that we must purge
This world–our star–of tyrant's scourge;
That when thus freed, 'twill shine as fair
And bright as any star up there.

This poem derives much of its force from a back and forth between the known and the unknown. The structure allows the poet to fill his composition with assertions about the righteousness of the war and to lend them a degree of certainty equivalent to his certainty as to the limits of his knowledge about interplanetary military affairs. We surely *don't* know if war is raging elsewhere in the universe; we surely *don't* know if ours is the "only backward star." But we truly *do* know that tyranny is a "scourge" at odds with the planetary harmony and, most importantly, that we must eliminate the source of disharmony if the world is to "shine" again and please those out there—God—who are paying attention. *The Stars and Stripes* poet did not turn away from the pain and suffering of war even as he turned his gaze skyward. He did not deny that war damaged men and their families. In trying to make sense of these facts, he invested the earthly reality of the war with a sense of metaphysical meaningfulness. Win this war, he wrote, and at least *our* world will be in tune with the cosmic good.[29]

Good and evil did not exist only in the abstract for soldiers and war workers. Rather, they gave both quite specific names and quite concrete religious identities. The Allies were synonymous with Good and were cast as fairly uniform in their Christianity. The Central Powers were, predictably, cast as apostles of a godless militarism when they weren't portrayed as minions of Satan (see figure 1.1). One particularly widespread way of describing the war's redemptive power was to draw strong connections between current military developments and moments from scripture and Christian history in which "evil" and "good" struggled with each other. Some of these episodes emphasized the adventure and romance of war; nearly all of them showed the soldier playing an active part in the latest chapter of salvation history. The Great War thus became an opportunity to put Christian faith into action, to join a long and distinguished line of Christian warriors in the Christian struggle to redeem the world.

Through most of its run, *The Stars and Stripes* portrayed the German enemy as not just anti-Christian, but as party to particularly notorious episodes from Christian history. An early article on war-time atrocities invoked the mythology of Jesus' infancy and Roman perfidy expressed in

Figure 1.1. A peasant "Germany" walks between the demon "Militarism" and the conniving "Kaiserism." Woodrow Wilson said repeatedly that the war was not against the German people but against their government. This cartoon in the July 5, 1918 issue of *The Stars and Stripes*, while not contradicting Wilson's position entirely, placed the common German in devilish company and authorized violence against him. Blows struck against the German soldier, the picture seems to say, are righteous blows against larger demonic forces. Image courtesy of the University of Illinois Library.

Matthew 2 by describing German conduct in occupied French and Belgian villages as a "Slaughter of Innocents." A subsequent editorial cartoon took the equation of Germany and Christ-killing Rome from cradle to cross, as it were, when it depicted the Crown Prince laughing at the crucified Christ and saying to the Kaiser, "Oh, Look, Papa! Another Of Those Allies."[30] (See figure 1.2.) These images told of an opponent who would not be content to achieve a military victory and to claim the political and economic spoils, but who would also strive to defeat Christianity. If they had had the chance, the picture argued, German leaders and soldiers would have killed Christ himself. In the editorial eye of *The Stars and Stripes*, the highest calling of the A.E.F. soldier was to wage war for Christ and thus save the world from an anti-Christian menace.

The private reflections of Americans at war include many instances of a similar framing of the war. In letters and diaries, soldiers and war workers depicted German soldiers as savage vicious Huns, and cloaked themselves and their allies in the mantle of Christian heroism. When Kenneth MacLeish, a native of Glencoe, Illinois and a student at Yale, sought permission from his parents to begin training for aviation in March of 1917, he wrote explaining his desire to enter the war. War was "terrible," he admitted, but Germany's actions and the "wanton murder of helpless American women and children" were worse. Contemplating what he should do, MacLeish took Christ as his model.

> There are many things worth giving up one's life for, and the greatest of these is humanity and the assurance of the laws of Christianity. Some people think that the only words Christ uttered were, "Resist not evil." Do you think for a minute that if Christ had been alone on the Mount with Mary, and a desperate man had entered with criminal intent, He would have turned away when a crime against Mary was perpetrated? Never! Religion embraces the sword as well as the dove of peace.[31]

Christ would have fought with "all the God-given strength He had," and so would MacLeish. Adrian Edwards, a lawyer from Carrolton, Illinois, wrote in his last letter to his mother that this war "to save civilization, to prevent future wars . . . and to make the world safe for democracy" was also being waged to "punish the Germans, who have disregarded every law of God and mankind, whose only god is the god of war and military force."[32] Villains and heretics embraced war for gain or, worse, war for war's sake. Heroes and Christians stood against them.

When, in the summer and fall of 1918, the struggle between good and evil, God and Satan, moved to already sacred terrain, *The Stars and Stripes* and Americans both in France and at home connected their own moment to past ages of undeniable soaring religious meaning and imagined the redemption that would result from recapitulating crusade history.

Figure 1.2. The Crown Prince and Kaiser Wilhelm demonstrate at once their anti-Christian nature and the true Christianity of the Allied cause in this editorial cartoon from the June 14, 1918 issue of *The Stars and Stripes*. Many soldiers and war workers expressed sentiments similar to those presented so starkly here. Image courtesy of the University of Illinois Library.

In 1918, British General George Allenby fought a number of battles in his eventually successful Palestinian Campaign. On the American home front, pre-millennialist Christians—Christians who believed that the thousand-year period of peace promised in the Book of Revelation would be inaugurated by Christ's dramatic second coming—interpreted this news as validation of prophecy and an indication that the end of history was nigh. Allied armies had "cleared the path for the fulfillment of the predicted return of the Jews to Palestine"—an important sign of the end times.[33] Discussion of this development dominated prophecy conferences in 1918 and helped pique American evangelicals' interest in the war.[34]

The Stars and Stripes was also publicly thrilled that British forces had planted their flag in the soil once walked by Jesus and the last successful crusaders. "The victory in Palestine means that the Holy Land, the golden quest of three disastrous crusades in the Middle Ages, has been snatched from Turkish rule," the paper reported on September 27, 1918. Two subsequent editorials published in the fall of 1918 connected these military developments to crusading lore and wove the accomplishments of contemporary crusaders into biblical accounts of the final stages of history. Hopes for the fulfillment of Christian history dominated an editorial titled "Nazareth," penned one week after the report of Palestine's capture. The author began by quoting John 1:46, "And Nathaniel said unto him, Can there any good thing come out of Nazareth? Philip saith unto him, Come and see." All were aware, according to the editorialist, that the first "good thing," was Jesus, who "grew to manhood" in Nazareth. The land from which Jesus emerged had long ago sunk back into darkness, but war meant that redemption was now at hand. "And today we know that, for the first time in centuries upon centuries, Nazareth is under the rule of the Christian, civilized power, and freed forever from the domination of the Turk." According to the writer, the two events, separated by nineteen centuries, shared a geographical locus and a commensurate level of religious meaning.

> Nearly 2,000 years ago it was that the religion of humanity, of right, of justice came out of Nazareth. Now, after years of Saracen and Turkish administration, a good thing has come again into Naareth [sic] in the shape of the forces of humanity, of right and justice. . . . The shades of Godfrey de Bouillon, of Richard Coeur de Lion and of the good St. Louis of France must look down with envy upon the forces of our British Allies who, in the twentieth century, have made the great dream of Christendom come true.[35]

This editorial presented in close proximity three points on an axis that ran from Christ to Couer de Lion to the Allied soldier. The "good thing" that had come forth from Nazareth long ago had spawned a great history of struggle against evil—a history in which many had fought to bring about Christ's promised reign of peace. At last, in 1918, that goal was achievable.

These strands of Christian meaning—the conquering of an anti-Christian foe and the redemption of the Holy Land—came together publicly again on October 4, 1918 as *The Stars and Stripes* reported on further British progress against Ottoman forces. According to an editorial, a British communiqué received in the autumn of 1918 provided remarkable substantiation of beliefs in the war's Christian meaningfulness. The communiqué read, "On the north our cavalry, traversing the field of Armageddon." Having received this report, *The Stars and Stripes* published "Armageddon In Fact And In Allegory," which began by describing the numbing effects of war. The physical and emotional strain of waging war was apt to make even the most wide-eyed soldier "spiritually calloused" to the experience of fighting where Clovis and Charlemagne, and "Caesar before them" fought. The author admitted, though, that the war was still able to "provide an occasional thrill that sets the mind ringing," as evidenced by the message regarding Armageddon.

> The words set the blood pulsing. They conjure up two pictures–one of an embattled Israelite host fighting for the land and liberty into which it had entered after generations of slavery and oppression; the other of a simple, inspired hermit, looking out over the blue Aegean from "the isle that is called Patmos" and visioning the ultimate battle of battles, the victory of the legions of Heaven over the legions of Hell, the final triumph of Good over Evil.[36]

For those unfamiliar with either Armageddon narrative, the editors recounted both—though with greater initial attention paid to the warring "Israelite host" than to the "inspired hermit." The editorial's conclusion, however, drew a closer connection between the Great War and the "ultimate battle" for cosmic renewal described in the Book of Revelation. Though the fighting in the Holy Land was closer to the fighting of the Israelites, the end result would be more like the visions of John: "And I saw a new heaven and new earth; for the first heaven and the first earth were passed away . . . "[37] The author did not explicitly equate the Great War with "the ultimate battle of battles;" he did not say who, in this historical moment, were "the legions of Heaven" and who "the legions of Hell." He did not need to.

A discursive amalgam of Christ, crusader, and British soldier, Israelite, Hermit, and Apocalyptic warrior, American fighting men shouldered quite a load of holy expectation. But while the historical particularities of these identities faded into irrelevance, their imagined core qualities— a willingness to wage war (or at least imagine a war) for world redemption—remained profoundly appealing to soldiers and war workers. As they pondered what lay ahead of them, many soldiers and war workers imagined themselves as modern crusaders, recapitulating what they believed to be a noble—if heretofore mostly unsuccessful—history of Christian warfare. They understood themselves to be part of a modern fight to rid Christian Europe of the Hun, to redeem the Holy Land from the Turk, and to forge "a new heaven and [a] new earth." While walking an early morning beat among sleeping soldiers in France in June of 1918, Private Clarence Lindner found himself torn between admiration of the sleeping men, "dreaming on the edge of the supreme adventure," and speculation as to "when the dreads and misgivings of the present would ever again give way to the rare securities of the former days." He wrote of this moment in a letter to his family, and described a sudden feeling of assurance that he would do "the appointed thing." He continued, "I felt a part of a great army of an ancient crusade, with all the pomp of armored men and prancing steeds, and the romance of the thing came to me as it had not before."[38] Leo Jacks, a member of the 119th Field Artillery, 32d Division, also found the crusader a fitting type of the American soldier. "Since the days of Peter the Hermit and Bernard of Clairvaux there has not been an army so blindly devoted in general to its ideals, so little given to counting the cost, and so little affected by adverse propaganda as the A.E.F."[39] United in a Christian cause, fighting for world redemption, American men and women found inspiration and meaning. They knew that death and suffering might touch their lives. They also knew that they were heroically carrying a Christian tradition to the brink of consummation.

Of course, not all soldiers and war workers imagined the war in identical ways or held identical views about its Christian meaning. Some, like Clarence Lindner, Leo Jacks, and Kenneth MacLeish, emphasized the heroic Christian nature of the struggle. Others, like Marine aviator Walter Poague and African American war worker Addie Hunton, harbored doubts. Addie Hunton was one of only three African American women working to support African American troops in France during the war. She described her experiences with a mixture of excitement and dismay. Her dismay grew from the realization that Jim Crow segregation and racial discrimination had followed her and every African American to France. Her excitement sprang from the belief that war service would be a springboard to equality and would repair the United States' broken democracy.[40] This mixture of views and experiences led her to invert—not abandon—the crusade trope and to revise—not dismiss—the notion that the Great War was a redemptive enterprise. She wrote of herself and her companion Kathryn Johnson, "We were crusaders on a quest for Democracy! How and where would that precious thing be found?"[41] On Hunton's account, the task for the properly holy warrior was not to make the world safe for democracy, but rather to find true democracy and bring it back to a needy United States. America's crusade might well redeem the world from tyranny; in the process, she hoped, America itself would finally be redeemed.[42]

Walter Poague's understanding of crusading and redemption in the Great War was also complicated, though for different reasons. Poague attended Chicago's University High School and the University of Chicago before joining the Marines in June of 1917. After completing his training, Poague was sent to the Azores to fly seaplanes on anti-submarine missions. He was killed on November 5, 1918, six days before the Armistice, when the plane he was flying hit a sea wall. During his service, Walter Poague kept a diary and wrote letters to his family in Chicago. His writings include a range of voices on the topic of war and its redemptive potential. In an entry dated Sunday, January 13, 1918, Poague wrote not of Christian triumph and of a world made new, but of the senselessness of the war and of how warring was at odds with his aspirations. "I'm tired and blue, for the whole War is such a useless thing. I don't want to waste my time as I am doing—my years are too few. Art is too long, and this is all so useless and idle. Way down inside of me is a power that is bigger than I am. It's a good power for creative work and all this War business is killing it, and [is] senselessly useless."[43] While writing that Sunday, Poague imagined that his contributions to the world would come in the realm of art—poetry, must likely—and that war was taking him away from his life's work and possibly killing the very impulse that could drive him to create and do good. Four days later, though, he seems to have been feeling differently. Writing in his diary on Thursday, January 17, he noted he was not afraid of death "at least not yet," and that while he "love[d] life madly," death was truly a "splendid gamble." He appears to have been helped to this view, or at least the articulation of it, by the recently famous American war poet, Alan Seeger, whose poem "The Sultan's Palace" Poague then paraphrased ("I find no fear in death // No horror to abhor."). Perhaps Poague had realized that some members of his generation, Seeger for one, were finding in war just the vibrant muse they needed.

In mid-February of 1918, Poague wrote to his mother in a still different voice, this one much closer to MacLeish, Lindner, Jacks, and *The Stars and Stripes* (which, incidentally, he likely had not yet seen since it was first published in Paris on February 8, 1918). Poague's letter to his mother on her birthday announced "This is not a terrible war. It is the most wonderful war in the world. It is the war which means the real salvation of the world." Citing "eternal peace" as "the prize" for which he and others might give their lives, he proclaimed it was "a privilege to fight in such a war even if it takes valuable years." The letter contains nothing of his previous, ostensibly private skepticism; no rumblings of an internal battle between war and art. Instead, one hears only the major cords of Christian adventure and triumph epitomized in his pronouncement: "We are the truest Crusaders who ever lived."[44]

Poague presents an interesting case. His use of a wide range of voices in discussing the war could point one in many different directions. One could certainly argue that the letter sent to his mother is an "inauthentic" expression of his true feelings and reflects most clearly an attempt to put his mother and the military censors at ease. One could also follow Mark Meigs and Elaine Scarry in arguing that, though "authentic" in so far as it represents Poague's thoughts at that time, Poague's letter to his mother shows that the traumas of war (which had been comparatively mild for Poague) had rendered him an essentially passive receptacle for propaganda—a drone for the government and the military.[45] Yet it seems most accurate and most respectful to the complexity of soldiers' views of the war to hold that Poague (and many others like him) owned all of his opinions of war fully, or as fully as anyone can. War did seem a waste, a splendid gamble, and a true crusade. By serving in the Great War, he betrayed his muse, courted a hero's stature, and did his part to secure eternal peace. One day, the light could hit his corner of the war and show it to be an abysmal bore; another day it could appear to be "the most wonderful war in the world . . . the real salvation of the world." Put differently, Poague exemplifies the human tendency to harbor a variety of views of a person or an event and to hold those views in tension in spite of others' calls for consistency. Further, Poague expresses with beautiful precision the internal structure of the Great War as a religious experience. Lives would be wasted—Poague's life would be among them—and individual creative impulses snuffed out. Those confronting the potential loss of their own life did not, however, leave it at that; they reached for frameworks of meaning grand and simple to help them think about the broader implications of their own mortality. In some cases, death became a "splendid gamble" to be embraced and not feared; in others, it became a redemptive sacrifice for the prize of peace. In some cases death was both, and war was tragedy and triumph, horror and thrill all at once.

A War to Redeem the Nation

As the testimony of Addie Hunton indicates, the American women and men involved in the Great War did not all see America as a perfect nation. Hunton had ample reason to point to the United States' need for redemption, but she was far from the only one to do so. Some saw Wilson's reluctance to enter the war as sinful; others focused on a United States divided by ethnic diversity, sectionalism, and various other violations of God's will. Still others, Hunton among them, saw America's unwillingness to treat all citizens equally as a sin. For many of these men and women, American history, like Christian history, provided a rich vein of sacred images with which to relate war experiences to a grander framework of meaning—a framework of national redemption.

There is a distinctly jeremiadic tone to the public and private attempts of American soldiers and war workers to see themselves recapitulating and adding to sacred American history. Their words, like those of Edwin Abbey quoted earlier, indicate a sense of falleness and crisis at the same time that they reveal normative visions for American society as such and for America's place in the world. The vision of how American society ought to look and function shared much with John Winthrop's oft-cited sermon of 1630, *A Model of Christian Charity*, in which he noted that God had structured society hierarchically and smiled upon those who lived in harmony, according to this structure. "[W]e must be," he wrote, "knit together . . . as one man." Many hoped that the fires of war would burn away the divisions caused by immigration and sectionalism. Another common wartime vision of America in the world echoed Winthrop's description of the Massachusetts Bay Colony as a "City upon a Hill," a model for other nations, but went beyond this model and portrayed America as responsible for defending and promoting "American" values in the world. Having lost touch with or never fully understood this covenant, America could ratify its terms by fighting the Great War. In short, the war would redeem the war generation and their country from the sins of isolation and internal division, and might well launch an exciting new chapter in America's historically intimate relationship with God.

Such readings of the war were in keeping with widespread views of America as a society in crisis. People from a wide range of political and religious persuasions (progressives and anti-modernists, muscular Christians and Social Gospelers, proto-fundamentalists and Pentecostals) sensed that the early twentieth century was a time of crisis and at least impending decline. Many argued further that pervasive cultural "effeminacy" and over-civilization played a part in the deteriorating situation, and that going forth boldly to act would help place American society back on a track that would lead to vigorous leadership in the world.[46] The United States' claim of neutrality in the war's early stages, often attributed to Wilson alone, and widespread popular apathy drew the ire of two figures, Elizabeth Banks and Alan Seeger. Banks and Seeger were more cosmopolitan than most, but summarize nicely the nature of America's covenantal crisis.

Elizabeth Banks was a pioneering muckraking journalist who, though born and raised mostly in Wisconsin, made her career living and writing in England. In her memoir of wartime redemption, *The Remaking of an American*, Banks recalled her distress at American inaction in the years 1914–1916, her embarrassment at the cowardice of fellow London-based expatriates, and her own determination to seek the cause of America's tragic turn from the world. According to her memoir, the *New York Times* piece written about her journey back to the United States noted that Banks "refused to sail from England under the American flag because she considers that flag has shown its inability to protect those who have a right to protection." The article continued, noting that she had come to the United States "to see myself whether it was true that Uncle Sam had lost his spinal column."[47] In Banks' eyes, there was no such thing as principled neutrality. In the Great War, there were only noble warriors and feckless cowards.

Banks' travels took her to the American Midwest and West where she found, much to her disappointment and horror, that in 1915, whole swaths of the country appeared not to care about the Great War.[48] In a church not far from her childhood home in Wisconsin, she sat through hymns, prayers, and a sermon on the evils of Darwin, all of which she found trite. "The thing I had waited and watched and listened for did not come. I wanted to know if any mention would be made in prayer or sermon of the greatest war the world has ever known. There was nothing."[49] Banks made clear that this was no isolated incident. "In Michigan, Wisconsin, Illinois, the burden of the cry is . . . 'We've got nothing to do with it!' In the village churches, the people and the services are like unto those in the neighborhood of [my childhood home] Experiment Farm. The war is something afar and apart from these people, moderately prosperous, kindly, intelligent. They have no understanding of its causes or its issues and cannot be convinced at present that it will affect them." Elizabeth Banks was dismayed but remained curious enough to seek explanations. If rather rare in her desire to understand American neutrality, she was far from alone in her dissatisfaction with it.

The young American men who went to war of their own volition in 1914, 1915, and 1916—whom Banks would later exalt in a special editorial—also speculated in their letters and diaries as to whether America under President Wilson had lost touch with its sense of duty and right.[50] Was the land of freedom, liberty, and divine mandate really allowing evil to run roughshod over fraternal nations England and France? Was this acquiescence in the face of evil a failure of leadership or was it a sign of weakening national character? Alan Seeger's 1916 poem, "A Message to America" offered a diagnosis and a cure. While serving with the French Foreign Legion and, thus, already doing "his part," Seeger expressed concern that his nation had forgotten the principles for which it stood, and was losing credibility and honor worldwide by staying out of the war.

You have the grit and the guts, I know;
You are ready to answer blow for blow
You are virile, combative, stubborn, hard,
But your honor ends in your own back-yard;
Each man intent on his private goal,
You have no feeling for the whole. . . .
Unmindful that each man must share
The stain he lets his country wear. . . . [51]

America was like a talented prize fighter ignoring an attack on an innocent shopkeeper, justifying non-intervention in terms of selfish interest.[52]
This narrow and self-serving application of principle was, in Seeger's eyes,
sinful. And as clear to Seeger as the stain on the United States and its
citizens, was the solution that would remove it. "I would go through fire
and shot and shell / And face new perils and make my bed / In new privations if Roosevelt led." A leader prepared to fight and, more importantly,
intent on preparing the country to fight, would solve the problem in an
instant.[53] In the eyes of Seeger and Banks, America could only purge its
sin of omission through the redemptive act of war.

When America entered the war in April of 1917, and in the following
months, many American women and men both in France and preparing
to deploy wrote of relief, revival, and redemption. In so doing, they expressed beliefs similar to those of Banks and Seeger, that America had
been pursuing a course contrary to its appointed role in the world. Reactions like those of Esther Root, Vinton Dearing, and Thomas Slusser to
the American war effort are best read against the backdrop of America's
once sinful neutrality. Esther Root, who aided war refugees in Paris, wrote
on April 8, 1917 that the "long-waited-for news of our actually going to
war had rejoiced us all yesterday." The news brought a sizable number
of Americans in Paris to a "Patriotic Service" at the American Church.
She continued, "The American Church was full–men from the American
Ambulance Service sat in uniform in the front rows and the church was
decorated in flowers and flags. Dr. [Ernest W.] Shurtleff preached a fine
sermon. He said that to lose life was to gain it, and that this war was
fought that war should cease–that the world should know Christ's
peace."[54] Root bore witness to the feelings of thrill associated with war
and to one clergyman's attempt to cloak the war and America's entry in
Christian garb. When Root's friend and co-worker Marjorie Crocker finally saw American troops in Paris, however—when the war effort took
on a human face—she felt little urge to rejoice. Writing of the scene in a
July 4, 1917 letter, Crocker admitted, "I hate to think that our country
has come into it finally, and I couldn't help thinking all the time that these

men, who are walking down the streets so gayly [sic] now, will probably go to the front and be killed soon; what for?"[55]

Long after the American parade through Paris, though, optimism, revival, and redemption were on the minds of many American participants in the war effort. First Lieutenant Thomas A. Slusser, of the Thirty-second Division, demonstrated how thoroughly Christianity and Americanism could be woven together when he wrote to his wife of the redemption that war was accomplishing. In a letter from May of 1918, Slusser shared the belief that America had been sinfully slow in entering the war and predicted that God would not hesitate to show displeasure. "If it shall be that all of our chatter . . . and folly must be paid for with blood and tears, we as a people can only bow our heads and say to God who leads us through, 'Just and righteous are Thy Judgments altogether.'" He continued:

> American citizenship must mean something. It has come too easy. Perhaps the American people will only be brought to a realization of their blessings when they have gone through the Valley of the Shadow of Death. We value highly only those things that have cost us dearly. You remember the Roman Centurion who stood in awe before the Apostle Paul, who was a native born Roman citizen, and said, "This Citizenship I bought with a great price." It will be well if we feel so as a nation.[56]

There would be pain and there would be victory, Slusser wrote, ("We shall win for the righteousness of our cause is . . . certain.") and both would redeem the fools and chatterers from their ways while redeeming all from a watered-down sense of citizenship and nationhood. On June 3, 1918, infantry officer Vinton Dearing echoed Slusser, but without the minor chords. He wrote, "Oh, mother, what a lot has happened in the last five months! Isn't it a revelation how America has awakened! She surely is doing wonderful work here."[57] America's willingness to fight for "Right" signaled a renewal of the old covenant, and redemption from the general sins associated with non-involvement in a righteous struggle.

Many hoped that war would also bring redemption from the more specific "sins" of ethnic and regional division.[58] The strength of these hopes as well as the frequency of their articulation is testament both to the depth of the divisions that marked American society and to the concern within and without the government for how such division might undercut the war effort. America's burgeoning racial and ethnic diversity generated a tremendous amount of concern in the pre-war era. In the harshly assimilationist, "anti-hyphenate" sentiments of President Wilson, the mob violence against German-Americans, cultural reassertions of the superiority of Anglo-Saxon masculinity, and the attraction of the newly popularized "melting pot" image, one sees reflected the fear that, if left "untreated," diversity would bring weakness or destruction to America.[59] The nation was rather clearly not, in John Winthrop's words, "knit together . . . as one man." But war offered a way back to the mythic days of covenanted harmony. It also allowed men and women of diverse ethnicities the chance to "own" the America covenant and promised to dissolve the significant cultural differences that so concerned America's custodians of culture. President Wilson himself publicly anticipated a "more perfect union" forged by war.[60]

A clear articulation of war's ability to make immigrants into covenanted Americans came from *The Stars and Stripes* editorials published on May 3 and May 10, 1918. The first editorial described a quasi-baptismal moment in the war involving a "Russian Pole" by the name of Frank Savicki. Savicki, the editorialist explained, had escaped from a German prisoner of war camp and, in fleeing to Switzerland, encountered one final obstacle, a stream, between him and freedom. He readily swam the stream and emerged "not Frank Savicki the Russian Pole . . . [but] Frank Savicki, the American."[61] The piece proclaimed further that "those who used to talk of 'da old-a-country' " were now united with sons of the settlers, fighting on behalf of "the ever new country, the ageless country, that draws all manner of men from all manner of races to itself, and makes them proud and glad to champion its cause, to give their toil and blood to that cause's furtherance."[62] The second editorial, published one week later, showed that this new, diverse, covenanted community could fight effectively against the heathen. Reading through the list of "117 men of the 104 Infantry who were decorated with the Croix de Guerre for the fight they fought at Apremont Wood" the author wrote, "[gives] fresh evidence of how infinite is the variety of that blend of peoples which we call America." The list of names included Desvalles, Murphy, Levine, Christiansen, Waskewich, Weiser, Amaral, Penn, Perednea, Stefanick, Donnissoni. "Why," the author continued, "it reads like a roll call of the peoples of the world." The list was also a testament. "It was all the world that went to war with Germany when America came in."[63] According to *The Stars and Stripes*, war both revealed the consensus of diverse peoples against German barbarity, and demonstrated the ultimate and essential unity of the American people. The United States faced many internal challenges, but the age-old covenant could be renewed, expanded, and resanctified through the violence of war. As stylized and contrived as these editorials may seem, they reflect a long-standing belief in the relationship between service, manhood, and citizenship—a view reflected frequently in the personal writings of American soldiers and war workers.

As Elizabeth Banks watched A.E.F. units parade through London's Trafalgar Square, she and some of her fellow onlookers found the ethnic diversity of the group jarring. But the diversity seemed to Banks momentous. She saw something new and hopeful. "As line after line passed, I scanned the men's faces. Now I know what had made me almost jump in my surprise when I had seen the first line. It was that they looked like a new race, difficult, indeed, impossible, to name."[64] The fires of war would indeed be the ultimate melting pot.

At the same time that they argued for war as a solvent of hyphenate Americanism, the editors of *The Stars and Stripes*—and much of its readership—had to confront the fact that the memory of war in America was itself divisive along regional lines. Barely fifty years prior to the Great War, the nation had been torn by a civil war framed on both sides, ironically, as a noble effort to keep the terms of the United States' covenant. War could unite, to be sure, but war had rather recently and horrifically divided. In 1917, memories of the American Civil War could still evoke powerful emotions as the tumultuous release of D. W. Griffith's 1915 *The Birth of a Nation* amply demonstrated. Those who thought that regional tensions between "white" Americans had been laid to rest learned how easily "dead" hatreds could be reanimated when state-based National Guard units were called into federal service and brought together for training. Albert Ettinger, a private in New York's Fighting Sixty-ninth, recalled one confrontation between members of New York– and Alabama-based regiments. While the units were training at Camp Mills, Ettinger wrote, the Alabamians took exception to the presence in camp of the "Fifteenth New York Guard (Negro)." They harassed and picked fights with the African American unit and with members of the white Sixty-ninth.[65] As tensions increased, members of the African American unit were required to surrender their ammunition, but violence erupted anyway when members of the Alabama unit attempted to attack and tear down the New York unit's camps. Ettinger described a scene in which the military police of the Sixty-ninth had to "fix bayonets" and drive the Alabamians back.[66] The white senior officers and soldiers of the Fifteenth New York found themselves in the middle of many potentially explosive situations both on base and off while training at Camp Wadsworth near Spartanburg, South Carolina, and were only too happy when the orders came sending them first to Camp Mills (and the tension with the Alabama unit) and then on to war.[67]

Memorial Day, 1918, gave *The Stars and Stripes'* editors a chance to reflect on the connection between their moment and the Civil War—to imagine the Great War as at once a recapitulation of the noble aspects, and a redemption from the sinful aspects of that conflict. To this end, the paper ran an illustration on the front page of the May 24, 1918 issue, titled "In France–Memorial Day, 1918." Above the text of the Gettysburg Address was a large illustration of Uncle Sam and Lady Liberty, heads bowed, holding a wreath with a ribbon that read "1861–1865 and 1917–1918." Behind them stood the ghost of Abraham Lincoln with a hand outstretched to bless the scene. (See figure 1.3.) The messages of this tableau were that sacrifice for the nation had been and continued to be noble, that the call of duty was sacred, and that to heed this call as Union and Confederate soldiers had, was to share in a sacred American tradition. This set of images was, however, as complicated as the war it invoked. The very presentation raised painful, perhaps incendiary, questions even as it asked the children and grandchildren of victors and vanquished to forgive and forget. Had the Confederates once been the equivalent of the anti-Christian Hun? Was the cause for which they had once fought and died as demonstrably Satanic as the German cause? Were sacrifices made to sunder the Union and preserve slavery equal in value to those made to preserve the Union and end slavery? Had the editors reflected on the divisive potential of their Memorial Day tableau or given thought to the commentary it provided on wartime assertions of absolute good and absolute evil, they might have filed it away. Instead, they worked to establish that the storied Civil War and the Great War were of equal gravity, and implied that this new war would redeem the nation from its past sins.[68]

Widespread belief in war's redemptive powers might have been tempered by the divisive and volatile issue of racial discrimination. Though inextricably bound up in understandings of region, racial "troubles" proved far from regionally contained in the second decade of the twentieth century. Jim Crow, share cropping, and lynch law were powerfully Southern phenomena, but the consciousness of racial hierarchy that undergirded each was increasingly drawn forth in the North by the redistribution of the African American population during the war years. As whole communities of African Americans moved from the rural South to the urban North in search of "the Promised Land" of economic opportunity and at least a measure of racial harmony, white northerners confronted new neighbors with old prejudices and mob actions that seemed to shock all involved.[69] Deadly riots in East St. Louis, Illinois and tensions between black soldiers in training and the community of Des Moines, Iowa where their segregated training camp was established, put the lie to treatments of race as a "Southern" problem.

White Americans were, however, not particularly interested in redemption from the many "sins" of racial discrimination. Government officials chose to segregate African American troops in undertrained, undersupplied, underfunded "Negro" units and, in most cases, sent them to France to work as stevedores and in burial parties.[70] As noted earlier, white ambivalence over African American service was nothing new. White Ameri-

Figure 1.3. Uncle Sam and Lady Liberty bow their heads while holding a wreath labeled "1861–65, 1917–18." The ghost of Abraham Lincoln offers his blessing from the background. This front-page illustration from the Memorial Day 1918 issue of *The Stars and Stripes* used sacred American figures, a martyr President, and the memory of the Civil War dead to sanctify the struggles and deaths of American soldiers and war workers. While clearly an attempt to unify the American Expeditionary Force and infuse their fight with national religious meaning, the artist's use of Lincoln would also certainly have reminded some of division and defeat. Image courtesy of the University of Illinois Library.

can men had not been prepared in 1865 to grant that African American men were their equals, and were no more ready in 1918. Still, African American heroism was war news. When Henry Johnson and Needham Roberts, two New York–born soldiers fighting with the 369th Regiment under French Army command, were awarded the Croix de Guerre for repelling a German raid on their trench, *The Stars and Stripes* put the story on the front page. But the paper tempered the tale of heroism with racist language internal to the article and with racist imagery elsewhere in the same issue. The Johnson/Roberts headline read, "Two Black Yanks Smear 24 Huns; Big Secret Out / *Station Porter* and *Elevator Boy* Win Croix de Guerre / Negro Unit In Trenches / Great Boast Is That They Don't Need Lampblack for Patrol Work." As if the front-page assertion of the relevance of the African American soldiers' home-front professions wasn't insulting enough (you may be a war hero now, but you will always be an elevator boy), a mere four pages later *The Stars and Stripes* ran a photo of two smiling African American soldiers, leaning out of a train window, with the caption, "Yais, suh; we's de cooks, we is. We's de vittlers on de hos-pittlers train, dat's what we is. What's dait? What's our names? Whah, bless yo' soul, honey, we ain't got no names. Dey all calls us 'de Gold Dust Twins!' "[71] (See figure 1.4.) Needham Roberts and Henry Johnson had encountered war and emerged triumphant, but contrary to hopes for permanent advancement based on the "opportunities and advantages which our race acquired" in the war—hopes expressed by Emmett J. Scott, W.E.B. Du Bois, James Weldon Johnson, and others—"white" America and the American Expeditionary Force viewed Roberts' and Johnson's triumphs and sacrifices, and those of thousands of other African American soldiers, through a thickly, relentlessly racist lens.[72]

A War to Redeem the Soldier

American soldiers and war workers hoped that their sacrifices and struggles would redeem a fallen world, unite a fractured country, and bring a just and lasting peace. Whether imagining themselves as crusaders against the Hun, owners of a new national covenant, Civil War soldiers, or craftsmen of eternal peace, soldiers invested the outcomes of war with tremendous religious significance. But there was also a dimension of the redemptive effects of war that had little to do with the achievement of particular religio-political goals. Soldiers and war workers of all ranks and races wrote frequently of their war experiences as individually redemptive *as such*. Encountering combat, weathering the storm, exerting oneself in new ways and to new extremes, they wrote, revealed new truths, and transformed atrophied souls. War, they wrote, revealed the insignificance

JES' DE TWO OF US

Yais, suh; we's de cooks, we is. We's de vittlers on de hos-spittlers train, dat's what we is.

What's dait? What's our names? Whah, bless yo' soul, honey, we ain't got no names. Dey all calls us "de Gold Dust Twins!"

Figure 1.4. In the same May 24, 1918 issue of *The Stars and Stripes* that used Lincoln, Liberty, and Uncle Sam to connect the Great War and the Civil War came front-page reports of the battlefield heroics of African American soldiers Henry Johnson and Needham Roberts. The paper's staff published a photo and commentary that offset news of black soldiers' martial exploits and demonstrated the A.E.F.'s enduring concern for racial hierarchy. Soldiers who may have been upset that black men were being tested in the trenches were reminded that not all familiar roles had been abandoned. Image courtesy of the University of Illinois Library.

of individuals and, therefore, of distinctions among them; how one stood up to combat was, likewise, indicative of one's true nature.

Belief in the redemptive power of war was abroad in early-twentieth-century America. The words of Theodore Roosevelt are particularly illuminating. In a rhetorical flourish, the Rough Rider juxtaposed the insufficient, insufficiently patriotic, shrinking man with the stern man of military and imperial vision.

The timid man, the lazy man, the man who distrusts his country, the over-civilized man, who has lost the great fighting, masterful virtues . . . whose soul is incapable of feeling the mighty lift that thrills stern men with empires in their brains–all of these, of course, shrink from seeing the nation undertake its new duties; shrink from seeing us build a navy and an army adequate to our needs . . . I preach to you then, my countrymen, that our country calls not for the life of ease but for the life of strenuous endeavor. . . . Let us therefore boldly face the life of strife, resolute to do our duty well and manfully.[73]

The river that separated the slacker from the true American—that baffled the soul of one while nourishing the soul of the other—was the "mighty life" of "strenuous endeavor." Young men's organizations, American literature, and popular culture oozed with the mythology of militarism and violence. In individual and group activities and renderings of battles past, present, and looming, "true men" were those bold enough to leave the constraining structure and familiarity of society, returning only after developing and exercising their "savagery" on an imagined frontier.[74] In a world viewed as existentially, physically, and religiously restrictive, soldiers and their spokesmen treated the male camaraderie and the adventures and strains of war as metaphorically, sometimes truly, salvific.[75]

The young American women and men who volunteered or were drafted to serve in the Great War had heard from an early age that war and the life of the warrior burned away the accretions of over-civilization and *transformed* men, giving them a deeper understanding of themselves, their friends, and God.[76] An editorial cartoon published on May 10, 1918 in *The Stars and Stripes*, captured and conveyed one of the "finer realities" of war by depicting the many ways that preparation for war revealed a man's true character.[77] The cartoon depicted seven young men "before" and "after" entering the army. The army reveals a "civilized" man who wore padded clothes to be, in truth, scrawny and weak; a well-coiffed man to be, in reality, unsightly with his head shaved; an apparently fat man fills out a uniform quite well; and two clearly wealthy men become vulnerable and humble once their fancy clothes and facial hair are removed. (See figure 1.5.) These public embodied examples of war's presumed power to reveal essences harmonize well with the sentiments of individual participants in the war effort.[78]

Serving refreshments to soldiers just out of combat, canteen worker Marian Baldwin wrote on October 4, 1918, "Artificiality was for once forgotten, every one was dealing simply and unconsciously with the elemental things of life and no one was ashamed of wearing his heart on his sleeve." Wearing hearts on sleeves allowed men to evaluate not only those

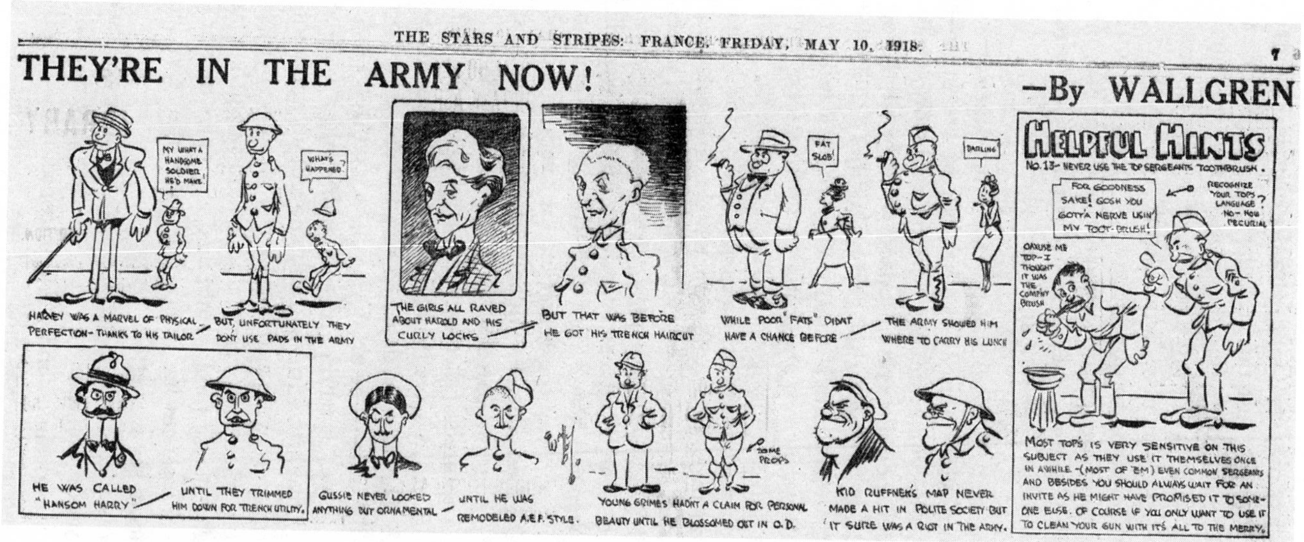

Figure 1.5. This cartoon from the May 10, 1918 issue of *The Stars and Stripes* shows the many ways that war service reveals essences. The trappings of wealth and class, such as fancy clothing, styled hair, and other adornments are removed, revealing the true and vulnerable state of their wearers. By contrast, war service reveals those less attractive in civilian life to be true and virile men. Image courtesy of the University of Illinois Library.

around them, but themselves as well. William Thomas of Richmond, Virginia was a private in the Thirty-sixth Regiment of the African American Ninety-second Division. Reflecting on the "mental effects" of combat, he wrote that he had learned "There was more metal [sic] than I really thought I possessed myself."[79] Infantry officer Vinton Dearing, writing to his "sister" Peggy on March 5, 1918 expressed his belief in the personal revelations that war forced: "We get the real thing here as regards uncovering what men are made of. We all have our petty failures, but whether we have the stuff that stands under real strain proves in the end. May your brother have this when the time comes."[80] War was the ultimate test, the true revealer and gauge of one's "stuff."

The potentially subversive power of this view of war experience, hinted at in *The Stars and Stripes* cartoon's pictures of class inversion, is also evident in the words of "Rick," an acquaintance of *New Republic* writer Elizabeth Shepley Sergeant, and Christopher Watts, a sergeant in the 369th Regiment of the African American Ninety-third Division. Rick, a pilot who was thoroughly convinced that war was "the only reality amidst all the pale mirages of experience I have known" told Sergeant "I never knew what brotherhood was before. Never really got outside my class. War is human. It's more than that—it defies human relations."[81] War upset that which was static and called into question things once accepted. Christopher Watts agreed with Rick and with *The Stars and Stripes*, though to ends that the paper, at least, would not have supported. His experiences in combat taught him that "all men are the same."[82] While *The Stars and Stripes* published plenty of material that showed the wealthy and favored cut down to size, it was unwilling to question prevailing notions of racial hierarchy.

But war did more than simply reveal. American participants in the Great War claimed that war transformed and redeemed. Those who approached it, wrote Hervey Allen, Francis Reed Austin, Isabel Anderson, James Lark, and Julia Stimson, would almost certainly be changed.[83] Hervey Allen, an officer in the Twenty-eighth Infantry described an encounter with a comrade, Lieutenant Shenkel, that made the transformative power of combat abundantly clear. Allen had not yet seen action, but Shenkel had just returned. Allen noticed immediately that his friend was changed. He wrote, "Shenkel was still alive by a series of miracles. His face was flushed, and his eyes wide and brilliant with excitement. He was a different man. Something had come to him which had not yet come to us. It was the trial of battle. No one who passes through that is ever quite the same again."[84] In Allen's account, the effects of having experienced the "trial of battle" loom larger than the tale of the action itself. Shenkel had not merely fought and survived, he had been perceptibly added to and transformed. That which had transformed him, "the trial of battle," remained a mystery in everything but the knowledge—the faith—that "[n]o one who passes through . . . is ever quite the same again."[85]

Francis Reed Austin recorded his thoughts on the benefits of combat as he, like Allen, stood on the edge of war. He relished the chance to wage a righteous war and be refined by it. "To-night I am going up to the *Front Line for my first real time*, and I assure you it is very fine to be so near and to have the chance to stand up for the ideals I believe in and be on the side of Right and Justice." American soldiers weren't only on the side of Right and Justice, he continued, they were themselves right and just. In the same pen stroke, Austin reflected on the individual purifications that war would accomplish. Those whose selflessness and self-sacrifice had brought them to the edge of civilization would be purified even further by the fire.

> Believe me, I am proud to be an American, because there never could be a more unselfish cause than the one Uncle Sam has openly supported to the limit. His boys have come over with absolutely one idea,–namely, to crush cruelty, barbarism, and make the world a happier, safer, and more peaceful place to live in, and then return home to their loved ones and leave untouched what there they found with "Freedom to Worship God." I know these men will return finer, cleaner, straighter men.[86]

For Austin as for many, war promised to build a stronger America not only by unifying the nation in an act of selfless goodness, but by strengthening and purifying individual Americans.[87] African American soldier James Lark testified that he too had been "refined" by war. Lark, a graduate of the University of Chicago and teacher in the Richmond area, looked back on his service in the medical department of the 336th Labor Battalion and wrote, "I have a wider view of life. . . . I have a deeper love and respect for mankind."[88]

Julia Stimson saw the same redemptive effects among the nurses whom she led to war. Stimson left her native St. Louis and her job as Superintendent of Nurses at Washington University when her Red Cross nursing unit was mobilized for the war. She brought her team of nurses into the war zone, became the Chief Nurse in British Hospital Number 12, and was eventually named Chief Nurse of the American Red Cross in Paris. Stimson wrote letters regularly during her service, often reflecting on the enormity of the events in which she and her unit were involved. Writing on December 8, 1917, she emphasized the benefits, indeed the blessing, of war service. "I believe there is more real peace on earth in men's and women's hearts now in the midst of this world turmoil than has ever been known before. . . . Oh I wish I could tell you what all this is meaning as I see it. . . . We talk about it from time to time, some of us, . . . and oh, dear people, no greater thing can ever come into any one's life than this chance of ours–to get away from little things and self and to know what the things of the Spirit are, and what true values really are."[89] War's revelation of the insignificance and impermanence of "little things and self" and the contrasting greatness and permanence of the Spirit and Truth could not but change her. (The title of Stimson's memoir, *Finding Themselves*, indicates she believed she was speaking for her unit in describing war's revelatory, redemptive power.)

Did soldiers and war workers view the transformations of which they wrote as *de facto* religious? Certainly not. To borrow a phrase from Rudolf Otto, the transformation was "a sort of shadow or subjective reflection" cast by diverse soldiers and war workers standing in the flashing light battle.[90] But their collective "shadow" indicates both an expectation and an experience of moral refinement, physical and mental development, and, as indicated already, an improved ability to discern both true natures and Truth.

American soldiers and war workers expected redemption from war. They expected to redeem through war. They fought and served within a vast framework in which their experiences of service, suffering, and death were profoundly meaningful. Aspects of the war were indeed intoxicating, rejuvenating, and fully compatible with Progressive muscular Christian notions of the benefits of struggle. Other aspects of the war, sometimes a different side of the same coin, could provide more difficult lessons about efficacy, progress, and "redemption." Among the many experiences of war that might have undermined this framework, soldiers' and war workers' encounters with the industrialized violence of the Western Front was potentially the most devastating. Chapter 2 will focus on their attempts to theologize this violence.

CHAPTER TWO

Chance the Man-Angel
and the Combat Numinous

> The daemonic-divine object may appear to the mind an object of
> horror and dread, but at the same time it is no less something that
> allures with a potent charm, and the creature, who trembles
> before it, utterly cowed and cast down, has always at the same
> time the impulse to turn to it, nay even to make it somehow his
> own. The "mystery" is for him not merely something to be
> wondered at but something that entrances him; and beside that
> in it which bewilders and confounds, he feels something that
> captivates and transports him with a strange ravishment, rising
> often enough to the pitch of dizzy intoxication.[1]
> —RUDOLF OTTO, *The Idea of the Holy*

THIS CHAPTER EXAMINES two kinds of reflections on combat common
among soldiers and war workers. The first type consists of attempts to
answer the question of design in a world where devastating violence shattered some and not others. The second—touched upon in the previous
chapter—includes descriptions of battle as invigorating and revelatory.
Theories of battlefield order and beliefs in battlefield redemption are
linked, I will argue, by the Great War's diminution of the individual—by
its myriad, often devastating, assertions that individuals were not in control. American soldiers and war workers could have found in this wartime
catechesis a dramatic refutation of Progressive-Era celebrations of the individual and individual efficacy. They could have cursed the modern war
machines that depersonalized killing and death. Instead, they often wrote
of finding in radical objectification an experience of Truth and religious
invigoration. Thoughts that move clearly in the direction of human inef-
ficacy in the Great War resolve themselves, finally, in a belief in the redemptive power of momentary powerlessness.[2]

When historians of the American experience of the Great War have
considered soldiers' and war workers' reflections on the nature and design
of modern warfare, they have noted a rupture between the combat soldiers imagined and the combat they experienced. Both David Kennedy
and Jennifer Keene describe the industrialized depersonalized violence of
the Western Front as jarring to soldiers and tell of struggles to reconcile

this reality with mythic notions of combat; they treat those struggles as basically pathological, as exercises in denial.[3] According to Keene: "Few combatants squarely confronted the irrationality of their situation, in which men died indiscriminately every day. Many remained adamant in believing that order could be discerned in the chaos of frontline life."[4] Soldiers and war workers were clearly shocked by the machines and materials that tore flesh, shattered bone, and wrought death, but their attempts to make sense of their violent world were other than simple denial. These efforts were theological.

To describe soldiers' attempts to order their chaotic and deadly world without some sensitivity to the religiousness of that task is to grasp only partially their experiences and the effects of those experiences on individual men and women, and on their culture more broadly. By attending to the ways that soldiers expressed helplessness and impotence, by attempting to make sense of the multivalent language they used when they wrote of omnipotence and the ordering principles responsible for death or survival, we can begin to understand why they also wrote of the transforming thrill of confronting such forces and, after the war, wrote longingly of their experiences. Scholars and students can certainly read these texts as evidence of denial or self-deception. But such readings are in their own way superficial and reductive. When death strikes suddenly on the battlefield or off, during war or during peace, few concern themselves with material causes alone. To say that a bullet, a bomb, an illness, or an accident killed someone is to provide, at best, a partial answer. Many think and ask further: Why did this happen? Why now? Why him? Soldiers' answers to these profoundly human questions, their attempts to engage the "irrational," asserted and defended the meaningfulness of life and death and war in the moments when meaning was most in jeopardy.[5] The identification of an ordering principle that governed life and death in war was their response to war's unpredictability and death's persistence in the face of earnest efforts to ward it off. Theologizing combat was, most importantly, a preemptive assertion of meaning in the face of deaths that might be deemed avoidable or, worse, meaningless.

THE DESIGNER: WAR'S QUESTION, SOLDIERS' ANSWERS

Speculation as to the design of combat was virtually inevitable given the conditions under which soldiers fought and died in the Great War. Only the narrowest of margins separated those who lived to tell about the war from those who did not. Shells launched from miles away, heard but not seen, reduced some men to pieces of flesh and bone while leaving those merely yards away soiled but physically unscathed. Snipers killed single targets from great distances and spared those nearby. Pilots finished missions and turned perfectly functioning aircraft over to others, only to watch both crash to the earth seconds later, brought down by a catastrophic failure.[6] Death "chose" some and not others. Privates Wayne A. French of the Fifth Regiment, U.S. Marines and Larry Wolff of the 319th Machine Gun Battalion were both wounded in the summer of 1918, but lived to recount the moments at which death missed them by inches. French wrote, "Well, I was wounded by a H[igh] E[xplosive] shell while coming out of Belleau Wood. The same shell killed my best friend, within reach of my hand."[7] Private Wolff's experience was similar. He and some fellow soldiers took cover under a bridge during an artillery barrage. Wolff wrote, "I was standing in among a few fellows, when a shell hit a Buddy of mine and he fell into the stream. Yet I, who stood right beside him, escaped injury. I don't understand it, but those are the mysterious things that happen in war."[8]

In attempting to make sense of death and survival in war, soldiers and war workers asked the obvious questions: How did I survive? Why did I survive? The answers to these questions began to emerge as the questions were asked. In their answers, we frequently see soldiers lifting their eyes and minds above the immediate and obvious answers—a well-aimed bullet or shell, a well-timed attack or overzealous commander—and offering deeper, more theological explanations. But who, if not the combatants and their weapons, was responsible for death? Who decided who would live and who would die?

Many soldiers testified that God was the author of individual fates in combat; that it was God who was everywhere at work. Edmund Genet was the great-great-grandson of "Citizen Genet," an infamous French ambassador to the United States, recalled in 1793 for political indiscretions. High-minded though the namesake was, he too involved himself in scandal. Genet's enthusiasm for war led him to desert the United States Navy in 1915, make his way to New York City, and to book passage to France intending to join the French Foreign Legion. Waiting to sail, Genet wrote to his mother to thank her for the cross she had sent him, and to let her know that he had a copy of the New Testament. He added, "God will take care of me, Mother. I trust in Him with all my heart and soul. May he keep you well and safe and happy and guide me back to you some day. I am not afraid if He sees fit to take me. I am His and He will do with me as He sees fit." Once in France, Genet, of Catholic and Quaker blood but a practicing Episcopalian, continued to write his mother letters filled with references to divine guidance and providence.[9] Two letters, one dated December 22, 1915, and one dated January 19, 1916, capture his beliefs regarding the "designer" before and after a costly engagement. Genet expected that he and his unit of the French Foreign Legion would spend Christmas *en repose*, but they were, instead, sent forward into the lines. Having marched through rain and mud and cold to a forward position, he wrote to his mother a letter that could have been his last. In it, he enjoined her, "And *DON'T* worry about me. If God means me to die fighting for France worry isn't going to keep me alive."[10] Genet survived the battle, but only barely. He and fellow Legionnaires came under an artillery attack, which Genet recounted for his mother.

> Somehow we felt that huge shell coming; how, I don't know, but we all just threw ourselves flat into the mud. If I had been one little hundredth of a second late I wouldn't be telling the tale now. I felt that monster hurl directly over my head; the intake of air raised me at least an inch out of the mire which I was gripping with every finger and with all my might. The shell burst not more than three yards behind me and killed four of the section and wounded several others. My heart had one of the quickest jumps of its life.

His survival, Genet continued, was not due to reflex or luck. "I thanked God then and there for His mercy and He must have heard me, for no other shells came our way though they kept bursting to our left among the Second Regiment in endless numbers."[11]

A. L. Bartley also testified to God's authorship of life and death. Bartley recalled the experience of combat quite graphically: "the thunderous explosions, the fumes of gas, the cries of the wounded, the wading through the blood of our fallen comrades and trampling on bits of their flesh scattered here and there, all combined to form a perfect hell on earth." He then attributed his survival with great certitude to his mother and his God. "There is no shadow of a doubt in my mind that Mother was at that moment asking God to protect and care for her son and although we were thousands of miles apart her prayer was answered, for no human effort could protect a man through such a downpour of bullets, shells, shrapnel and gas as was showered upon us during this drive . . . "[12] Genet and Bartley encountered the "hell" of battle and survived. When violence and destruction overwhelmed them and "no human effort could protect a man," they wrote, the grace of God kept them alive.

Soldiers and war workers were not, however, bound by the language and ideas of a particular religious tradition in imagining the author of their fates. Many wrote of alternate designing principles. Soldiers who attributed death and survival to "luck," "chance," and "fate" stepped away from explicitly Christian understandings of the designer, but not always from the belief that some principle was in control. Writing to his wife in December of 1917, one Major Denig of the Marine Corps described the art of survival in the trenches, "If you are out [in the trenches] you keep to the enemy's side and trust to luck."[13] As far as Denig was concerned, luck determined life and death. If luck was with a solider, he lived; if it was not, he died. Reflecting on the death of his friend Greayer Clover in a letter to Clover's parents, James Crowe invoked an all-powerful "chance": "If so good a flyer as Greayer had to fall I know that it is all chance and what happened to him may happen to any of us, any time."[14] Chance either favored a person or not; the evidence of its blessing was, to Crowe, unmistakable. "Fate" was another widely acknowledged author of life and death on the battlefield. Soldiers and war workers, such as John Kautz, acknowledged the power of Fate in their frequent discussions of fatalism. Kautz, who served as a camion driver in the American Field Service hauling weapons and supplies to French forces, wrote in his diary on July 3, 1917, "I suppose we are all to become fatalists by now with regard to life and death. It is well, for the philosophy will let us love each day with all the fervor in us, and it leaves no place for cowardice."[15] Kautz's opinion was shared by the anonymous author of *A Red Triangle Girl in France*, a collection of letters written by a female canteen worker with the YMCA. She asked her correspondent to tell "G." not to worry about her fiancée, "So far as the actual fighting and falling goes, one must turn into a fatalist. It's the only way."[16] Vinton Dearing wrote to his mother of the "great spirit" of fatalism the soldiers in France developed, making clear to her how liberating belief in "fate" could be. "The soldier . . . says there is a shell over in Germany with his name on it, and when that comes there is no use dodging it, for it will find him out in the deepest dugout, but until it comes, what is the use worrying about the rest of them."[17] Fate chose the time and place of one's death and always kept its appointments.

One could divide these views of the designer of life and death in war into "theistic" and "non-theistic" answers. By such a dichotomy, the soldiers who looked outside the created order for controlling principles were "theologians" and those who looked within it were "philosophers."[18] But such a distinction, when applied to this group of laity, is problematic for at least two reasons. First, distinctions between theism and non-theism rely on language, and soldiers' and war workers' descriptions of the design of death and life in battle often mixed terms and concepts such as God and fate to such a degree that it is impossible to determine which they saw as primary. Luck, Chance, and Fate bore "earthly" names but acted in god-like ways. Second, such a distinction does not acknowledge the capacity of some lay men and women to embrace "theological" and "philosophical" answers simultaneously. In addition to his letter-perfect definition and praise of fatalism, Vinton Dearing also wrote to his mother, "I thoroughly believe that God has a way of working things out for the best, and though lots of us have to suffer in our own individual way, it is all for the best."[19] These words indicate that Dearing, the son of Baptist missionary parents, lived in a world large enough for both God and fate as he understood them. The fatalism described by the "Red Triangle Girl" as "the only way" was also not all-encompassing. She discussed fatalism exactly two pages after describing a flood of "sixty or seventy" "superstitious" pilots who asked her to sew their wings onto their uniforms. The reason, she explained, was that "none of 'my' aviators have been hurt."[20] Calm resignation to one's fate and a rather more activist indulgence of superstitions could and did inhabit the same mind.

Hamilton Coolidge described a cosmic gumbo that also points quite clearly to the problems with a too rigid differentiation between "theistic" and "non-theistic" designers. Coolidge was a pilot who enjoyed great success in training and combat, and advanced quickly to the rank of captain. One day, a slight puff of wind separated the rudder from the tail of an aircraft he had just landed. Such a failure in flight would have resulted in a loss of control and, almost certainly, a fatal crash. He wrote to his mother on April 14, 1918.

> I do seem to live with a horseshoe around my neck, though. It's all luck and God's good will whether one lives or dies, so why worry, that's the way I look at it. . . . Heaven only knows why [the rudder] waited till I came down before coming off. That's only one of the six cases like it, but it illustrates the kind of incident that develops a fatalistic point of view and strangely enough it has just the opposite effect of making one worry. It merely inspires a calm feeling of dependence on one's Maker![21]

Both "luck" and "God" were at work in Coolidge's world. That the rudder of his plane held through the tremendous force of acrobatics only to snap in a gentle breeze once he had landed could have been the work of either or both. Similar equipment failures, both harmless and fatal, were, he wrote, commonplace and led those affected by them to "a fatalistic point of view." But the presence of fatalism did not push God from the picture. Instead, Coolidge was moved "strangely enough" to "a calm feeling of dependence on [his] Maker[.]" It seems likely that Coolidge saw God as the author of life and death and wrote of horseshoes and luck neither as a legitimate means of influencing outcomes nor as competing or subordinate principles. Yet the fact that his theistic order allowed for the mention of both and, as described by Coolidge, resulted in "a fatalistic point of view," ought to warn those who might approach these terms with fully developed assumptions regarding their theological valences.

A soldier or war worker did not have to be explicitly theistic in the traditional Christian sense to believe that a designer was behind life and death in combat. The Christian God certainly fit well into the role but had equally omnipotent counterparts—Chance, Luck, and Fate—on the Western Front. The handiwork of all these forces demanded comment and reflection. And in moving from thoughts about the identity of the designer to reflections on the reach of the design, soldiers again blurred the boundaries between God and other principles. Those who identified themselves as Christian often used language that obfuscated their Christianity, while those whose writings contain little or no religious sentiment could write with a convert's conviction of the omnipotence of Chance or Fate.

THE REACH OF DESIGN

Edwin Abbey, the Philadelphia native who fought and died with a Canadian unit at Vimy Ridge, provided a clearly Christian account of the reach and power of a designing principle. He harbored no doubt as to God's influence on life and death. "Life, here, is such a feeble little thing, so uncertain from hour to hour, that one cannot help knowing that it is a gift and entirely in God's hands."[22] Christian Blumenstein captured another expression of this belief in his account of the first talk his company commander gave to the troops after embarking for France. The commander, Captain Prentice, invoked the image of the Book of Life when discussing the question of design with his war-bound men. "Here is the way I look at it: If your name is written down in that Big Book up above, you are not coming back, and if your name is not down in that book, you can go through hell snapping and cracking, and you will live through it all."[23] Though using different language and invoking different images, Abbey and Prentice voiced similar sentiments: God's design for individual fates in battle is *all determining*.

Those who believed God's plan to be all controlling offered one Christian, or Judeo-Christian, explanation of the relationship between the divine will and personal fates in war. They did not, however, exhaust all "Christian" and "non-Christian" approaches and terminologies. As noted earlier, Vinton Dearing set forward a near perfect definition of fatalism: ("[T]here is a shell over in Germany with [a soldier's] name on it, and when that comes there is no use dodging it . . . but until it comes, what is the use worrying about the rest of them."[24]) while also professing belief that God was "working things out for the best." Dearing was sure, as were others according to his account, that death and survival depended *entirely* on a principle, Fate, described as the personalization of an artillery shell that could not be altered once set in motion. Whether consciously distancing God from a war that was claiming his friends, or simply relying on and relaying what was common parlance, Dearing appears to have been comfortable with the existence and operation of a God-like principle whose reach was unavoidable, even in "the deepest dugout."

Belief in an all-encompassing design, a kind of wartime double-predes-tinarianism, was not only the province of the explicitly Christian, or even of practicing Christians writing in a more generally applicable idiom. Some American soldiers who went to war with no identifiable faith and who were not inclined to see God's hand in the war as a larger enterprise, came to recognize an order to life and death that was immutable and everywhere in force. In his memoir, Hervey Allen described his belief in a principle of design that, though inscrutable, was all determining. Allen and his men, under intense artillery fire, found their fates governed not by a guiding Lord, but by "chance."

> [W]hite-faced men digging like mad or standing up under it according to the temperament–some cool, some shaking, some weeping; a few grim jokes, but mostly dull endurance; a hunching of the shoulders when another comes, and the thought–"How long, how long?" There is nothing to do. Whether you get through or not is just sheer chance and nothing more. You may and you may not.[25]

The design in this case appears to be no design at all. The governing principle seems to be capricious. Yet that principle, "sheer chance and nothing more," is reliably at work in *every* death and life. Jack Wright held a similar view. Despite writing to his mother of "all the atheism I contain," Wright invoked the semi-divine when discussing the design of life and death. "[Y]ou get to be a Fatalist out here; in fact, it is necessary that you do, that when you're up, you realize that if Fate intends you to live you shall, and reciprocally–that gives you great courage, and with the help of the roar of the motor and hurricane blast of the wind as you split the space, all fear becomes quite humble; it must."[26] If we take Wright at his word, the act of placing death and survival in the hands of another force gave him courage, humbled his fears, and, at least in theory, made him a more willing combatant. If we look beneath the words, we can hear him telling his mother (and himself): If I die, know that it was my fate and that I could not have avoided it.

The agreement among all voices in this section that the design of com-bat determined all deaths and survivals is worthy of notice. Abbey, Dear-ing, Allen, and Wright came from different religious backgrounds and used different religious language to express their understandings of the forces at work in the war. Yet, prompted by the violence and apparent disorder around them, they each wrote of a world in which every tragedy and triumph was ultimately controlled by a non-human being or force. The inescapable reach of the designer—Chance, Luck, Fate, God—is, in the end, where these confessionally diverse accounts agree, and in this agreement we can see, as Keene noted, an "adamant" belief that some "order could be discerned in the chaos." Why, then, was order so important? Why were so many soldiers and war workers not content to see death as the product of the rather obvious confluence of fragile flesh and dense metal, poisonous gas, or heart-stopping concussion?

We can begin to answer this question by looking at one important divergence among the voices cited so far, and at two moments of convergence. Hervey Allen wrote that "just sheer chance" was separating those who would die and those who would not. While "chance" was to him all-determining, it was apparently without telos—it was a roll of the dice, not a sentient, active demigod. Allen's order differs clearly from Abbey's and Dearing's on this point. By contrast, when James Crowe wrote that his friend Greayer Clover's death was due to "chance," he preceded the statement with an interesting turn of phrase. "If . . . Greayer *had* to fall," he wrote, "I know that it is all chance . . . " Similarly, Jack Wright wrote, "if Fate *intends* you to live you shall, and reciprocally . . . " Behind Wright's "Fate" and Crowe's "chance" is intent, the kind of personal quality absent from Allen's order. Here, both men might just as easily have written, as many did, of providence or God. By naming principles as they named them and by giving those principles the power to elect, soldiers and war workers were not only discerning order in the chaos, they were allowing themselves and others to find meaning in death. If Abbey, Dearing, Crowe, or Wright were to die in the war, as all four did, those left behind could echo their words: Abbey's life was "entirely in God's hands;" Dearing's death was God's way of "working things out for the best;" Crowe "had to fall;" Fate "intend[ed]" Wright to die.

"I LEFT IT ALL TO CHANCE":
THE THEOLOGICAL ANTHROPOLOGY OF THE GREAT WAR

The theological valences and meaning-making power of terms such as chance, luck, fate, providence, and God are important for understanding soldiers' uses of these terms. So too are their anthropological valences; namely, whichever principle was at work, human actors were very restricted in the amount of influence they exerted over outcomes. Edward Lukens expressed this connection between the language of design and conclusions about human efficacy when recalling an event in mid-October of 1918. "When I rejoined my men at the northern edge of the woods, I learned that no one had been hurt during my absence, but that a few minutes after I had left a sharp fragment, like a railroad spike, had driven itself deep into the bank just where my chest had been. Call it Luck or call it Providence, it was with me on the Eleventh of October, or I would not be alive today."[27] Lukens use of the apparently contradictory terms "luck" and "providence" expresses the essence of the Great War's theological anthropological catechesis. Something helped me survive.

American soldiers entered the Great War with a well-developed sense of the connection between masculinity and the ability to command, control, and determine the outcome of a situation. Physical strength, pluck, and determination, they had been told, would bring triumph to individuals and their society. But war experiences taught even the stoutest disciples of Progressive Rooseveltian masculinity harsh lessons. Soldiers' answers to the question of what role they could play in authoring their own survival provide fascinating and compelling testimony to the theological and anthropological effects of war experiences. More than any Calvinist or Lutheran catechist or anti-Modernist polemic ever could, modern warfare gave them a taste of the radical subordination of individuals to higher powers, in this case the principles (God, Fate, chance, luck) governing war. When the whistle blew and the barrages began, rugged individuals saw firsthand that their survival did not depend on works, merit, or muscularity. "Grace" in its many names, bestowed by God or by some other principle, was what separated the living from the dead.

Briggs Adams and Kenneth MacLeish, both pilots, went to war sounding very much like disciples of rugged individualism. Adams was born May 6, 1893 and attended Harvard as a member of the class of 1917. He served as a camion driver, transporting supplies along the Western Front, before transferring to the aviation service. Substantial passages of Adams' correspondence from aviation training express his belief that survival at the front had everything to do with individual skill—that the fit would survive the war. Adams clearly considered himself to be among the fittest. He wrote to his mother in October of 1917: "I am determined to be as good as any and better than most, for only so can I expect much of a chance of coming back. The dubs and boneheads get picked off quickly."[28] Adams had completed acrobatic flight training and felt confident that he was prepared to survive.

> I feel quite gratified that I have [finished acrobatics], for now no matter what happens I can't feel afraid and get rattled. Many fellows have been killed by being thrown accidentally in a bad position and getting scared and rattled, I can't be killed flying now. You see, when I get to fighting, not having to think of my machine, I can concentrate every attention on the fighting and so bring down an adversary.[29]

Briggs Adams' interpretation of the relationship between skill and survival was not without basis. Aviation training was quite risky and, as he noted, was frequently fatal. In the course of the war, 199 American pilots died in training, a rate of roughly one per eighteen graduates. Those who were training in air-to-air combat, as Adams was, died at twice the overall rate.[30] According to Adams, these young men fell due to insufficient skill, fear, weak nerves, or a combination of the three. Adams believed that he was beyond such a point—above the "dubs and boneheads"—and would not meet their fate in training or in combat.

In December of 1917, prior to deploying, Adams reiterated his belief in his ability to determine his own survival and explicitly rejected dependence on the "gods" of chance and luck. He wrote to his mother, "And my chances are really good that I can return; for I have learned my work well and driven into myself a course of conservation, unwavering determination, which is going a long way toward bringing me back. I haven't relied on hunches or chance or luck; and if I had, I should have as good chances as any other. This way I believe better."[31] To Adams, the ultimate designer of a soldier's fate was the soldier, of which he was a particularly rugged, well-trained, and therefore durable example. On March 14, 1918, Briggs Adams put his aviation training to use in a combat mission. It is unclear whether an accident or enemy fire brought his plane down. In either case, he was killed less than three weeks after reporting to his squadron.

Before even leaving the United States, Kenneth MacLeish developed a theory of how death was meted out in combat. He was just beginning his aviation training in Palm Beach, Florida in the spring of 1917 when he wrote to his parents:

> I never try foolish things, however, because I'm a firm believer in the Laws of Chance. I believe that a man has only a certain number of chances to take before he fails to "get away with it." If he takes them in rapid succession and gets into trouble, he is said to be reckless or unlucky. If he uses them slowly, he's all safe. There surely seems to be a well-defined and infallible formula connected with all chances.[32]

MacLeish treated "Chance" as a principle that was observable and predictable—that acted according to laws. The intricacies of Chance's behavior yielded themselves to the properly scientific mind and could be reduced to "well-defined and infallible" formulae. At the center and in command of the world MacLeish described was a man who could, through observation, analysis, and proper action, control his fate. MacLeish survived his first combat tour but was shot down in the midst of his second.

Though many men entered the war thinking like Adams and MacLeish, experiences of combat led them to believe that "works" were of little value in attaining survival. Their Luck, their God, their Fate, their Chance had authored a plan and would not respond to their input. Regardless of what Rooseveltian prophets or military trainers told them, they were helpless on the landscape of modern warfare. Elmer Harden wrote a unique but instructive account of how this belief came to him and how his life was saved by an embodied "Chance." A native of Massachusetts, Harden was a relatively late volunteer for the French Army. He enjoyed the romance of his first few months of service greatly. His sunny tone changed, however, with his first experience of combat in the summer of 1918. In an early-summer letter to his mother, Harden reported his unit's advancement to the front line, his experience of an artillery bombardment, and his thoughts on the design of death and life.

> A soldier's life is a series of miraculous escapes, or else we must believe in fatality and know we are immortal until our name is called. I have talked with so many soldiers who have fought since the beginning of the war and not a scratch to show for it, and I've heard of others who were killed in their first attack. Is it all luck or is it fatality, or do the two words mean the same thing?[33]

Seven days later, Harden entered combat.

Harden's friend and captain, "Pete," was wounded after one day of battle. Even more painful for Harden was his realization of the horror of the enterprise in which he was involved. Writing from a "calm corner" in which he found himself after helping Pete to an aid station, Harden confessed, "My escape has been a miracle; we have been shelled for hours–and gassed–and shot from the German *mitrailleuses* and the devils in the air. . . . I am crying hard inside. It is more terrible than any one has written or told."[34] Battle was clearly traumatic for Elmer Harden. Such emotional prose is extremely rare in the personal literature of American soldiers. With regard to his own survival, Harden wrote not of predetermined outcomes and the "fatality" of which he had written a mere seven days earlier. That he was alive and unharmed was, to him, "a miracle." Whether he wrote of miracles purposely to exclude "fatality," as one reading of his earlier passage might indicate, or whether he believed at the moment that "the two words mean the same thing," is unclear. What becomes clearer in a subsequent passage is the absolute externality of the forces on which Harden's welfare depended. Nothing within his body or within his power had done him any good at all.

While recovering from wounds sustained on July 21, 1918, Harden wrote home extensively, describing his combat experiences and the actions and attitudes of those with whom he served. In one letter, dated September 7, 1918, he shared general observations on the design of personal fate, along with specific details of how his fate was determined on the day he was wounded. He began the letter by writing in generalities: "Soldiers are fatalists. Chance is the fighting man's God." Other soldiers and war workers support these general conclusions. The "fighting man's God" had many names, but worked in ways that limited human efficacy and confounded analysis. When Harden's focus shifted from general sentiments to his own encounter with combat, his description moved from the common to the fantastic.

> During the infernal barrage–daybreak, July 21st–I was vividly conscious of Chance–my Chance–my protector–scurrying around me. It was something with abnormally long legs–it was male–so much is certain; vaguely I think it was more like a devil in appearance than an angel, but it may have been a man-angel whose face was tortured by excitement. Anyway, I knew it for Chance and knew also it was working to save me. *I did nothing*–I left it all to Chance.[35]

Here, Chance is something larger and more animated than an "ivory image"—something external, visible, and absolutely integral to his survival. But Harden again paints a representative anthropological and theological picture. That which determines outcomes, in his case "something with abnormally long legs . . . a man-angel whose face was tortured by excitement," is alien and intervenes on a person's behalf when it so desires.

This "Chance," an anthropomorphic ordering principle *cum* guardian angel, protected and amused Harden, giving him nothing to do but marvel at a creature who "reminded me of a jumping jack, his legs were so long and active." Its spectacular, grotesque presence gave Harden a sense of security and ease. "The thicker the high explosives the calmer I became. I examined the pebbles in the rut–I quietly bandaged the wounds of a man who fell nearly on top of me. Chance was straddling around–this side, that side, over me–like a maniac."[36] While Chance was near, Harden was safe. But when Chance proved an inconstant companion, Harden knew he was in trouble. At one point, Harden wrote, the man-angel moved away, prompting him to cry out, " 'I'm still alive. I'm still alive' . . . perhaps to tell Chance not to lose heart; perhaps I fancied he might miss sight of me and mistake another soldier for me." Finally, in a turnip field where Harden saw other demigods including "the God of War" and "Death . . .a crumpled thing dressed in blue and green and khaki," Chance took his leave saying, "Now E., you must scuffle for yourself." Shortly after being left to scuffle as a masculine soldier should, Harden was shot. He then began a perilous walk to the rear to receive medical attention, but was joined again by Chance the Man-Angel.

> He was before me, looking over his shoulder–kept zigzagging the path–now to the right, now to the left–as the "marmites" fell now here, now there. My faith in him during that return was complete. He was my God. I walked tranquilly behind him–and he gently disappeared as I neared the [aid station].[37]

Once in view and guiding Harden, Chance again became the object of his complete faith, and the source of tranquility. As if to preempt the dismissal of his account, Harden closed the letter by stating, "Cherie, you think this is all a fancy–a joke? Its every word is out of my deepest consciousness."[38]

Harden's consciousness and his recollection are so vivid as to be unique, but his understandings of the operation of design and man's dependence on the force of design in battle are common. Chance—which could also be called Luck, Fate, Providence, or God—was an external guide, a guardian angel of sorts. It saved and let fall according to its will. When present, Chance was a mighty protector; its long legs working feverishly, straddling Harden like a maniac, setting out a path for him to follow to safety. But when it vanished—and it did *vanish* on Harden's account, it did not become *bad* or *ill*—Harden was alone and vulnerable. There is little sense of omnipotence in Harden's account of his man-angel Chance, but the relationship between Harden and Chance was clearly one of dependence. Chance the Man-Angel determined death, survival, and injury by both presence and absence.

The theological and the anthropological lessons that soldiers derived from their war experiences were, as they had been in pre-war American Christianity, inextricably linked. The Great War forced men to reconsider the mythic millennial efficacy of the masculine man with which they were so familiar. As they pondered the design of death and survival on the Western Front, as they searched for order and meaning, they nearly unanimously acknowledged their dependence—often complete—on a supreme supernatural ordering principle. How did some survive while other "fellas" did not? According to a great many, strength, skill, goodness, wisdom, pluck, vigor, and industry played no part. "Someone was regulating the stride of my step."[39] "Chance worked like a Trojan–a mad Trojan." "[O]nly Providence knows."

The first three decades of the twentieth century saw many debates, some of them acrimonious, as to the relationship among God, history, and humanity. These debates pitted those who saw human activity as vitally important to the establishment of the kingdom of God in history against those who saw humanity as playing little or no role in the achievement of God's plans for the world. Theological liberals, the former group, generally embraced an immanent God for whom human works were of great importance while theological conservatives, the latter group, looked to a transcendent God whose grace did not flow in predictable ways.[40] The theological experience of waging the Great War challenged liberal theological impulses while also, it seems, providing a rather sound experiential basis for theologies of divine transcendence. At war in a world of depersonalized industrialized violence, American soldiers and war workers confessed that some supernatural principle was at work, that its reach was unavoidable, and that men could influence it only minimally if at all. This is not to argue that soldiers and war workers emerged from war ready to carry the banners of fundamentalism—a great many roundly rejected the moralism of religious arch-conservatives—or a budding neo-orthodoxy. It is important, however, to note that the challenges to religious liberalism that emerged during and after the Great War were not felt only in seminaries, divinity schools, and in denominational conferences.[41] Young men and women waging war in France felt quite powerfully, and quite simultaneously, their insignificance and their dependence on a higher power.

CONFRONTING THE COMBAT NUMINOUS

The preceding discussion has, I hope, provided a framework for thinking about soldier's reflections on non-human ordering principles in combat, and underscored what I take to be the most important consequence of this insistence: the diminution of notions of human efficacy. The wartime realization of the limits of human action and of the unalterable nature of the design of war could certainly have troubled American soldiers and war workers deeply. An encounter with such an all-determining uncontrollable force in an arena in which "masculine" virtues were supposed to reign could have been treated as a refutation of the value of those virtues. But the writings of American soldiers tell a different story. They tell of men and women aware of and largely comfortable with their powerlessness; they attest to perceptions of telos, mostly unknowable, in the ordered disorder of combat. And out of these reflections on the limits of human efficacy emerges another set of insights on the forces present in war and the effects of encountering them.

Many participants in, and writers on, war have noted that war is attractive and invigorating. Within twentieth-century America alone, thinkers ranging from William James to J. Glen Gray to Jean Bethke Elshtain have conceded and, in Gray's case, testified that war is exciting, enlivening, capable of calling forth greatness in otherwise ordinary women and men.[42] Many American soldiers and war workers serving in the Great War shared this view and expanded it into theological territory. They approached war with a sense of awe, expecting and experiencing a transformative power. Some believed that the explosions and exertions, the devastations and the daring, revealed Truth.

It may seem perverse, indeed heretical, for men and women, mostly Christian, to have seen in the violence of war the essence of their faith. While there is plenty of off-putting theology in the writings of Americans at war in France, one can hardly fault soldiers and war workers for embracing and developing the connection between faith and war that, to be fair, also seized American and British clergymen, and reached into Germany as well. Indeed, the German theologian and scholar of religion Rudolf Otto wrote in a voice often eerily similar to that of the soldiers. Though problematic as an interpreter of all religious experience, Otto provides a helpful point of reference in interpreting soldiers' religious experience. His thought illuminates interesting corners of the powerful feelings that accompanied and gave religious counterweight to the chaos and horror of war, and may suggest the outlines of an answer to the question of why men and women who encountered combat believed themselves to have been transformed, and in some cases redeemed by it. Further, by keeping Otto's work in mind while reading the words of Americans at war, we can see more clearly how experiences of powerlessness in combat became the basis for critiques of American Christianity and assertions of the religious authority of the American soldier.[43]

Rudolf Otto published his landmark work, *The Idea of the Holy*, in 1917—the year the United States entered the war—and in it attempted to cultivate in Christians of his day a deeper appreciation of the non-rational holy. On Otto's reading, Christians in the late nineteenth and early twentieth centuries had come to understand "the holy" as primarily, even exclusively, moral and rational. Their faith, he believed, was the poorer for it. Along with the rational, he argued, Christians had to engage and experience the non-rational in their God to have a full and proper faith. Otto deployed the term "numinous" to describe the holy "minus its 'rational' aspect altogether."[44] The numinous was, on his account, that ineffable, mysterious, powerful, wholly other aspect of the divine that made it both frightening and fascinating. Otto believed that a Christian encountering the numinous faced something that (1) was beyond comprehension and articulation, (2) engendered a "creature-consciousness"—an existential humility that he described as "the emotion of a creature, submerged and overwhelmed by its own nothingness in contrast to that which is supreme above all characters,"[45] and (3) through a combination of "awefulness," "overpoweringness," and "urgency" filled the believer with an attractive holy terror or *mysterium tremendum*, at once terrifying and fascinating— dangerous and powerfully magnetic. Those who encountered and experienced the numinous, Otto wrote, could no longer be satisfied with dry rigid Christian rationalism.

The numinous was, to Otto, "wholly other . . . that which is quite beyond the sphere of the usual, the intelligible, and the familiar, which therefore falls quite outside the limits of the 'canny', and is contrasted with it, filling the mind with blank wonder and astonishment."[46] The historian necessarily falters when attempting to report "blank wonder" except as it is made partially not blank by an author's pen. The words of Louis

Ranlett, Marian Baldwin, James Hall, Charles Nordhoff, Elizabeth Walker Black, and Jack Wright accomplish this task while also conveying the sense of an unnamable, overwhelming, uncanny force present in war. When they wrote of combat, they emphasized the horror and the attraction, the immensity and the "awefulness," the tendency of war to put a soldier in rather immediate touch with his "createdness." In the face of war, not just agency but individuality and even identity melted away. Soldiers and war workers trembled in the war's presence, yet wanted to be near it, and they believed one had to experience war's forces to be changed by them.

Louis Ranlett, a native of Auburndale, Massachusetts and a student at Harvard, wrote eloquently of his war experiences and of occasional attempts to practice his faith. Ranlett began his war service as a corporal in the 308th Infantry of the Seventy-seventh Division—the ill-fated "Lost Battalion." During the Meuse-Argonne offensive of October and November 1918, elements of the 308th spent six days surrounded by German forces, completely cut off from support, and subject to withering fire from all sides. When American forces reached their trapped comrades on October 7, 1918, only 194 of the original 550 men were alive and uninjured. But prior to those tragic events, Ranlett was promoted to the rank of second lieutenant and left the 308th for the Twenty-third Infantry of the Second Division. While he and his men were heading into combat, they encountered a battalion making its way out. In recalling the scene, Ranlett wrote of the awe-filled aftermath of battle but faltered when he tried to describe battle itself.

> The slope of the ravine was riddled with shelter holes–"fox holes" they were called–and swarmed with men of the 9th, many dead, the rest more beaten out than any men I had yet seen. The faces of the living were gray, just a shade off the green of those who were dead. Their eyes seemed to stare, though their lids were heavy. Their shoulders were hunched in a permanent cringe as though they heard shells coming even in the silence. They passed hardly a word with us. We could not ask questions of men with faces like that. They had run into *It*–whatever *It* had been.[47]

Ranlett knew the physical reality that the men had encountered. He knew the shells and bullets, the grenades and bombs. But the physical event and the experience were two different things. Shells could be rendered linguistically. "It" could not.

Ranlett's own encounter with one instrument of "It," an exploding shell, left him first baffled—unaware that he had been hit—and then disembodied, his ability to speak, see, and act completely confounded by the experienced power of the combat numinous. He wrote, "I was speaking firmly, but my voice came out weak. There seemed to be two of me. Number One was well and willing. Number Two was wounded and weak. Number One looked on at Number Two–though I was wholly blind–and tried to speak and act through him. Number Two obeyed either feebly or not at all and Number One was puzzled, astonished at every failure."[48] This division of the subject into willing and unwilling, active and paralyzed parallels the contradictory emotions—enfeebling yet enthralling—that Otto believed attended encounters with the numinous. Attempts to describe such encounters, like the voice of Ranlett's "Number Two," would fail. Writing on July 22, 1917, canteen worker Marian Baldwin struggled similarly in attempting to describe her encounter with war, "It is all so inspiring and so tiring. . . . The emotional strain is terrific. . . . There is so much color and experience crammed into each day that I can't begin to write of. The whole situation is colossal; it is simply impossible to express it in words."[49]

Colossal and inexpressible as war was and enfeebling as encounters with it could be, soldiers and war workers still attempted to record their encounters with the combat numinous. And as many of those voices testify, the Great War cast soldiers headlong into a state of existential humility, a state analogous to Otto's "creature consciousness." James Norman Hall, whose fame as the author of *Mutiny on the Bounty* was presaged by the success of his wartime memoir of life in the British Army, recalled one night in the trenches during which the scale of his life became perfectly clear.

> I watched the rockets rising from the German lines, watched them burst into points of light, over the devastated strip of country called "No-Man's-Land" and drift slowly down. . . . The desolate landscape emerged from the gloom and receded again, like a series of pictures thrown upon a screen. All of this was so new, so terrible, I doubted its reality. Indeed, I doubted my own identity, as one does at times when brought face to face with some experiences which cannot be compared with past experiences or even measured by them. I groped darkly, for some new truth which was flickering just beyond the border of consciousness.[50]

This truth, "the tremendous sadness, the awful futility of war" came to Hall only later. In the moment that he came face-to-face with war, the truth that struck him most powerfully was the insignificance of his very identity. Another night attack provided the occasion for a similar reflection by Charles Nordhoff, Hall's co-author for the "Mutiny" series. He wrote on April 10, 1917, "A night attack is a wonderful thing to see; the steady solemn thunder of the guns, the sky glaring with star-shells and trails, the trenches flaming and roaring with bursting shell." The scale of the violence led him to think it beyond the ability of man to create. "It is like a vast natural phenomenon,—Krakatoa or Mount Pelee,—too vast and cataclysmic to be man's handiwork; and yet, into the maelstrom of spouting flames, hissing steel, shattering explosions, insignificant little creatures like you and me will presently run—offering, with sublime courage, their tender bodies to be burned and pierced and mangled." In Nordhoff's eyes, the immensity of combat and the relative insignificance of man provided the occasion for genuine metaphysical heroism. "To me that is war's one redeeming feature—it brings out in men a courage that is of the spirit alone—above all earthly things."[51]

Nordhoff's language here is striking in its combination of romantic notions of war and modern realities. He sees wonder and solemnity in the attack. Soldiers display "sublime courage" and "offer" their "tender bodies" as sacrifices in the "vast and cataclysmic . . . maelstrom." But modern war does not receive the soldiers' offerings like a polite predictable God; instead it burns them with "spouting flames," pierces them with "hissing steel," and mangles them with "shattering explosions," driving home the insignificance of these "little creatures." But having approached and described the dark heart of modern combat, Nordhoff pulls back. Rather than dwelling on the horror, he describes "war's one redeeming feature"—its ability to draw forth in men an unearthly spiritual courage. As much as the romantic and the modern view of war may seem to be in tension here, and in previous accounts as well, in fact they rely deeply on one another. The vastness of the manmade cataclysm and the horror at its swirling center are what make the courage of the "little creatures" so sublime. The unpredictable violence of the combat numinous and its unwillingness to recognize the significance of the individual make encounters with it both annihilating and redeeming.

American soldiers and war workers also converged with Otto in the belief that direct experiences of the war were the best means for bringing about rejuvenation and redemption.[52] Red Cross nurse Elizabeth Walker Black had been engaged in war work since the summer of 1917 and believed there to be "an exaltation about being under fire." Those who did not join the fight, she wrote, would never know this exaltation or its religious transformative effects. "[Shirkers] are left so far behind with their flabby souls and sluggish blood living selfish lives, while they let others die for their safety." Black herself experienced the reinvigorating transforming effects of encountering the combat numinous when she moved toward the trenches in December of 1917.

Something of that first strange thrill that had been with me when I began nursing at the front, but which had slowly vanished through the blessing of getting used to things . . . began to return and seize me with

renewed vigor as we sped nearer and nearer to the German lines. . . .
out there something stirred and quickened in my heart again, and I was
glad to feel a thrill of excitement.[53]

Black had slowly become accustomed to the once thrilling presence of
the war, but all she needed to revive the affective dimension of her experience was to approach once again the combat numinous. Even official
religious authorities, like a chaplain profiled in *The Stars and Stripes*,
found their standing among the soldiers and their understanding of Truth
indisputably deepened by encountering battle. A September 13, 1918
story describing "Doc," a Baptist pastor from Arizona, noted that "[l]ike
all good chaplains he was in the thick of things at the Marne and would
come out *wild-eyed and reverent* after each engagement." He always carried his own pack, went on foot, and never attempted to set himself apart.
"[N]one come out of such an adventure saying that Old Doc doesn't
know what it's like." The article reported further that in a recent engagement Doc had attempted to rescue his wounded colonel and had, in the
effort, been gassed and wounded by shrapnel. In the eyes of his men, Doc
had been revealed as one of them. "When Doc came to in the evacuation
hospital, he found that his outfit had stealthily cut-off and confiscated all
his Y.M.C.A. insignia and sewn on their own emblem instead."[54] Having
been revealed as a true man of faith by the light of the combat numinous,
Doc no longer belonged in a YMCA uniform. If his soldiering was not
enough, his willingness to lay down his life for another man, and the
deepened faith such a sacrificial act bespoke, certainly legitimated his
religious authority.

The war was, to American participants, variously, even simultaneously,
horrific and beautiful, repulsive and attractive. These qualities were not
de facto religious, but encounters with them were often treated as such
by soldiers and by *The Stars and Stripes*. An unnamed poem written by
Private Lloyd Luzadre and published in *The Stars and Stripes* on 15 November 1918, demonstrates well the elision of martial and religious experiences. A soldier speaking to and for soldiers, Luzadre made the beautiful
horrors of war "his own" and allowed those who had been there to claim
the "dizzy intoxication" of war as well. Luzadre summarized nearly perfectly soldiers' understandings of the meaning of an encounter with the
combat numinous. He described first a pre-war world that had lost its
hold on him and caused his very soul to atrophy. He then wrote of war
as the path back to life and God and Truth.

> He did not care if he ever returned
> Back to the world that he knew.
> He left it, a youth with shriveled soul,
> And his heart—it was not true.

But there on Flanders' blood red fields,
Where men are broken or made,
He fought the battles of flesh and soul
While he had red blood to wade.
He swallowed the acid taste of fear
That rankled up in his throat;
And fought the one great fight of man,
And crossed, with God, the moat.
Yes, crossed the moat and won his fight,
And went through the purging fire–
And a man like the pure white lilies afloat
Sprang out of the mire.
He did not know and could not see,
But war has opened his eyes;
It showed him the road to Heaven and Hell,
And how a brave man dies.
Yes, how he dies and how he lives,
And should fight the battles of peace.
So now it matters if he never returns
When this wild turmoil shall cease.[55]

Combining modern language and a thoroughly romantic sensibility, Luzadre treats combat experiences as primarily religious. Men with "shriveled" souls and untrue hearts had journeyed to war. There they found blood, violence, and "the holy." This combination purified and purged them, opened their eyes, made them men. War revealed not just their true selves and the true selves of those around them, but "the road to Heaven and Hell" and God's demands of men. The souls of those who had "crossed, with God, the moat" had expanded. Their hearts had been made true. Otto could not have described the effects of an encounter with the combat numinous more precisely.

Why do these voices of young Americans at war sound so similar to the voice of a German scholar and theologian? One answer may be found in the similarity between what Otto sought for his co-religionists and what American soldiers and war workers found in war. Otto wanted contemporary Christians to understand that God could not be ascertained only intellectually and that there was an aspect of divinity that dwarfed humanity to an awe-inspiring, terrifying degree. One can reject the notion that divine forces were at work in combat and still accept that the sometimes terrifying, sometimes invigorating experience of war sparked a realization of createdness and finitude very much in line with Otto's hoped-for outcome of encounters with the numinous. And though one needs to tread carefully when speculating about shared concerns, it is rather easy to see in both sets of writings a belief that modern ways of being, thinking, working, and believing had obscured the essence of life and faith, perhaps mediated that essence out of existence.[56] Modern society had flattened life as dogmatic Christianity flattened faith. Soldiers, like Otto, sought and found terrifying and invigorating experiences that cracked the bland façade.

When American soldiers and war workers described the design of combat and asserted that encounters with combat animated their souls and deepened their faith, they were doing more than musing. They were asserting order in the apparently disordered and, thereby, creating room for meaning in a space where life itself could seem to lose all meaning. They were also asserting authority over and against those who knew nothing of the combat numinous. Soldiers, war workers, and *The Stars and Stripes* would go further in their assertions of order and meaning; they would invoke the life and death of Christ as the paradigm for their struggles and sufferings. And when American clergy took issue with aspects of the soldiers' conduct, they would invoke the combat numinous and their status as imitators of Christ in a remarkable series of wartime attacks on moralist Christianity.

As with soldiers' and war workers' reflections on design, it all began with death.

CHAPTER THREE

Suffering, Death, and Salvation

> So if I should be killed I think you ought to be proud in
> knowing that your son tried to be a man and was not afraid to
> die, and that he gave his life for a greater cause than most
> people do--the cause of humanity. Otherwise, I may never do
> anything worthwhile, or any good to anyone after the war, and
> may live to regret that I wasn't killed in it.[1]
> —KIFFIN ROCKWELL to his mother, June 15, 1915

DEATH IN WAR is different from death as most will encounter it. War
brings particularly violent deaths to men and women who are relatively
young, enhancing the awfulness, the tragedy, and the sense of loss felt
by family and friends. War shatters healthy bodies, sometimes beyond
recognition. Yet in the experiences and the imaginations of both those
who have fought wars and those who have translated war experiences
into cultural memory, these very same qualities of war death—the violence, the youth of its victims—enhance its glory, beauty, and meaning.
War and stories of war would be far less compelling were the individual
stakes not so high.

The letters, diaries, and memoirs of soldiers and war workers record
quite clearly attention to both the ghastliness of war death and affection
for symbols and narratives that asserted, often poetically, the metaphysical meaningfulness of death in the Great War. This convergence of horror
and beauty, dread and exhilaration, brokenness and redemption are central to this chapter; indeed they are central to this whole work. For one
of the most striking dimensions of the wartime literature is the extent to
which Americans involved in the Great War embraced violent death in
the war effort as salvific. Though shocking and awful and presumably
quite painful, a war death was treated by the young men and women
waging the war as the key to a hero's memory and, in many cases, the key
to heaven. Americans involved in the Great War were certainly capable of
seeing the obliterated bodies of those killed in war and of thinking their
lives wasted, but most saw something else. They looked upon twisted or
still-writhing bodies as meaningful sacrifices, whether on the altar of a
righteous cause or a neighboring altar of heroic selflessness. Pilots who

fell from the sky were martyrs. Soldiers, bleeding, broken, and dead, were imitators of Christ.

There are as many ways to interpret such language today as there were ways to understand it in the midst of the war. The historical meaning of any one particular "Christ-like" death or wartime "martyrdom" could vary according to different notions of Christ-likeness and martyrdom among readers. As African American soldiers' reflections (the focus of chapter 4) make clear, soldier-authors imagined and embraced different Christs. The importance of allowing for the multivalent nature of words and images, and attempting to account for multiple meanings is undeniable. These texts were, however, more stable than most in that their authors and audiences were focused on death in war. When soldiers applied ideas of martyrdom, heroism, and Christ-likeness to war death, they narrowed the range of potential meanings considerably. The lowest common denominator of these accounts is that death in war meant something special—it would purchase a hero's memory, model commitment to a cause, or help bring salvation to the world. Soldiers and war workers often made such equations in letters to family and friends, but they were clearly also writing to themselves, reassuring all that if they never again saw their homes, wives, children, or parents, their sacrifice would not be meaningless.

Because not all Americans involved in the Great War embraced Christian faith or practice at all, let alone uniformly, it might seem odd or inappropriate to place their understandings of death in a framework as religiously charged as martyrdom, let alone *imitatio Christi*. This framework is, however, an accurate expression of many soldiers' beliefs regarding death. Whether death was presented as an expression of the Christian martyr tradition or couched in classical heroic terms, the effect was to make death a crowning moment, and to make the dead soldier an object of admiration. Some exponents of this view saw or placed a suffering Christ among the soldiers, implying a comparison between the two when not making it explicit. In the spaces where it is wanting for descriptive reasons, the framework is useful for interpretive reasons. Beyond the many ways that soldiers expressed a positive value-giving relationship between the death one died and the life one had lived, the themes of martyrdom and *imitatio Christi* illuminate the fact and the power of postwar exaltations and invocations of the war dead. Families, communities, veterans' organizations, and politicians described these "sainted" dead as a group whose vision was righteous, whose "cause" demanded continued vigilance, and whose salvation was assured. Such was the power of the fallen soldier that surviving comrades invoked their memories frequently and to wide-ranging ends, sometimes even seeking to imitate soldiers' wartime sacrifices.

DEATH AND ORDER ON THE WESTERN FRONT

The American soldiers and war workers who encountered the Great War thought and wrote extensively of death from the moment of their enlistment until well after the guns fell silent. With actual combat an ocean and many months away, they recorded premonitions, fears, and assurances.[2] As they sailed for France, they wrestled with consciousness of their finitude and pondered the reordering of loved ones' lives that their deaths might bring about.[3] Their accounts bear the marks of different experiences and beliefs but share the realization that, in war, death and the dead loomed larger and loomed *differently* than they did at home.

The young American men and women who went to war in France were less prepared than previous generations to face death on a scale so profound. As already noted, cultural trends in early-twentieth-century America valorized the masculine, vibrant, progressive man and inclined young men toward activity and achievement in life over the contemplation of death. In terms of experience, previous generations had known death far more intimately. Those who had lived through the Civil War had experienced and sensed death on a scale unmatched before or since.[4] On a more prosaic level, the turn of the century saw a physical distancing of the living from the dead. As cultural historian Gary Laderman explains, where death had once been a family affair with corpses being handled in the home, in the early twentieth century death and the dead were increasingly the business of hospitals and funeral homes. "For many . . . Americans at the turn of the twentieth century, it was easier to imagine the dead than to actually encounter them in everyday life . . . a 'mortality revolution' in the early twentieth century contributed to the gradual disappearance of the corpse from the lives of Americans."[5] Beginning in 1914 for some Americans, and in 1917 and 1918 for many others, this "revolution" was suddenly, stunningly reversed.

No amount of anticipation could have prepared soldiers and war workers for their encounters with death and the dead in war. In spite of their many anticipations of death, they struggled to make sense of what they saw, heard, and smelled. Some, like James Norman Hall, were horrified by the new proximity between the living and the dead. "The worst of it," he wrote, "was that we could not get away from the sight of the mangled bodies of our comrades . . . Men look about them and see the bodies of their comrades torn to pieces as though they had been hacked and butchered by fiends."[6] Others, unprepared to see death in new contexts, were unable to recognize the dead as dead. Louis Ranlett was accustomed to seeing the dead presented solemnly and found war's more casual presentation confusing. Reflecting on his encounter with dead German soldiers,

Ranlett recalled, "Some lay about the big shell holes, some in the trench bottom, some on a parapet or half-buried in it. All had been turned face down, all lay with legs, arms, and necks bent or twisted in unnatural, impossible attitudes." What impressed him most about the scene was less its "unnatural" appearance and more its impossibility. "All looked like little more than bundles of green gray cloth and seemed but natural parts of a scene that was all wreckage. Though they were the first bodies I had seen, I hardly thought of them as men and was not in the least awed by them."[7] For Ranlett, awe in the presence of the dead depended more on the presentation of the dead—their likeness to the men they had been—than on the absence of life. An anonymous soldier stuck in cognitive limbo between death as he was seeing it and death as he believed it ought to be seen was even more explicit, "They were not like the dead at home, washed and combed and faultlessly attired in awful dignity amid silks and flowers." In their informal imperfect wartime poses, the dead appeared to the author to be something other than human, "the forest was not a death-house, but a monstrous wax-works; and some of the figures were broken."[8] Because this new reality was so dissonant with what was familiar, the author experienced it as unreal.

Hall and Ranlett speak from opposite ends of the continuum of possible reactions to war's reconfiguration of relations between the living and the dead. Both men, like all who waged the war, were asked to live and move in a landscape populated by dead bodies. Hall responded with graphic haunting reflections, "One thinks of the human body as inviolate, a beautiful and sacred thing. The sight of it dismembered or disemboweled, trampled in the bottom of a trench, smeared with blood and filth, is so revolting as to be hardly endurable . . . "[9] Ranlett responded by thinking of the dead as something else. Hall wished he could escape the sight of men he had once known; Ranlett imagined the dead into non-existence. Most American participants in war, however, occupied the space between these two points. They recognized the dead for what they were and who they had been, and felt the need to confront and make sense of death and the suffering that preceded it. Some longed for previously held ideas of the human body as "sacred" and "inviolate," ideas that war made it difficult, if not impossible to hold. Most longed for a return to a landscape in which the differentiation between the living and the dead was firm.

But in the absence of familiar relationships and firm physical boundaries between the living and the dead, soldiers and war workers joined ranks with scores of figures from scripture and myth who thought violent death profoundly meaningful. In its frequent reduction of healthy young men to broken, wounded, dying, and dead bodies, in forcing the living to "lie down with the dead to save ourselves," as one Marine wrote, Great

War experiences made appealing, even necessary, the embrace of new old understandings of death's meaning.[10]

SOLDIERING, DEATH, AND THE WARTIME MARTYR IDEAL

The soldiers and war workers who saw their dead as martyrs embraced two related beliefs. The first belief was that death in the war, specifically in combat, would transform one's life and memories of it. Exit this world boldly and for a righteous cause, both Christian and non-Christian exponents wrote, and your life will be recalled as meaningful and heroic. American pilot Kenneth MacLeish wrote in a March 19, 1918 letter that death in the war would be miraculous in that regard. "To me, the finest miracle in life is to be able, in the last few moments on this earth, to revolutionize one's own entire existence, to forget a life of failure, and weakness, and to die a hero. The Gates of Honor are opened to us, those lucky ones who are over here."[11] In an August 1917 letter to a female correspondent in Boston, Elmer Harden described the war as a this-worldly "opportunity" for him and for her. "I cannot fail–or, rather, even failure in this case has its touch of nobility. Do you understand? We are alive–we have become part of our generation–I have my role to play and you have yours."[12] Both he and she would be illuminated "forever and ever" by the glory of war. Similarly, the editors of *The Stars and Stripes* referred frequently to the "good fortune" of those involved both in the war effort and in particular battles. The paper described those "in the thick of it" as the lucky ones. In the imaginations of many Americans, the prospect of death in war, however terrifying, had a strong and lasting "up-side"—die on the field of battle and the world will honor your memory.

The second belief was that one's lot in a future life depended on the way one departed this life—in other words, one's eternal life was directly linked to the style of one's death. This element builds upon the views set forth by MacLeish and Harden but differs in its metaphysical focus. Paul Rockwell expressed it clearly in a letter to Edmund Genet's mother following Genet's death.

> I think that one enters eternity with the same force and strength that one quits the world with, and that one falling in battle in the full bloom of youth and energy has a better place in the next world than those who linger here and die of illness or age. Anyhow I would change places with any one of the boys who have died so gallantly.[13]

The tragedy was not that "one of the boys" had died. In so doing he had, after all, won himself "a better place in the next world." The true tragedy, heroically averted in Edmund Genet's case, would have been survival and a pedestrian exit from this world at a ripe old age. As Elizabeth Shepley Sergeant explained, "the friends who have vanished during the smoke of battle . . . are the ones who in the far future will remain most vividly alive for me . . . while the 'survivors' . . . will transform themselves into everyday citizens, gradually losing their identity with the Great War, drifting away into unknown paths."[14] Rockwell, MacLeish, Harden, and many more agreed with her. It was best for one's earthly legacy *and* for one's eternal fate to exit the world in a blaze of glory and a hail of bullets.

The most famous wartime apostle of this martyr tradition was Alan Seeger, Harvard-educated poet and soldier of the French Foreign Legion until his death near the northeastern French village of Belloy-en-Santerre during the Battle of the Somme in July of 1916. Seeger's apostleship was prototypical. He spread his beliefs about death through his poems and letters, but, as we will see, was also associated with a number of similarly inclined men whose ideas and idealism he captured, refined, and exemplified.

Alan Seeger argued relentlessly in his poems that death was neither tragic nor to be feared. Indeed, death to Seeger could be both an object of love and a way to new life. This relationship is evident in the most famous American poem of death to emerge from the Great War, Seeger's "I Have A Rendezvous With Death," in which Death becomes Seeger's wartime love and a life-giving springtime presence.[15]

> I have a rendezvous with Death
> At some disputed barricade,
> When Spring comes back with rustling shade
> And apple blossoms fill the air—
> I have a rendezvous with Death
> When Spring brings back blue days and fair.
>
> It may be he shall take my hand
> And lead me into his dark land
> And close my eyes and quench my breath—
> It may be I shall pass him still.
> I have a rendezvous with Death
> On some scarred slope of battered hill,
> When Spring comes round again this year
> And the first meadow-flowers appear.
>
> God knows 'twere better to be deep
> Pillowed in silk and scented down.
> Where love throbs out in blissful sleep,
> Pulse nigh to pulse, and breath to breath,
> Where hushed awakenings are dear . . .

But I've a rendezvous with Death
At midnight in some flaming town,
When spring trips north again this year,
And I to my pledged word am true,
I shall not fail that rendezvous.[16]

One striking feature of this poem is Seeger's insistence that in the midst of industrialized violence and mass anonymous death there remains something deeply personal about dying in war. Indeed, Seeger envisions a lover "Death" who is not a ghoulish dreaded presence, but a gentle, caring, and personal companion, indeed the only respectable companion for a man living in a time of war: "It may be he shall take my hand / And lead me into his dark land." Later in the poem, Seeger recalls past amorous moments, moments for which he longs. "Pillowed in silk and scented down, / Where love throbs out in blissful sleep, / Pulse nigh to pulse, and breath to breath." But having taken a new lover, he must turn to a more honorable comfort. In Seeger's eyes there was little reason to "fail" his rendezvous. Not only would the experience be generally pleasing, avoiding it would constitute a violation of honor.

The imagery of spring woven into Seeger's ode to Death points toward his belief in war death as redemptive. He anticipates that he will meet with Death "When Spring comes back with rustling shade / And apple blossoms fill the air," "When Spring brings back blue days and fair," and, lest their be any confusion, "When Spring comes round again this year / And the first meadow flowers appear." The season of rebirth will be the season of Seeger's death and rebirth.[17] The literary merits of this poem aside, the effects of these sets of images—Death as lover, death and springtime—are to paint war death in a highly favorable light and to imply that death will bring the soldier life.

Like most relationships between lovers, Seeger's relationship with Death had many facets, some contradictory. He wrote of death as natural and rather meaningless; he also wrote of death as a metaphysically significant opportunity. In his poem "The Sultan's Palace," Seeger described death as natural and quite terminal, emphasizing humanity's participation in the realm of nature. "Flowerlike I hope to die as flowerlike was my birth." He wrote, further, that since his life was "Rooted in Nature's just benignant law," he wanted nothing more from death than what other living, dying things drew "from green Earth." Death, he imagined, would be easy and natural.

I see no dread in death, no horror to abhor.
I never thought it else than but to cease to dwell
Spectator, and resolve most naturally once more
Into the dearly loved eternal spectacle.[18]

By seeing himself as entirely contained within nature, Seeger transformed death from an object of "dread" into a natural resolution. To the Seeger of "The Sultan's Palace," life and death were best understood as natural processes—the rise and fall of a flower, with the "spirit" nourished by the body and, apparently, unable to move beyond it.

Seeger's view of death as "natural" stands in apparent contrast to his view of death as potentially heroic. He set forth the heroic view most clearly in his poem "Maktoob," but also in "Liebestod" and "Ode in Memory of the American Volunteers Fallen for France." These poems, all written during his participation in the war, convey the belief that death is a test of masculinity with one's eternal fate at stake. Seeger made the same point in poetry that Paul Rockwell made in his letter to Edmund Genet's grieving mother: It is best to die with "force."

> So die as though your funeral
> Ushered you through the doors that led
> Into a stately banquet hall
> Where heroes banqueted;
>
> And it shall all depend therein
> Whether you come as slave or lord
> If they claim you as their kin
> Or spurn you from their board.[19]

Die like a man, he wrote, and great men will welcome you. This is a clever assertion of the hidden mythic nature of the war in the face of evidence to the contrary. The violence around you is devastatingly modern, Seeger seems to be saying, but if you approach death as mythic heroes did, you will soon sit among Trojans, Romans, Vikings, Crusaders, and Arthurian knights. Seeger emphasized elsewhere how rare and wonderful was the opportunity to die so nobly. In his "Ode in Memory of the American Volunteers Fallen for France," he inverted the standard expressions of gratitude extended by a "nation" to those who have died in its defense. After asking whether France owed his fallen "brothers" gratitude for giving everything they could in the war effort, Seeger answered: "Nay, rather, France, to *you* they render thanks / (Seeing they came for honor, not for gain), / Who, opening to them your glorious ranks, / Gave them that grand occasion to excel, / That chance to live the life most free from stain / And that rare privilege of dying well."[20] The man seeking the transformative, stain removing "privilege of dying well" in war could only thank France (and Germany, I suppose) for the opportunity to gain both.

Seeger's views of death—the naturalistic and the heroic—offer different, perhaps irreconcilable, interpretations of death's ultimate meaning. Death in the course of nature has no great meaning and is to be expected if not welcomed. Death to the hero, on the other hand, is a test, something to be met with relish and vigor, to be neither avoided nor mourned. In spite of their divergence, these views share one crucial insight: A war death is no tragedy at all.

Many Americans who fought in the Great War agreed. Kiffin Rockwell, who fought alongside Seeger, wrote in a nearly identical voice. Rockwell and his brother Paul, sons of a southern family and grandsons of two Confederate Army officers, were among the first Americans to offer their services to the French government. Kiffin volunteered to fight on August 3, 1914, and he and Paul sailed for France on August 7, 1914.[21] Kiffin Rockwell and Alan Seeger served together in the French Foreign Legion. They were members not only of the same regiment, the *2eme Etranger*, but of the same company and stood sentry duty together, once coming under near fatal attack.[22] Rockwell and Seeger shared a uniform and an experience. They also shared similar (and similarly contradictory) beliefs that death was entirely natural—a metaphysical non-event—and that death was intensely meaningful.

Having been wounded in the spring of 1915 while advancing on the northern French village of La Targette, roughly five miles outside of Arras, Kiffin Rockwell knew something about encountering death in combat. He described that experience to his brother Paul in a May 13, 1915 letter, and conveyed the view that death was nothing exceptional, nothing to be feared—nothing more than natural. "While I was lying there, three shells exploded within ten meters of me, each time covering me with dirt. The last one landed within five or six meters of me. I would hear them coming and would say to myself, 'Well, it is over,' and shut my eyes."[23] Yet in writing of the same event in a May 18, 1915 letter to his friend the Vicomte de Peloux, Rockwell shifted voices and wrote of the transformative redemptive power of a war death. Though concerned that Peloux might think him "cold-blooded," Rockwell emphasized anyway the "pride and admiration" that surpassed the "horror" of his comrade's deaths. "This life does not hold such great value in my eyes as it does in some people's, and I feel that those men who died that day, died having made a success of their lives in their own little way."[24] Death was not the failure of life, but its culmination. When his friend Victor Chapman died, Rockwell wrote to Chapman's father in a similar voice, emphasizing the glory that a man derived from the way he died.

[Victor] died the most glorious death, and at the most glorious time of life to die, especially for him with his ideals. I have never once regretted it for him, as I know he was willing and satisfied to give his life that way if it was necessary, and that he had no fear of death, and there is nothing to fear in death.[25]

The death that Victor died—he was shot down by a German airplane—was gloriously violent; Victor was both gloriously young and gloriously willing. These would-be martyrs, Seeger and Rockwell, made sure that others knew (and made sure to tell themselves) that death in war offered earthly and metaphysical benefits unattainable in times of peace, indeed unattainable in survival.

The dialectic at work in these views of death is not terribly complex. If one exists in a landscape crowded by death and sees friends dying nearly every day, it is not surprising that death becomes in poetry and prose something natural and common, not to be celebrated or feared. The death of a human being is as natural as the death of a flower, as banal as an appointment to be kept. At the same time, death came and was met in many ways by the men on the Western Front. Youth and vigor did not shield men from fear. While death was a natural and common occurrence, so were death-ways important. One could find in death either honor or shame. To meet death boldly was, in the eyes of these early apostles of the Great War martyr tradition, to find salvation from otherwise ordinary lives. Though Seeger and Rockwell were not unblinking in their conviction, most consistently and most publicly they described death in such a way as to find in it not great tragedy, but an opportunity to sacrifice themselves for a cause in which they believed, and thus to purchase lasting glory.[26]

In the years immediately following Alan Seeger's death, his poems provided the framework, sometimes even the syntax that many American soldiers employed when writing of death. Seeger's book of poems, published posthumously in 1917 and reprinted ten times during the last two years of the war, grabbed the attention of young men involved in the war and drew praise from Teddy Roosevelt, among others.[27] Seeger's influence, though impossible to gauge perfectly, is evident in American soldiers' personal writings. Ambulance driver Henry Kingman described his unit's library to his parents and mentioned the recent purchase of "Alan Seeger's poems."[28] As noted in chapter 1, Marine aviator Walter Poague wrote in his diary for January 17, 1918, that he was not afraid of death "at least not yet," and that despite loving life "madly," he agreed with "Seeger" who wrote: "I find no fear in death, no horror to abhor. / I never thought it aught but just to cease to dwell / Spectator, and resolve most naturally once more / Into the dearly loved eternal spectacle."[29] More common than this paraphrasing of an entire stanza of Seeger's *Sultan's Palace* are views reflecting the core beliefs of the wartime martyr tradition, such as Briggs Adams' reflection on death in a letter to his mother dated October 24, 1917. "Death is the greatest event in life, and it is seldom that anything is made of it. What a privilege then to be able to meet it in a manner suitable to its greatness!"[30] Words ascribed to fallen soldier Salter Storrs Clark struck similar chords. His comrade, Herbert C.

Randolph, wrote of a pre-combat conversation between the two, "[Salter] tried to cheer me up . . . he had come to the conclusion that it didn't make so much difference when a man died, as how he died, and that he knew of no other cause more noble to die for."[31] Seeger's stamp is not everywhere apparent, but the widespread appeal of his views of death, and the interplay between them and the Christian faith of many American soldiers is clear.

Perhaps the most eloquent exponent of the wartime martyr ideal to fight under the American flag was Kenneth MacLeish. MacLeish was raised in Glencoe, Illinois, the youngest son of a wealthy and devout Baptist family. He was a junior at Yale University when, in the spring of 1917, he joined the First Yale Unit and began training for aviation in Palm Beach, Florida. Kenneth's father Andrew was an executive with the department store Carson, Pirie, Scott, and his mother, Martha Hillard, once head of Rockford Seminary, was a regular volunteer at Jane Addams' Hull House.[32] Archibald MacLeish, Kenneth's brother, gained fame first as a poet and later as a scholar and statesman. The family was, by any measure, distinguished.

Kenneth MacLeish was in many ways the ideal American soldier. Well educated, raised in an established and accomplished Christian home, Kenneth wanted nothing more than to fight the war. He gave extended attention to the potential for contradiction between his participation in the war and his Christian faith, and resolved the question in favor of fighting.[33] MacLeish was convinced that entering the war involved acts of *imitatio Christi* both real (sacrifice) and hypothetical (armed defense of the innocent). He also saw Germany as sinful, a criminal nation deserving of harsh punishment. Kenneth MacLeish sailed for Europe believing he was joining a righteous battle.

MacLeish's experiences upon arrival in France seem to have enhanced his already well-developed sense of the romance, nobility, and Christianity of the war. France had felt the sting of war for three years, had already lost approximately 900,000 men, and endured in 1917 a summer of mutinies and strikes among its front-line troops.[34] If MacLeish saw this side of the French war experience, he did not report it. He wrote instead of heroism. In a letter to his aunt, Mary Hillard, MacLeish described an atmosphere imbued with "such magnificent courage and such a wonderful spirit," in which "[d]eeds that would astound the world five years ago are as common as rain." This environment was also characterized by what he saw as a remarkable approach to the loss of one's life: "There is no fear of death. It is accepted when it comes as quite natural and quite right."[35] Though views of death among the French were surely not as one-dimensional as MacLeish believed, he was affected by the equanimity (or the numbness) he perceived.

MacLeish breathed this view of death in and made it his. In a December 9, 1917 letter to his family, he wrote of the possibility of his death, the value of his life, and the need to sacrifice for victory, "It isn't a question of when we die, it's *how*! You people at home will have to make your sacrifices before the nation wakes up. . . . I feel sometimes that you value my life more than I do. I don't think it's worth a darn, just now, but it will be, in some capacity, before I'm through here." He concluded by asking his family to pray not that he would avoid danger, but that when it came he would have the martyr's courage that he saw displayed around him.[36] Confronted with his own finitude, MacLeish thought about the relationship between the war and the value of his own life. He concluded that war would transform a life not "worth a darn" into a life of glory and triumph.

The fact that death in war would give value to his life led MacLeish to embrace the "opportunity" of war enthusiastically. When he was engaged in "the scrap," he wrote giddily of his experiences. After an early April 1918 combat mission during which his aircraft came under heavy fire from the ground, MacLeish wrote to his friends of the exhilaration that the experience gave him and of his mild disappointment that it had not been a closer call. "When I got back I expected to find that the 'bus' [his aircraft] had been riddled with bullet holes, but to my surprise there wasn't one. I was disappointed and tickled to death at the same time–this combination causes one to itch violently."[37] As his experiences of the war broadened to include the loss of friends, he came to see death in the war as perhaps the ultimate proof of the value of one's life, an event that could cover or cleanse past sins and convert one to heroism. He wrote to his brother of the miraculous and redemptive effects of a war death, in which "a life of failure, and weakness" would be ended and a "hero" would be born. We cannot know the degree to which MacLeish imagined himself to be weak and a failure. What is clear is that he longed to become, if not a martyr, at least a hero.

MacLeish's understanding of a war death's redemptive potential led him to face death, or at least write of facing death, boldly. It also led him into depression. In a letter to his brother Henry written during MacLeish's long tenure at a desk job in London, he admitted nearly overwhelming feelings of hopelessness. His words are those of a desperate man whose dreams of heroism, indeed whose hopes of salvation, are slipping away. "All the hope or enthusiasm I ever had of helping out in this war has left me–left me in an I 'don't care' mood . . . This constant discouragement has got under my skin so deeply that I'm sick absolutely sick, mentally and physically." War had promised invigorating bouts with evil, exhilarating near misses and, possibly, deadly wounds. What war was giving him instead was the enervating emasculating experience available to any clerk in any city in America. His body and his spirit were, as Teddy Roosevelt might have predicted, shriveling at his desk. "I've lost eleven pounds, and all the 'pep' I ever had. . . . With the exception of those two glorious months when I was really doing something, I've been discouraged and misled for six whole months."[38] Without the possibility of a rendezvous with death, war was no more than boring business.

Alan Seeger, Kiffin Rockwell, and Kenneth MacLeish saw plenty of death and acknowledged the feelings of sadness, emptiness, and horror that came with the loss of friends and comrades. All three also insisted, finally, that death in war was heroic. All expressed—sometimes strongly, sometimes faintly—the wartime martyr ideal. When, as Kenneth MacLeish and Alan Seeger did, soldiers connected the heroic death to a heroic heavenly afterlife, they took another step along the well-worn path of the martyr tradition, the Christian manifestation of which is defined by the life and the Passion of Christ. Like MacLeish, many believed and were told that involvement in the war was an imitation of the masculine Christ's approach to His world's problems. As troubling as it may be, it should be no surprise that as these men entered and ordered a world in which death and young life intersected so regularly and terribly, they frequently connected both their lives and their deaths to those of the paradigmatic Christian martyr.

DYING THE GOSPEL:
THE AMERICAN SOLDIER AS IMITATOR OF CHRIST

The casting of the American soldier as the exemplary imitator of Christ did not sprout *sui generis* among the poppies and the wheat of wartime France. For decades prior to the war, American Christianity had been fertile ground for the masculinization of Christ and the Christian ideal as well as for the valorization of the soldier and his willingness to struggle, suffer, and die. The two trends converged quite easily. Christ was a man of action; the soldier was a man of action. Christ fought for justice in His day; the soldier was fighting for justice in his. Christ suffered and died that people could be saved; soldiers were suffering and dying for one another and for the world. Christ descended into hell and rose again bearing the marks of his passion; no less exalted an American warrior than Civil War General William T. Sherman had famously declared that war was hell, and soldiers bore the signs of their descents—etched by metal into flesh, sewn by thread onto a sleeve—to answer all who doubted their status as saviors. Christ the man, Christ the warrior, and Christ crucified helped soldiers to frame and find comfort in their sufferings, and to relate painful experiences to a durable metaphysical structure.

Among the four million Americans who volunteered or were drafted into service, Joyce Kilmer stood apart as a poet, essayist, and literary critic. His work was published in *Harper's Weekly*, *The Nation*, and *Outlook*. He became a staff writer for the *New York Times Sunday Magazine*, served as poetry editor for *Literary Digest* and *Current Literature*, and held the assistant editorship of the Anglican *Churchman*. He followed his first book of poetry, *Summer of Love* (1911), with the acclaimed *Trees and Other Poems* (1914), and *The Circus and Other Essays* (1916). Kilmer's young career was nothing short of spectacular. His religious life was also quite remarkable. Raised in the Episcopal Church, Kilmer was not satisfied with its spiritual and devotional rigor and, with his wife Aline, began studying Catholic dogma, completing their conversion to Catholicism in 1913.

The comfort of their new religious home was spiritual for both Kilmers, but for Joyce it was emphatically not physical. Physical and spiritual comfort were, to him, something approaching antithetical. In a letter to Reverend James Daly, S.J., Kilmer claimed a need "to have some of the conceit and sophistication knocked out of me" and longed for "a stern medieval confessor . . . who would inflict real penance."[39] He also hoped that his rise in the literary world would give him the opportunity to write of and spread his faith—to talk "veiled Catholicism to non-Catholics." "I have no real message to Catholics," he wrote "I have Catholicism's message for modern pagans."[40] The messages of Catholicism and "paganism" converged in the spring of 1917 and Joyce Kilmer, like many other men of all faiths in New York and the United States, felt the tug of war. In late April of 1917, he enlisted in the Seventh New York, National Guard. He requested and gained transfer to another National Guard unit, New York's historically Irish Catholic Fighting Sixty-ninth, in September of 1917.

Joyce Kilmer's wartime poems "The Peacemaker" and "A Soldier's Prayer" demonstrate how easily the life and suffering of the soldier could be interwoven with the life and suffering of Christ. In "The Peacemaker," Kilmer looked upon his fellow soldiers and the many contradictions they faced in waging a war for peace and wrote: "That pain may cease he yields his flesh to pain, / To banish war he must a warrior be. / He dwells in Night, eternal Dawn to see, / And gladly dies abundant life to gain."[41] The American solider, he wrote, submits himself to suffering and death that the world might be saved; he is glad to die to gain "abundant [earthly] life" for all and, presumably, "abundant [eternal] life" for himself. That Kilmer's poem could accurately describe both Christian and non-Christian views of the war should not obscure the implied comparison between soldiering and Christ's Passion that becomes far more explicit in "A Soldier's Prayer." This poem is a prayerful back-and-forth in the voice of a soldier who is reflecting on his daily struggles and comparing them to the events of the Passion.

> My shoulders ache beneath my pack
> (Lie easier, Cross, upon His back).
> I march with feet that burn and smart
> (Tread, Holy Feet, upon my heart).
> Men shout at me who may not speak
> (They scourged Thy back and smote Thy cheek).
> I may not lift a hand to clear
> My eyes of salty drops that sear.
> (Then shall my fickle soul forget
> Thy Agony of Bloody Sweat?)
> My rifle hand is stiff and numb
> (From Thy pierced palm red rivers come).
> Lord, Thou didst suffer more for me
> Than all the hosts of land and sea.
> So let me render back again
> This millionth of Thy gift. Amen.

Kilmer here describes an intimate relationship between the soldier and Jesus in which the soldier's sufferings for the world—sore shoulders, aching feet, numb hands—are an echo of the Passion. While Kilmer would clearly like to impart "proper" humility to the soldier who might get carried away in this comparison—he describes soldiers' sufferings as comparatively minor and the soldier's gift as only a "millionth" of Christ's—the framework does not lend itself to restraint.

James Anderson Winn has argued that poetry like Kilmer's transgresses against the art of poetry and against true religion as well. The bases for these judgments are his normative views of poetry and his belief in the essential pacifism of Christ and Christianity. It should be clear by now that large numbers of soldiers and war workers wrote poetry that exhausted their muses. It should also be clear that many did not share Winn's view that their faith and their savior required pacifism. But as we can see by looking carefully at Kilmer's poems and those of less renowned writers, neither were all soldiers comfortable with a warrior Christ. Kilmer's "Soldier's Prayer" captures something of the soldierly via media through its focus on suffering. By comparing experiences of pain, Kilmer is able to connect Christ and the soldier without directly raising the issue of violence and, further, to solidify the relationship between the two. Indeed, Kilmer's Christian framing of the soldier's experience was but one poetic manifestation of a set of beliefs widely held and expressed in the American Expeditionary Force. Not all subscribed, but many made reference in images, turns of phrase, and scriptural quotations to the Christ-likeness of the lives and deaths of American soldiers.

Infantry officers Hervey Allen and Harold Speakman, Red Cross Nurse Carolyn Clarke, and war volunteer Katherine Blake, like Kilmer, saw much of Christ in the American soldier. Allen, whose memoir documents the Twenty-eighth Infantry's disastrous advance on the town of Fismes in August of 1918, recalled that while tending to men wounded during that push, he attained a level of insight into Christian truth that had eluded him previously. "The feel of warm human bodies and blood and the quiet patience and confidence of the men brought a realization of life to me in that hour that I shall never forget." What did Allen realize in that moment? The horror of war? The reality of suffering in combat? These he knew already. In this moment, he continued, he came to know Christ. " 'This is my body which is given for you.' What that really meant, now I knew."[42] The broken bodies and flowing blood brought Allen to a deeper understanding of the Last Supper and its sacramental recapitulation, as well as the Crucifixion to which both point.

Harold Speakman, serving with the 332nd Infantry Regiment in northern Italy after a brief stint in France, composed a poem entitled "Christ in the Trenches," and published it in his memoir *From A Soldier's Heart*. Speakman described a dream in which he saw "the Master" walking toward him in a trench and, initially, mistook him for a soldier: "O Sir, take cover when you pass this way; The Hun shoots well–a man must guard his head. . . . " After speaking to the apparently careless apparent soldier, however, the author recognized him to be Christ and saw that in addition to wounds on "his brow" and hands—"Hardly there was a place he had not bled!"—then Christ spoke.

> "Laddie, this cheek has felt the shame anew,
> This temple, torn by every falling spire,
> Is crucified afresh on no-man's wire;
> Yet high my head is, for the souls of you
> Rise in a new-born glory–cleansed by fire."[43]

Though it is tempting to read this verse as Christ's revelation that all war does damage to Him and His Church, to do so would be a mistake. Speakman wrote from within a discursive realm defined overwhelmingly by belief in the unity of the Allied cause with Christ's cause, and characterized by repeated descriptions of German atrocities as affronts to Christian civilization. Speakman's Christ imitated the Allied soldiers' Christ imitations when He hung "afresh" on the barbed wire of No-Man's Land. His body—His "temple"—like their bodies had been torn. The struggle of the Allied soldier in the trenches, Speakman wrote, was a recapitulation of the struggle of Christ's Passion, and would grant those who experienced it the glory and respect of a Christ who declared them "cleansed by fire."

In July of 1918, Carolyn Clarke was thrust with little warning into the fiercely contested region around Chateau-Thierry and could hardly have been prepared for the sights she would see. She seems, however, not to have doubted the meaningfulness of the suffering and death. Seeing wounded soldiers lying still with small crosses (actually the letter "t") marked in iodine on their foreheads—an indication that they had received anti-tetanus serum in the field—Clarke commented that the marks "seemed symbolic of something more than a treatment."[44] The men before her were, if not Christ's imitators, at least marked as suffering saviors of civilization. In a letter to friends in the United States dated September 22, 1918, Katherine Blake reflected on the exploits of a "son of a Pittsburgh millionaire, graduated from Groton, who had looked death in the face and lived through the kind of agony which the gospel [sic] calls 'Bloody Sweat.' In the Litany it says: 'by the Bloody Sweat.' "[45] Soldiers, war workers, and chaplains did not simply attach a vague sense of religiousness to the war and to their labors. Rather, they found in their actions and in the actions of those around them multiple recapitulations, grand and subtle, of the pivotal event of Christian history.

Throughout most of its run, *The Stars and Stripes* also described the American soldier as an imitator of Christ. Images, articles, and poems emphasized the Christ-likeness of soldiers' sufferings and the atoning regenerative effects of their spilled blood. *The Stars and Stripes* motives in connecting the American soldier to Christ are far clearer than those of the soldiers themselves. The staff of the paper sought to valorize soldiers and to elevate them above all temporal and, it seems, all eternal critiques. One consistent voice in this forum was that of Catholic chaplain Thomas F. Coakley. Coakley was a Pittsburgh-area priest who, after the war became pastor of Sacred Heart Church and a prolific author and pamphleteer for the Catholic Truth Society.[46] While in France he was an equally prolific poet, repeatedly making clear that the American soldier was an imitator of Christ *par excellence*. His poem, "A Chaplain's Prayer," appeared in the paper's popular "The Army's Poets" section on June 21, 1918.

> Oh Lord, I am not worthy to
> Be found amid these reddened hands
> Who offer an atoning due,
> Themselves, to Thee, great martyr bands.
> Let me but kiss the ground they tread
> And breathe a prayer above their sod,
> And gather up the drops they shed,
> These heroes in the cause of God.[47]

Coakley used the language of atonement and self-sacrifice, as well as the preciousness of the soldiers' spilled blood, to draw the soldier and Christ into a relationship so intimate that it was beyond, indeed above, him. "These heroes in the cause of God," Coakley wrote, whatever their faith backgrounds and qualities positive and negative, were a company in whose presence he was not worthy to stand. Another of Coakley's poems, "The Holocaust" appeared on October 25, 1918, again telling the soldier-readership of connections between the suffering and death they witnessed and endured, and Christ's Passion. In this bit of verse, Coakley took the fact of soldier *imitatio Christi* to its soteriological conclusion.

> Not since Thine own most bloody Sacrifice
> Upon the sacred hill of Calvary,
> Has such a flood tide set towards Paradise,
> The countless millions slain to make men free.
>
> They are the pure in mind, the clean of heart
> Unspotted holocausts who kept Thy law,
> Our first born sons who played the victim's part
> Thy Judgment, Lord, will find in them no flaw.[48]

This is not a particularly clear poem in its detail, though its message is unmistakable. Coakley is comparing the Great War and the Passion, and the basis for comparison is twofold. The first similarity is the "flood tide" of souls that each event sent toward paradise. Christ's sacrifice purchased salvation for sinners; the war was sending "countless millions" to heaven. The second point of comparison is the sacrificial death at the center of each event. Coakley uses this comparison to answer any question as to the soldiers' eternal fates. Just as Christ was an unspotted unblemished sacrifice, so too are the soldiers pure and heaven-bound. The poem, formally directed heavenward, was truly directed to soldier-readers and its message was clear: The soldier's work and his death are Christ-like; God will admit all of the Allied fallen to "Paradise."

As off-putting as Thomas Coakley's poetic voice may be to the twenty-first-century ear, his words cannot be dismissed as only bad art and/or bad theology. Coakley's poems were published in a highly popular section of the most widely read soldier-authored newspaper in the A.E.F. The precise effect of these poems on soldiers' understandings of the war cannot be known, but his poems were repeatedly placed before American soldiers at times of great personal uncertainty and his verse not only valorized soldiers' involvement in the war—a task undertaken by many—but also sanctified soldiers as martyrs and imitators of Christ. Coakley spoke in terms that made sense to many American Christians in the early twentieth century. Muscular Christians worshipped a manly, active, often athletic Christ. They marveled at Christ's struggles for "Right" and his willingness to act. They called the modern Christian man to do the same.

When war tore those bodies, the Passion restored meaning. There was victory in defeat, strength in powerlessness, life in death.

Some soldierly accounts of war experiences relied heavily on Christ imagery while articulating a kinship of suffering and death less direct than *imitatio Christi*. "Battle Prayer" written by Major Brainerd Taylor and published in *The Stars and Stripes* on November 29, 1918 (the third issue published after the Armistice), found another figure present on Calvary to be a more apt type of the contemporary soldier. The poem is vivid and horrific, obscuring neither the violence of war nor the collapse of boundaries between the living and the dead. "Alone upon a hill I stand / O'erlooking trench and No Man's Land; / In night's black skies the Northern Lights, / Pale flashes rise to mark the heights / Where Death's dark angels bear away / The souls of men who die today." Standing above the valley of the shadow of death, Taylor paints a dark picture of war and suffering. He then enjoins Christ to be with those caught in the maelstrom.

> Jesus of Nazareth from Thy cross
> Look down and comfort those who toss
> And scream in pain and anguish dread
> In No Man's Land among the dead;
> Have pity for the wounds they bear,
> Jesus of Nazareth hear my prayer.[49]

To this point, Taylor, though twice invoking the name of Jesus, focuses on No Man's Land and the suffering of soldiers. Some men "toss and scream in pain;" others are dead. Some cry out for mercy from a sea of anguish scoured continuously by "Death's dark angels." He then shifts historical scenes, reminding the reader and Christ that such pain was not without precedent. "On Calvary as the hours dragged, / From cruel nails Thy body sagged / Yet in that agony, Lord, / Thou didst give blessed comfort t'ward / One suffering soul who with Thee died; / He who for sin was crucified." These soldiers are not Christ's imitators, though their suffering may be Christ-like. In Taylor's view, they are more like the thief who, justly condemned, hung next to Christ. According to the Gospel of Luke, the thief recognized the lordship of Christ and received assurance of his salvation.[50] With this scriptural precedent in mind, Taylor petitions Christ for mercy. "Out there lie men who die for right–/ O Christ, be merciful tonight; / Will thou who stilled the troubled seas / Stretch forth Thy hand their pain to ease, / Thy sons whose feet so bravely trod / Earth's battlefields, O Son of God?" Taylor's Christ is above rather than in the fray, yet the poet makes a very public case for Christ's ability to identify with soldiers' sufferings and to grant comfort and salvation to those dying "for right."

Thomas Coakley, Joyce Kilmer, and Brainerd Taylor, like *The Stars and Stripes*, had wide audiences. And though the precise influence of the regular placement of Christ among the soldiers and war workers is, ultimately, unknowable, Coakley and Taylor were not editorial staff. Kilmer, though a poet of some distinction, was a sergeant in his regiment's reconnaissance unit.[51] Harold Speakman, Hervey Allen, Katherine Blake, and Carolyn Clarke seem to have written and thought independently. This suggests that the equation of the American soldier with the suffering Christ was an attractive one to soldiers, war workers, and to many of the clergymen serving with them. One explanation for the appeal of Christ imagery among American soldiers and war workers is the meaning it imparted to violent, traumatic events. Another explanation is the salvation that it implied for America's un-resurrected saviors.

KILLED IN ACTION, SAVED IN ACTION

Soldiers and war workers often scoffed at those who gave extensive thought to matters of religious doctrine.[52] But some questions of belief found them and demanded their attention. As we have seen, one such question had to do with the forces designing life and death in combat. Another was the question of salvation. Soldiers could no more turn from the question of salvation than they could turn from death. And in response to this question, soldiers embraced a doctrine of immediate salvation for the fallen.

The words of many Americans—including Alan Seeger, Kenneth MacLeish, and Thomas Coakley—gesture toward a view of death in war as redemptive both of the memory of one's earthly life and of one's eternal soul. In the heated engagements of 1918, the doctrine of immediate salvation for the war dead became a matter of editorial concern for *The Stars and Stripes'* staff, which embraced, explained, and defended the doctrine in a series of articles and editorials. Though not the only voice speaking of death in war as salvific, theirs was the loudest. Driven by an understandable desire to bring comfort to a group of men confronting a sensually and existentially disorienting circumstance, *The Stars and Stripes* reported on soldiers' Christ-like willingness to suffer and die for others. How, they asked, could the eternal consequences of suffering and death be other than glorious?

Doctrines of immediate salvation for those dying for "the cause of God" have ample precedent within the Jewish-Christian tradition. Within the Christian Church itself such beliefs have the support of the martyr tradition and were most famously articulated in association with the Western Church's Crusades. During the Great War, there were many contemporary forces contributing to the development and prevalence of this teaching. One factor was war's lethality. Over the course of nine months engaged in front-line combat, American forces lost more than 115,000 men to hostile fire, illness, and accident.[53] (This equates to approximately two-and-a-half Vietnam wars in nine months of front-line service.) That figure grew at an average rate of over fifteen thousand per month. To paraphrase Shirley Jackson Case, the sky hung low over American soldiers in the summer and fall of 1918, and traffic was heavy on the highway between the Western Front and heaven.[54] The fate of this ever-growing "martyr band" demanded comment, and *The Stars and Stripes* provided it. A second important factor influencing the doctrine of salvation was the moralist voice of Christian America and those who carried its message to the Western Front. In spite of repeated protestations from *The Stars and Stripes* and its soldier-readers, concerns over the moral state of American soldiers found their way into the press, onto the desks of *The Stars and Stripes* writers, and into the hands of the troops. Religious authorities representing these positions emphasized not the Christlike suffering of the American soldier, but moral degradation, weakness before temptation, and the need for clergymen to help save soldiers' souls. As the casualties mounted and as these voices persisted, *The Stars and Stripes* answered them, furiously bringing their view of the relationship between death and salvation into the open and granting heretics and dissenters no quarter.

Before the shouts, however, came whispers. During Easter week, 1918, *The Stars and Stripes* used a conversation on the topic of soldiers' religious practices between an anonymous, possibly fictional, Salvation Army worker and a soldier-reporter to raise and answer the question of a soldier's eternal fate. "If any of them want to talk of God and their souls, they find us ready enough," the "Sallie" told her interviewer when asked about holding worship services for the soldiers. "But this is usually just a quiet chat with one or two of them." She concluded, "They are all fine boys, and I don't think they have to worry much about their souls, do you?"[55] We don't force religion upon those fine boys, she said. Their souls seem safe to us. One page later, on an editorial page containing a reprint of John 20 titled "The First Easter," *The Stars and Stripes* offered the Salvation Army worker a supportive exegesis. Easter, an editorialist wrote, provided the perfect opportunity to reflect on the position in which soldiers found themselves and on the promise of Christ to his imitators.

He will come to judge the living who have championed his cause–the cause of justice and freedom–and to judge, in His infinite mercy, those who have died in defending that cause. *And no man who lives or dies striving to bring about His peace need fear His judgment.* The Christ loved and preached peace; but He loved justice and freedom more, and for them He laid down His life. Ours is His fight; His peace, when it comes, will be ours.[56]

The editors had worked out in their minds if not fully on their pages that salvation had nothing to do with abstaining from vice, but rather came as the reward for a physical struggle, perhaps a sacrifice of the body, for the causes of peace, justice, and freedom. Dying as a result of this imitation was unquestionably salvific.

Having made such an assertion of doctrine, however, the paper's editors fell silent on the topic. Had it been an Easter device? Was it merely a bit of rhetorical excess to provide comfort for the growing A.E.F. in France? Two additional editorials argue for something more substantial. As the Allies launched the Meuse-Argonne offensive in late September of 1918 and American soldiers attacked long-established German positions through exceptionally rough terrain, the editors of *The Stars and Stripes* joined in. The roughly two million men under arms could handle the uniformed enemy in front of them. The Bible-toting enemy in the rear was another story.

"There is a man touring the A.E.F. entertainment circuit with a good speaking voice and the art of using it," began an editorial entitled "Salvation" in the September 27, 1918 issue. The man traveled with a band and a few well-worn sermons. He had come to bring religion and salvation to the soldiers.

> He told a story about a little soldier in barracks who, kneeling beside his bunk to say his bedtime prayers, was hit in the back with a shoe flung by a big, burly soldier, and wound up with a stirring appeal for orthodox Christianity with a request for those of his audience who wanted to come to God to "stand up."[57]

Many had already heard the story of the "shoe flinging," a staple of muscular Christian literature.[58] Hearing it again, the editorialist wrote, "took us back to our boyhood literature. . . . We recollected that [dime-novel heroes] Jack Harkaway or Dick Merriwell, or some one of our school boy idols, had done the same thing." In this narrative, Harkaway, Merriwell, the school-boy idol, or whoever played the role of protagonist, was hit by the flung shoe, finished his prayers, and invited the assailant outside to fight. The Christian protagonist—a formidable combination of faith and physical power—then bested the antagonist, thereby demonstrating the complementary nature of Christian faith and physical toughness.

The editorialist, familiar with this tale, took a lesson not from the story but from its repetition. The story, he concluded, was a fabrication and the teller a man of questionable status in the community—"we doubted

... if the man who told the story knows very much about this Army that he has come to save." The man with the good speaking voice was nothing more than another representative of an American Christianity seized by the false convictions that the men of the Army needed saving, and that tired devices could accomplish that end. He recognized neither the religious effects of war experiences nor the soldiers' imitations of Christ. In response to this affront, the editorialist explained and defended the soldiers' beliefs.

> There are a good many men in this Army who hold the belief that a man who, with a gun in his hand and a smile on his face, takes his chance in the battle line in this war, who faces death for the principles for which we are fighting, is working out his own salvation, and that he doesn't have to stand up in an entertainment hall in a back area to accomplish that salvation, either.[59]

Entertainment halls behind the zone of combat or churches across the Atlantic offered nothing like the eternal opportunity offered by the war. According to *The Stars and Stripes*, the cheerful soldier, the embodiment of the muscular Christian ideal, needed no sacrament, no anxious bench, and no sawdust trail. His willingness to die for the cause of Christ was sufficient to ensure him eternal life.

The editors repeated this defense, yet more forcefully, in another editorial, "Soul Savers," published on October 25, 1918. Again they described a direct relationship between proximity to battle and knowledge of religious truth, and claimed eternal life for Christ's imitators. The piece began by identifying another heretic and the nature of his heresy. "All the way across on a ship that docked at a certain base port the other day, a certain Pharisee among the passengers unctuously let it be known that he was coming to France 'to save the souls of our boys.' "[60] The editors elaborated for all who missed the force of the label "Pharisee." "For this man, and for every one of like breed, this newspaper has no words sufficiently strong in which to express its contempt. They are men, having ears that hear not, eyes that see not, brains that think not, hearts so filled with their own smug self-righteousness that they have not the faintest conception of the *ever-recurring miracle of the Allied battle line*."[61] Their religion was and always would be false. Like the Pharisees against whom Christ railed, this "breed" knew nothing of a new and miraculous revelation, knew nothing of the glory and effect of a Christ-like death.

> Because they have never really comprehended the teachings of the Master they profess, they cannot know that the smiling, cussing, battle-stained doughboy needs no help in saving his soul. They cannot know

that in offering and spending his life in a righteous cause the American soldier finds it. They can never comprehend that in saving the soul of the world, the soldier saves his own.[62]

The soldier needed no clerical assistance. Having participated as an imitator of Christ in "the ever-recurring miracle of the Allied battle line," his faith and his heart, in the paper's opinion, could be nothing but true. Those suffering and dying in the war could truly count themselves among the righteous.

The Stars and Stripes editors were not alone. Three soldiers recorded moments when the doctrine of immediate salvation for the fallen, or something approaching it, was articulated publicly, once by a chaplain, twice by senior officers. Lieutenant Frank Holden remembered the morning of October 6, 1918, when his unit's chaplain, Lieutenant Daniel Smart, gathered the troops for a worship service. They were camped in the Argonne forest near the village of Varennes. Holden recalled a beautiful autumn morning, a "hillside...covered with boys," and Chaplain Smart's sermon on 2 Timothy 4:7, "I have fought a good fight, I have finished my course, I have kept my faith."

He was preaching next to the last sermon he ever preached to many boys who listened to the last sermon they ever heard on this earth, for that night we marched into the fight and some of the boys who sat there on the hillside that Sunday morning died for America before the sun went down the next day, and a few days afterwards our Chaplain lost his life, too . . .

St. Paul's words were, in Holden's opinion, "fitting" to the moment and the location. Death was near at hand for the "boys" as it had been for Paul. They were asked in that moment, facing death, to reflect as Paul had on the goodness of their fight, the solidity of their faith, and the completion of their course. Chaplain Smart told the men what Paul had told himself, Timothy, and eventually the whole Church, "Henceforth there is laid up for me a crown of righteousness."[63] We cannot know whether the chaplain viewed fighting the good fight and finishing the course as evidence of a faith well kept. It is not unreasonable to assume that many of his listeners did, and believed that if they fell, they would gain their crown of righteousness.

Edward F. Lukens, who served as a second lieutenant in the 320th Infantry, wrote in his memoir of a memorial service that his battalion was ordered to hold "one Sunday." The battalion chaplain was fighting influenza and the effects of exposure to gas, which left Major German Horton Hunt Emory, the man to whose memory Lukens dedicated his memoir, "[to conduct] the service himself." The fact that Emory was standing in, Lukens thought, increased attendance beyond what it would have been "for any chaplain in the world." The service began with a few hymns, after which the major rose and delivered a sermon "simple and dignified, without a trace of sanctimoniousness or of apology." " 'Killed in Action' was his text and in beautiful and eloquent language he showed us the glory of such an epitaph above all others that man could earn or his friends could write for him." The messenger's war experience, style, and knowledge of the soldier—not to mention his rank—all lent authority to the message. "He spoke out clearly and frankly what every man of us held deep but vague in his heart–the eternal things for which we were fighting and living and (some of us) dying–the things that we all knew in our hearts were the real things and his tone was not that of mourning but rather almost of envy of the men whose lives had come to such a glorious climax."[64] Emory did not offer an explicit pronouncement that death in battle meant salvation, but the climactic glory of death in action, the eternal nature of the cause, and the envious tone that Lukens noted bespoke an understanding that something glorious and eternal awaited the fallen.

Finally, American soldier A. L. Bartley wrote in his memoir of an unnamed officer delivering a similar message on November 12, 1918, the day after the war ended. That officer lent the certainty of sunrise to the salvation of fallen soldiers.

> Some of our comrades have fallen, some of our boys have made the supreme sacrifice, but you know and I know that they have not died in vain, that their names, their deeds, their actions are immortal, and just as surely as the sun will rise tomorrow to proclaim that God still rules, just as surely are those boys now sitting on the right hand of God, for they died that the ideals, beliefs, and the religion taught to us by Jesus Christ, the Son of God, might rule the world.[65]

The speaker concluded by asking the question that *The Stars and Stripes* had answered so forcefully, "Could God do otherwise than to love them and bedeck their crowns with stars?" According to the dominant public voice of the A.E.F., as well as some, if not all, of its soldiers, the answer was a resounding "no." Vices could leave no spot, no blemish. Any soldier dying on the front would go directly to heaven.

There is no question as to the strength of *The Stars and Stripes'* conviction regarding salvation for the battle dead, no doubt as to the existence and appeal of a doctrine of immediate salvation beyond its pages. The paper did, however, publish a dissenting view. This came in a letter to the editor written by Chaplain Thomas C. Peterson and published on November 22, 1918, eleven days after the Armistice. Chaplain Peterson was responding to the "editorial (?) entitled 'Soul Savers' " published in the "religious department (?)" of *The Stars and Stripes*. (Peterson included the parenthesized question marks as an indication of his skepticism.) He began by endorsing the "flaying" of "a certain self-styled soul saver," and the characterization of him as a Pharisee. In short, Peterson agreed that such voices had no place among the soldiery. Then Chaplain Peterson changed his tone. The remainder of the "Soul Savers" editorial, he wrote, had been "foolish," and would have been "unworthy of answer" were it not styled as "the literary expression of Old Glory in France."

> But this much must be said, that when the writer contends that "the smiling, cursing, battle-stained doughboy needs no help in saving his soul" it does not sound like any of the great statesmen, either past or present, from the country represented by the Stars and Stripes. Nor is he voicing the opinion of the hundred million people in Christian America, nor the religious workers in khaki, nor of the doughboys themselves.[66]

Rather, Peterson continued, "The religious belief that every soldier who goes over the top thereby redeems his soul is not American, but Turkish-German . . . And it will surely not make our American soldiers any *less brave and courageous and fierce* in battle to hold them a clear, sound presentation of patriotism and religion." Peterson's response to *The Stars and Stripes'* demonstrates his concern both for the willingness of soldiers to fight and for the integrity of Christian doctrine and clerical authority. Bravery, courage, and ferocity in combat would not be compromised, he believed, by a soteriology that asked more of the faithful than that they die in the war.

Chaplain Peterson's critique of the soldiers' "Turkish-German" doctrine of salvation was an attack on the conflation of service to nation with service to God and, as such, struck at the foundations of the framework within which the war was experienced as redemptive and religiously meaningful. He called not for a focus on soldiers' sins as a "Soul Saver" might have, but for an interpretation of Christianity that did not assume death in combat to be the supreme expression of devotion to Christ, and a view of war that allowed for some debate as to what constituted a righteous cause. Peterson was echoing centuries of Christian discomfort with killing and military service. He was also echoing Abraham Lincoln's insight, expressed most famously in his Second Inaugural Address, that Christian peoples at war with one another are an object lesson in the hidden God—a bloody call for an ounce of humility. The Germans were historically Christian and adopted the phrase "Gott mit Uns" to describe their war effort. Both nations read the same Bible. Both prayed to the same God. Both could be neither completely right nor completely vindicated. A strong America and its strong men, he argued, could surely tolerate strong theology.

The Stars and Stripes disagreed. But rather than attacking Chaplain Peterson as a heretic to the war and the nation, the editors went to what they believed was the source. Their remarkably succinct response demonstrates the editor's readiness to invoke Jesus, if also a somewhat slippery grasp of New Testament teachings: "He who loseth his life in a righteous cause shall find it, good Chaplain. Jesus Christ himself has promised it."[67] The Synoptic Gospels agree that Jesus promised those who would lose their lives "for my sake" that they would gain life. The drift from "for my sake" to "in a righteous cause," though predictable in the religious culture of the Great War, was the work of soldiers, war workers, and their newspaper, not of the authors of Matthew, Mark, and Luke.

The appeal of the martyr ideal, soldier *imitatio Christi*, and the redemption that both implied continued after the war ended. As survivors attempted to make sense of lives lost and spared, many expressed admiration for the Christ-like dead and despair over a missed opportunity to be counted among them. Paul Rockwell wrote of being willing to trade places with any of those who died so gloriously.[68] Walker M. Ellis wrote longingly of the war and its glory to the father of his fallen friend, Hamilton Coolidge. "The incalculably dear deaths which have come to some of them were the destiny of all of us . . . those of us who remain have missed our calling. [The dead] are merged in the greatest spiritual tradition the world has known since Christ . . . "[69] His destiny, his calling, as Ellis understood it, was not merely to face death for the cause, but to be "merged in the greatest tradition the world has known since Christ." By surviving, he had irreversibly failed his Seegerian "rendezvous" and missed forever the chance to consummate fully his imitation of Christ.

While Walker Ellis mourned that he and other survivors had missed their calling and their redemption, Spence Burton worked to convince the world that his ailing brother Caspar had not. Spence Burton was a priest of the Anglo-Catholic Society of Saint John the Evangelist. Caspar Burton, described by Spence as "a genial and witty loafer," attended Harvard before venturing to war in 1915. Caspar found glory and adventure in the British Army until he was severely wounded by shrapnel. He recovered, but was not fit to enter battle again. Caspar eventually applied for a transfer to the American Expeditionary Force, received a commission, and began a desk job.

Caspar Burton survived the war, but the effects of his wounds were more than the most advanced medical treatments of the day could counter and, one year after returning, he was facing death in an unremarkable bedroom of his parents' Ohio home. As his health deteriorated, correspondence poured in from concerned friends calling Burton back to the days he had hoped to erase. The famous Canadian missionary, physician, and Dwight Moody convert Wilfred T. Grenfell expressed his concern for Burton in a letter dated March 4, 1920. He also delivered a mild chastisement to the dying young man. " . . . we all want you to feel we think of you in your trouble–and *whether you value it or not*, we pray you may be given that comfort and peace which comes from faith in the dignity and value of life–as the forerunner of continuous life–and sons of the everlasting God." Sensing that Burton might bristle at this, Grenfell wrote, "*You can't get away from these things, so take it with good grace, that we are serious both in our affection and our prayers.*"[70] But Caspar found his situation hard to take "with good grace." He agonized over his fate, and was not comforted that he was, at least, surrounded by loved ones. Despairing, he reportedly asked his mother, "Why couldn't I have gone out over there like Dill and the rest?"[71] He knew the heroic earthly legacy that a battlefield death could have purchased him, and that the death he now faced offered no such promise.

The story of Caspar's death, told by Spence, attempts to accomplish quite explicitly what his war experiences did not, and demonstrates the enduring meaning-making power of the *imitatio Christi* idea in the face of such a loss. Spence Burton wrote that he first "realized" his brother's Christ-likeness when seeing the wounds that Caspar bore.

> When he undressed I demanded a private exhibition of his scars. While I examined his back he talked up all its "points of interest." Up by his neck, almost on the spine, there was a livid blue hole, where the bulk of the junk in his left lung had gone in. To illustrate what that was probably like he had me feel a loose piece of metal under the skin, just below his shoulder blade. It felt like a loose key in one's pocket.[72]

This gruesome, highly private moment moved from exhibition to exegesis when Spence noted first that scars left by operations to remove other fragments were "cruciform"—"I told him they looked like the crosses chalked on the shutter of Joe Jefferson's 'Rip Van Winkle' to show how many drinks he owed,"—and then that those crosses were arranged in a familiar pattern. "[A]s I looked at the crosses, I saw they were in the pattern of crosses on an altar stone. In a flash I saw Caspar, conviviality and sacrifice, Rip Van Winkle and our Savior."[73]

Caspar and those who knew him acknowledged that his pre-war life had been a less-than-ideal example of Christian practice, traditionally understood. But in light of his patterned, cruciform wounds—his bodily testimony of suffering and sacrifice—a new reality emerged. Spence recognized that Caspar, who "never appreciated the value of sermons, psalms, hymns, litanies, and all the devotions he found in what he called 'darling little pious books,' " held his conviviality in tension with a vital faith.[74]

"Caspar expressed his religion in kindness, prayer and sacrifice. . . . There was no divorce between sacred and secular in Caspar's sick room or in his mind. . . . On one side of his bed was the crucifix, on the other a card table."[75]

In spite of this duality, Caspar's last moments recalled to Spence, as thousands of deaths had recalled to observers in France, no less holy a moment than the Crucifixion. Caspar's deathbed was no bed at all. Caspar became Christ crucified, dying a glorious, sacrificial death. Spence wrote, "From his cross he cried out 'with loud voice.' His sacrifice was almost finished. 'Father, into Thy hands.' . . . At six o'clock the fight was over, the victory won."[76] Caspar Burton was dead. A war death had not verified him as a true and truly saved imitator of Christ, but his brother the clergyman had done everything he could to establish and solidify that connection.

In reading these accounts of death and dying and the eternal benefits of martyrdom or *imitatio Christi*, it is important to think about the audiences for which they were written and, based on what we know about the audiences, to think about potential motives for imagining the dead and dying as heroic and saved. Some accounts of war and death were written for soldiers by other soldiers, by chaplains, and by A.E.F. journalists; other accounts were written for families by soldiers and by other family members. There seem to be two motives behind these writings. The first, most clearly present in the pieces written for soldiers, was to try to take the edge off of natural fears of death. By reminding soldiers that death in the Great War was profoundly religiously meaningful, these voices (many of which belonged to soldiers) hoped to make soldiers less reluctant to die and less likely to see the dead around them as dead in vain. The second motive, related to the first but more present in words written to families, was to comfort the mourning—to convince those faced with images of death and an unbounded void that the friend or loved one who was dead had not gone from one hell to another. On the contrary, these accounts told family members that their soldier had followed Christ and was now in Christ's company. Produced by individuals living and dying at the swirling confluence of the powerful religious currents of early-twentieth-century America and the traumas of war, these depictions made perfect, if bloody, sense.

CHAPTER FOUR

Christ's Cause, Pharaoh's Army

> "Trench religion" yes! We who have been there know its
> meaning and terms. You sure will get next to God in them
> trenches, and if you have never prayed in your whole life you
> will find prayer to be very efficacious there. That is the place
> of all the places where the right to live is determined solely
> upon being 100 per cent a man. It is too bad we cannot use
> this test in our every day practice. It is too bad some of these
> miserable people who hate a man or a woman because of the
> color of their complexion could not be trained in the trenches;
> it would really prepare them to meet the judgment of a just
> and righteous God.[1]
>
> —Pvt. Erkson Thompson, 370th Infantry

African American men and women fought a different war than their
white counterparts. In addition to the German enemy they faced in the
fields of France, black soldiers and war workers were fighting an American enemy every bit as vicious and far more deeply entrenched. For African American soldiers and war workers, the Great War was a two-fronted
war. Every military skill that a black soldier learned, every box that a
black stevedore lifted, every battle that a black unit fought, every black
soldier who was wounded or killed, every body disinterred and reburied
by a black laborer was significant not only for winning a war against
militarism in Europe, but, African Americans hoped, for battling racism
in the United States.[2] And when African American soldiers and war workers used religious language to describe the war and their experiences of
combat and suffering, they did so in ways that embraced popular views
of the redemptive power of the war in Europe and expressed the more
specific belief that black soldiers' contributions to the war effort and their
Christ-like sufferings would facilitate the entry of "the race" into the
Promised Land of freedom and equality.[3] This chapter examines African
American soldiers' and war workers' religious responses to their war experiences, and places those responses in the religio-political context of
African American life in the early twentieth century.

W.E.B. Du Bois' notion of African American double-consciousness, articulated in 1903 in *The Souls of Black Folk*, is indispensable for under-

standing African American soldiers' and war workers' reflections on the war. Du Bois described the "double-consciousness" of "Negro" men and women as a product of unfulfilled promises and ever-present racism.

> It is a peculiar sensation, this double-consciousness, this sense of always looking at oneself through the eyes of others, of measuring one's soul by the tape of a world that looks on in amused contempt and pity. One ever feels his two-ness,–an American, a Negro; two souls, two thoughts, two unreconciled strivings; two warring ideals in one dark body, whose dogged strength alone keeps it from being torn asunder.[4]

As experienced and as recalled, the Great War pressed double-consciousness down upon black men and women like few other experiences. Because of the double nature of their war service, we must treat the sentiments of all African American veterans as historically, essentially double: embracing questions of citizenship and self, describing the meaning of an international war of liberation and a nationalist project of social justice. They are, to be sure, testaments to the religiousness of a particular war and of war more generally; they are also, in many cases, expressions of faith in the righteousness of the ongoing war for equality being waged by black men and women on the familiar battlefields of the United States. The quote that opens this chapter makes this clear. Private Erkson Thompson's reflections on war move seamlessly from the trenches to the streets of Chicago, from a German to an American enemy. The words of Sergeant Arthur Davis of the Eightieth Division are spare and somewhat more opaque. Responding to a post-war survey he wrote, "I do not regret the time I served in the Army at all."[5] The most obvious meaning of these words— that Davis had no negative feelings about serving his country in war—is, of course, significant and connects him to many other war veterans. But the possible deeper meaning, inextricably bound up in African American experiences of the war, demands our attention as well. Emerging from an Army that loved and hated his sacrifice, Davis was also likely saying: *In spite of all you did, I served. I survived.*

"I HAVE GAINED MUCH AND LOST MORE."[6]
THE DOUBLE NATURE OF SERVICE IN PHARAOH'S ARMY

Nominally, all American soldiers and war workers in the Great War had a single identity. They were *American* fighting men and women. Practically, however, there were two American armies; one was white and one was black. White army generals and white politicians believed that the fate of Europe and of civilization depended on the white army and, for the most part, trained and equipped it accordingly. The black army they grudgingly accepted, consistently neglected, and openly mocked. In its handling of African American soldiers, the American Expeditionary Force did everything that it could to maintain a distinction between the two armies and to ensure that African American soldiers and war workers understood that the principles of democracy for which they fought did not apply to them; not in America, not anywhere.

But the black army, eventually 370,000 strong, was there and willing to serve.[7] Black soldiers from all regions and of all faiths volunteered and registered to be drafted for war service. There were enough African American soldiers to populate eight segregated infantry regiments organized into two divisions. The 365th, 366th, 367th, and 368th Infantry Regiments were the foot soldiers of the Ninety-second Division. The Ninety-third Division comprised the 369th, 370th, 371st, and 372nd. Many more black soldiers were drafted to serve as unskilled laborers in the ports of France. The senior leadership of these units was entirely white; black junior officers served in some units, but faced numerous challenges to their authority and frequently found themselves being relieved of command on trumped-up charges of incompetence and inefficiency.[8]

Innumerable episodes during the war highlighted white America's antipathy toward black soldiers. When Secretary of War Newton Baker decided to draft black soldiers and train black officers for service in segregated regiments and divisions, the question of where to train them caused great concern in the white communities that surrounded potential training sites. White populations in the North and the South were deeply uneasy at the prospect of arming black men and training them to fight in their midst.[9] Some white officers and enlisted men proclaimed that they would not salute a black senior officer and refused to be led in marching exercises by African American officers, commissioned or non-commissioned.[10] When a black soldier training in Des Moines, Iowa caused a stir by exercising his rights as a paying customer in a movie theater and attempting to move to a better seat, he became an example in the eyes of his commanding general, Charles Ballou, of how soldiers ought *not* to behave. Ballou issued an order to his troops that read, in part:

> It should be well known to all colored officers and men that no useful purpose is served by such acts as will cause the "Color Question" to be raised. It is not a question of legal rights, but a question of policy, and any policy that tends to bring about a conflict of races . . . is prejudicial to the military interests of the 92nd Division, and therefore prejudicial to an important interest of the colored race.

You may have rights, the reasoning went, but you are wrong to exercise them. Ballou reminded his men that "White men made the Division, and can break it just as easily as it becomes a trouble maker," and then concluded, echoing centuries of paternalistic rhetoric "[a]ttend quietly and faithfully to your duties, and don't go where your presence is not desired."[11] At nearly every turn, the ideals of equality and democracy that all American soldiers were called to defend in the Great War were in tension with the reality of race hatred.

The situation was no better in France. Due to concerns that more open race relations in France would "corrupt" the minds of black soldiers, the General Headquarters of the American Expeditionary Force requested that French soldiers and citizens in contact with African Americans treat them in accordance with American, Jim Crow customs.[12] Though French units did not comply with this request, it is indicative of the thoroughgoing racism of the American Army. This "spirit" reached well beyond those wearing army uniforms. Black soldiers were regularly refused service and otherwise overlooked by the support apparatuses of the YMCA, the Red Cross, and the Salvation Army. African American port laborers, or stevedores, often suffered the triple indignity of wretched living conditions, scant supplies, and aggressive oppressive military police whose job it was to "keep them in line." *The Stars and Stripes* frequently published photos and cartoons making fun of black soldiers, and the wildly popular entertainer Elsie Janis sought laughs among white American troops by lampooning them as well: "Two colored soldiers [are] talking about Army Insurance. One says, 'I done took ten thousand dollars' worth of insurance.' Other says, 'Good Lord! Why! You ain't got no wife to leave it to.' 'No,' replies his friend, 'but you know Uncle Sam ain't going to send no ten thousand dollar nigger up to the front.' "[13]

Alert to the presence of African American soldiers in the trenches across from them, German propagandists tried to use the double-consciousness of African American soldiers against the American Expeditionary Force. They designed a flyer that read:

> Of course some white folks and the lying English-American papers told you that the Germans ought to be wiped out for the sake of humanity and Democracy. What is Democracy? Personal freedom; all citizens enjoying the same rights socially before the law. Do you enjoy the same rights as white people do in America . . . or are you rather treated over there as second class citizens? . . . Can you get into a restaurant where white people dine? Can you get a seat in a theater where white people sit? Can you get a seat or a berth in a railroad car . . . ? And how about the law? Is lynching and the most horrible crimes connected therewith, a lawful proceeding in a Democratic country?[14]

German propagandists understood the profoundly contradictory position in which African American soldiers found themselves. In response to the conditions highlighted by their enemies, black soldiers expressed understandable disgust and frustration. Sergeant Robert Thomas wrote of feeling that "the colored boy was being used not because he was an American, but because things had reached the stage where they had to be called upon in greater numbers than had been anticipated."[15] Sergeant James Crawley observed rightly that democracy was "[t]he cause we give all to gain for everyone but ourselves." The anger and frustration, were, however, only half of the story.

African American soldiers, war workers, and their communities also expressed hope for personal and communal redemption through war.[16] Their hopes had a history. During the American Civil War, African American units were a source of immense pride for black men and women in both the North and the South. Black Union soldiers played a significant and massively controversial part in the Civil War. Whites on both sides of the conflict acknowledged that war service, manhood, and citizenship were inseparable. Military necessity led Union generals and politicians to allow African Americans into service and citizenship; Confederate soldiers, violently acknowledging the implications of service, executed all black prisoners of war.[17] In the post-war South, black veterans were at the center of struggles among newly freed slaves, their former masters, and the white supremacist society seeking to recover from the traumas of war. The "black and blues," as they were known, served the practical purpose of protecting unarmed and vulnerable black men and women from those seeking violent retribution at the same time that they served the symbolic purpose of staking freedmen's claims to power and legitimacy in the re-forming societies of the American South. The black soldier had, for a brief but shining moment, defended claims to equality; perhaps black doughboys would do the same.[18] African Americans' attitudes toward the Great War also reflected the influence of the Wilson administration's efforts to connect war service and citizenship rights. Serve us in war, Wilson had proclaimed to "hyphenates" of all types, and you will be one of us in peace: "[You] must expect nothing less than the enjoyment of full citizenship rights–the same as are enjoyed by every other citizen."[19]

Perhaps more persuasive than history or a frequently maligned president, were the voices of African American leaders who saw in the war an opportunity to demonstrate the depths of African American patriotism. James Weldon Johnson used the pages of the *New York Age* to make public his healthy and justified revulsion with Wilson and, at the same time, enjoined black men to defend and exercise their "right to fight" in the Great War—to make every effort to fulfill "the duties of citizenship" and thus "keep [the] case [for rights] clean."[20] Isaac Fisher, gifted essayist and editor of Tuskegee's *Negro Farmer* (later the *Negro Farmer and Messenger*), wrote in a very similar voice. In a March 13, 1915 issue of the *Negro Farmer*, Fisher asked the question, "In Case of War, What Must the American Negro Do?" He answered:

So far, the Negro's record as a patriot . . . is CLEAN. . . . "Thrice is he armed that hath his quarrel just," saith the Scriptures. Many oppressive measures have been directed against us on the ground of our race. But these will not–can not stand forever . . . but if in any State, if in any Congress of the United States any man can rise and truthfully say– "The Negro failed the nation in its time of need, therefore, let us visit punishment upon him," what defense can we or our friends offer?[21]

From the time of the Revolutionary War forward, African American men had been willing to fight and die for the country. While urging black Americans to continue building this sterling record of service, African American leaders also reminded their audiences that opponents of black citizenship rights were poised to pounce on any indication of disloyalty and to cite it as further proof of the degraded state of "the Negro."

Reflecting these influences, African Americans often wrote of their experiences of the Great War in terms that expressed hope even as they took account of the travails of war. They wrote of complex experiences: awful and wonderful; demeaning and ennobling; dull and thrilling; enervating and invigorating. They expressed a positive attitude toward the war's aims and acceptance of the demands the government levied on its citizens in times of war. Private Ward Smith of Portsmouth, Virginia summarized this well when he told of his "anxious[ness] to answer the call of Government, [and] willing[ness] to sacrifice all." Their reactions to training and camp life ran the gamut from Isaac Sanders' "didn't agree with me very well" to James Crawley's "Helpful in every way, except that it lack [sic] the true democratic spirit." And while some African American soldiers found their overseas experiences "deplorable in most instances," others felt gratified to have seen "more than I had ever seen in my life and learned quite a great deal."[22] Fighting, they believed, verified their manhood, demonstrating to themselves and to others that "[t]here was more metal [sic] in me than I really thought I possessed myself."[23] Black Baptists, Methodists, Catholics, and Episcopalians expressed the feeling that war had deepened their love of democracy and "fixed [their] faith in the Holy Divine."

African American men and women had more than ample reason to abandon belief in the rhetoric and symbols of the United States. They could not have been faulted for rejecting the notion that violence could, under any circumstances, elevate or redeem the perpetrator. They might have been skeptical of attempts, like those directed at the German enemy, to portray a people as evil, subhuman, or "other." (See figure 4.1.) Yet in spite of a long and tortured history of violation and prejudice, African American soldiers and war workers saw hope in the violence that they waged and endured. Even in the bleakest of moments, engaged in the most grizzly of tasks, soldiers and war workers could see hope for redemption. The double nature of the war experience did not always

PEACE PRELIMINARIES —By Charles Dana Gibson

Reproduced by courtesy of "Life."

Figure 4.1. This cartoon ran in the second issue of *The Stars and Stripes*, February 15, 1918. The image of Uncle Sam preparing to lynch the Kaiser—blood and entrails dripping from his hands, a burning village in the background—would certainly have highlighted to African American soldiers the double nature of their war service. They understood themselves to be engaged in noble service to the nation and to be fighting a fiendish enemy. At the same time, they were fighting for a nation in which white mobs lynched black men and women (not the Kaiser) with impunity. Image courtesy of the University of Illinois Library.

lead to a more active militant stance against Jim Crow racism and the hypocrisy of the American democratic ideal. Only recently have authors begun to catch up to the double nature of soldiers' experiences in, and reactions to, war—to the fact that the war was both invigorating and disappointing and remained a contradictory experience for those African Americans who served.[24]

AFRICAN AMERICAN SOLDIERS, RELIGION,
AND THE VIRGINIA WAR SURVEY

Between 1919 and 1921, the Virginia War History Commission, appointed by Governor Westmoreland Davis (1859–1942), set out to "complete an accurate and complete history of Virginia's military, economic, and political participation in the World War."[25] Survey commissioners used a state-wide distribution network including schools, churches, policemen, and the postal service to circulate questionnaires among servicemen and women in every county in Virginia. Over fourteen thousand men and women responded to the survey; roughly twenty-four hundred of them were African American.[26]

The survey was four pages long.[27] The first three pages asked for biographic information, including place and date of birth, parents' names, marital status, religious affiliation, education, and the details of the subject's war service. Page four of the survey was the most open-ended. It contained a series of questions designed to gauge a soldier's reactions to the various stages of service. The questions address pre-war attitudes toward the military, reactions to camp life, the effects of overseas experiences, the effects of combat, and a comparison of the soldiers' pre- and post-war "state[s] of mind." In the middle of this set of questions lay one that may have seemed out of place: "What effect, if any, did your experience have on your religious belief?" Some of Virginia's leading citizens were, apparently, interested in questions like those taken up by the Federal Council of Churches' Committee on the War and the Religious Outlook. Was the faith of the soldiery strong enough to withstand war? If not, where was it weak and why? Responses to this particular question are one valuable source for reconstructing black soldiers' thoughts on religion and the war, but they are not the only source. Religious language and religious imagery are also woven into answers to questions about citizenship and about the war experience as a whole. Though religious sentiments are sometimes explicit in veterans' responses to these questions, just as frequently they flash, then fade, in terse responses and general talk of a struggle that "made me better."

There is certainly a risk of over-interpreting the words that many soldiers offered on war and faith. Where the evidence is thin, cryptic, or both, and where language is most ambiguous, I will offer a range of readings contextualized by the efforts of African American leaders who tried to make sense of patriotism and faith in the era of Jim Crow and in wartime. The writings of W.E.B. Du Bois and of Tuskegee-affiliated men, mainly Isaac Fisher, offer thoughtful, trenchant, often divergent insights into relationships between religion, individual, race, and nation.[28]

For all of its potential value, the Virginia War History Commission survey is also problematic as a source for African American attitudes about the war, the nation, and faith. The involvement of government officials in the dissemination and collection of surveys almost certainly raised suspicions among African American veterans. In Richmond, Virginia, for example, the local branch of the War History Commission collaborated with the police department in the collection of surveys.[29] Given the level of racial tensions nationwide and particularly in Virginia, the level of caution observed by African American veterans answering the survey was likely quite high. In the summer of 1919, nearby Washington, D.C. had been shaken by deadly race riots in which white veterans had been deeply involved in initiating violence and black veterans had organized an effective and deadly defense of their neighborhoods. The questions behind the survey questions may have been quite ominous: Did the war make you feel equal to a white man? Are you a threat to the Jim Crow order of Virginia and the implicit racial hierarchies of the United States? Do you need to die if America is to remain "free?" Under such circumstances one might expect veterans to modulate their responses to questions based on their perceptions of which answers might bring trouble. Both positive and negative feelings about the war could have been perceived as threatening by white society.[30]

On a more practical level, either method or necessity seems to have inserted men and women into the data collection process who may have changed or filtered soldiers' responses. One set of surveys shows rather clearly how answers may have been shaped by the methodology. Surveys reporting the war experiences of Eldo Roberts, Elijah Powell, Moses Parsons, Frank Nottingham, Jesse Mustgrave, Emanuel McCoy, and Charles Martin are written in identical handwriting and contain, in many cases, either the same or very similar responses to the open-ended questions on page four of the survey. The uniform hand suggests the presence of a third party who either re-wrote the soldiers' original written responses or took dictation. The uniformity of syntax indicates that the transcription or dictation by the third party filtered responses down to terse one- or two-word answers: Question: "What was your attitude toward military service and toward your call in particular?" Answer: "Favorable." Question:

"What were the effects upon yourself of your overseas experience?" Answer: "Beneficial." Question: "What effect, if any, did your experience have on your religious belief?" Answer: "Strengthened it." The individual soldiers are present in these responses, but it is obvious that their reactions have been shaped by the interlocutor more than by the survey itself. Such filtering is likely present in less obvious ways throughout the collection.

This is not to say that these seven survey responses and the broader collection are either so much patriotic dissembling or meaningless distillations of richer, more authentic sentiments.[31] While there is some uniformity across the seven surveys mentioned above, there is also tantalizing variety. For example, the respondents express a generally "favorable" opinion of "military service" and of their "call in particular," but offer different, if still reconcilable, assessments of the war. Asked about the effects of his combat experiences, Private Mustgrave of the 369th Infantry answered simply, "War is terrible," and Corporal Emanuel McCoy of the 540th Engineers noted his agreement with "General Tecumseh Sherman," presumably referring to Sherman's famous statement that "war is hell." Private Charles Martin, who also served with the 540th Engineers, focused less on the hellish terror of war and more on war's redemptive effects. Martin's response reads, "I am a broader minded man and more tolerant of faults in others by reason of these experiences." On the topic of religion, these seven surveys show a difference in the depth of responses though not in their general tone. These African American men, two Baptists, two Methodists, and a Catholic, found their faith improved by war. War made Elijah Powell "believe more firmly in a true God," and made Frank Nottingham's faith "stronger." Corporal Emanuel McCoy noted that having been to war he could "serve the Lord better."[32]

In addition to variation among the responses to the Virginia Survey, there is a vivid religio-political voice that African American veterans could have suppressed but did not. Some soldiers were quite explicit and quite angry about both sides of their double war experience, describing it as miserable as such and even more miserable having been rendered to a government that was blatantly racist and hypocritical. Herbert White, a lawyer and Howard University graduate, wrote that he "did not feel justified in going into the service to fight for so-called democracy which I could not myself enjoy as an American citizen."[33] Ellsworth Storrs expressed anger even while suppressing it. Asked to describe his attitude toward the military and toward being called to serve, he wrote, "I would rather not be quoted." These plainly negative reflections on the war experience—reflections that one would expect given the nature of that experience—make it difficult to explain away the more positive, more typical evaluations like that of veteran James Golden who explained that war "accentuated the desire which was dormant in me to have the full rights of citizenship."[34]

The words of African American soldiers Vernon Smith, Isaac Sanders, and Julius Mitchell demonstrate well the terrain shared by many soldiers regardless of race. They are representative both in their generally positive feelings about the war and in the more specific claims that waging war verified and enhanced manhood and solidified faith. Smith, Sanders and Mitchell, like many soldiers and war workers, black and white, expected and found redemption in war. Their statements, terse as they may be, are also an excellent guide to the contours of the war experience that were more specific to African Americans. In each of these responses, the importance of the war as a European event is matched or eclipsed by its importance for African Americans in the United States. In the thoughts of each soldier, the religiousness of war experiences, real and transformative, lent force to those in America who were struggling to realize visions of the Promised Land.

A DEEPENING FAITH IN MANHOOD

The black soldiers whose experiences of the war most closely approximated the experiences of their white counterparts were the volunteer members of the Fifteenth New York National Guard, nationalized as the 369th Infantry Regiment. The Fifteenth New York was organized through the combined efforts of the cultural, religious, and political leaders of black Harlem and New York City's progressive white elites. Still, it was clear from very early on that the Fifteenth New York would have a different and rockier path to war than white units. Organizers had to fight from the beginning to secure adequate space and equipment for training and to gain the support of a sometimes skeptical black population.[35] To the end of gaining that support, Colonel William Hayward drew on the influence and fame of black veterans, athletes, and the popular musician James Reese Europe, and eventually got the Fifteenth New York close enough to "fighting strength" (3,000 men) to proceed.[36]

The unit's training regimen took them to Camp Wadsworth in South Carolina, where the local population was, to say the least, concerned about their presence. Mayor John Floyd of nearby Spartanburg, South Carolina tried preemptively to dispel any ideas that black soldiers had about their status in the community: "I can say right here that they will not be treated as anything except negroes. We shall treat them exactly as we treat our resident negroes."[37] Mayor Floyd did not care who was fighting whom in Europe and what the soldiers coming to his town might encounter in the trenches. Of ultimate importance to him was the defense of the racist hierarchy in which he lived, and moved, and had his being. On at least two occasions, altercations between white locals and black soldiers perceived as disrespectful of local "ways" threatened to ignite racial violence of the kind that had erupted in Houston and East St. Louis earlier in the year.[38] While training at Camp Mills on the somewhat friendlier turf of New York, tensions between the Fifteenth New York and an all-white regiment from Alabama again almost boiled over into violence.[39] The war that the Fifteenth New York was to fight raged in Europe, but the fight against bigotry began on American soil.

Once the Fifteenth New York arrived in France and became the 369th Infantry Regiment, they were disowned by General Pershing and attached to the French Army. Race relations among French soldiers, though not always characterized by an egalitarian spirit, were not nearly as strained as they were in the A.E.F. and so, in a French fulfillment of American prophecies of war, the men of the 369th found that the heat of combat actually *did* melt false distinctions among men.[40] In the course of the war, the 369th spent more consecutive days in the front lines than any other American unit and claimed in Needham Roberts and Henry Johnson the first soldiers of the American Expeditionary Force to be awarded the French Croix de Guerre for gallantry in combat (see chapter 1). By the measure of those who count exposure to death and maiming as luck, the 369th was one lucky outfit. Private Vernon Smith of the 369th was among those who felt lucky. His service in the 369th put him in the middle of a great adventure and helped develop his manhood in ways that he thought of as religious.

Vernon Smith was born in Norfolk County, Virginia on January 4, 1900, but had covered a lot of ground by the time he reached his eighteenth birthday. Like thousands of African Americans in the second decade of the twentieth century, he moved out of the South and settled in a northern urban center, in his case Brooklyn, New York. Smith found work there as a cook on the Cunard Line. But the adventures of trans-Atlantic cruise line work gave way to the "adventures" of war on May 19, 1917, when the seventeen-year-old Smith joined the Fifteenth New York.[41] Smith joined for reasons expressed by thousands of other soldiers. He was motivated, he recalled, by the threat of German tyranny: "My attitude was to fight for democracy, because I felt like we did not want any Hun." "[E]very man," Smith declared, "should have his right."

After enlisting, Smith was assigned to Company D and trained with his unit in various armories around Manhattan and in upstate New York. He was then assigned to guard the Lehigh Valley Railroad for two months. If he was with his unit during the tense times at Camp Wadsworth, South Carolina and at Camp Mills, New York, he did not make note of either. Instead, Vernon Smith wrote fairly glowingly of his "experiences in each camp" describing them as "great, because a colored man in war . . . before did not have the knowledge of military science."[42] As he learned to fight as a soldier, he also learned to be proud of soldiering and of his unit's ability to bear up under trials. Smith recalled with pride the Fifteenth New York's reaction when their first attempt at crossing to France ended with a ship fire, and their second nearly ended after a collision with a British transport. He wrote, "we never lost our nerve . . . so by the good lord we arrive in Brest, France on the 27 day of Dec. [1917]"[43]

Smith "first went into action" on March 16, 1918 and, he noted, was also involved in battles on the 14th and 25th of September, during which he and his comrades "captured [prisoners] by [the] Battalion." Thinking back on the feelings that combat called forth in him, he recalled being impressed by the need to "fight for my country, and to kill as many Huns as I could . . . for the benefit of my people at home."[44] On February 13, 1919, the 369th Infantry Regiment returned to Hoboken aboard the "Vaterland." Smith was discharged at Camp Upton eleven days later. Just why he returned to Portsmouth, Virginia after the war and did not remain in Brooklyn is a mystery, but like so many veterans, Smith likely followed the work. While working as a ship-fitter's helper in Norfolk Navy Yard, his job when the Virginia War Commission found him, he recalled not only an *expectation* of redemption through war, but an *experience* of redemption as well. Asked if the experience of war had an effect on his *religious* beliefs, Smith answered that "going overseas . . . made me a better man."[45]

There are two points at which the double nature of Smith's war experience is evident; both intersect with broader notions of the religiousness of the war. The first of these is his assertion, made twice, of what I have called the redemptive effects of war for his community and "the race." Smith justified volunteering for the service on the grounds that "we did not want any Hun" and "every man should have his right." He also framed any killing he may have done with the thought that it was done "for the benefit of my people at home." Based on these comments, it is clear that, while Smith was willing to fight and kill German soldiers, he was at least equally interested in the potential for his actions to redeem and transform America. There is a telling lack of geographical specificity to Smith's comments about not wanting "any Hun" and every man having "his right."

The second point of double-consciousness emerges from Smith's response to the survey question on war's religious effects. Going overseas, he wrote, made him "a better man." Many American soldiers, black and white, expressed this sentiment. It can certainly be read as a gloss on Rooseveltian theories of masculinity; the religiousness that Smith perceived can be attributed to a broad sense of the redemption offered by rugged living on the "Frontier." But as a black man, Smith was also almost certainly thinking of his place as a "man of color" in America and how war had affected it. Both Booker T. Washington and W.E.B. Du Bois

hoped to "improve" African American manhood and argued from different perspectives for the importance of improved manhood to the future
"the Race." By describing himself as "better," Smith may have meant to
emphasize that life in the midst of war had elevated his morality, straight-
ened him up, made him a cleaner-living and more conscientious person.
This reading, which emphasizes the "better" in "better man," harmonizes
with the progressive thinking that suffused the white officer corps of
Smith's division. Such thoughts also characterize the discourse that
emerged from Booker T. Washington's Tuskegee Institute, which emphasized a man's responsibility to be a properly moral, self-sufficient and
productive member of the Southern agricultural commonwealth. Better
men, Washington believed, would elevate the race in the South and bring
about a gradual reformation to a more egalitarian society.

But Smith may also have seen improved *manhood* as religious *per se*.
That is, he may have meant that by expressing and developing specifically
masculine qualities in the cauldron of war, he was *de facto* engaged in a
religious exercise. This reading, which emphasizes the "man" in "better
man," approaches the muscular Christian view that physical fitness reflected spiritual fitness, the soldierly view that combat offered the ultimate
stage on which to demonstrate and refine masculinity and faith, and
the Du Boisian view that true black men stood up and fought against
injustice and demanded their God-given rights of self-determination and
full participation in American democracy.[46] The fighting and resulting
masculine refinement Vernon Smith encountered in Europe would, on this
reading, lead to a more effective, more masculine struggle for citizenship
rights in America.

We cannot know for sure, but it is most likely that Smith's sense of the
religiousness of his manhood was more closely tied to the Du Boisian,
activist reading than to the Washingtonian and the moralist. Given the
connection he made between fighting in France and giving "every man
his right," it seems likely he saw manhood as determined by equality before the law and by the ability to fight those who would systematically
oppress others. By waging a double war, Smith came to believe or was
reinforced in his belief—widely shared—that the sanctifying fires of
combat had forged in him a new, more militant, more Christian manhood, and that being a Christian man required struggling for equal
citizenship in America.

ENCOUNTERING COMBAT AND SEEING TRUTH

The story of Corporal Isaac Sanders, another combat veteran, points to
the double-consciousness that attended African American soldiers' en-

counters with the combat numinous. Sanders wrote of his war experiences with nearly untainted affection and made clear his belief that his time in combat had both strengthened his faith and, like most encounters with the combat numinous, revealed Truth. Black and white soldiers and war workers agreed about the principle, *in bello veritas*, but many black soldiers heard in the bloody cacophony a gospel of racial equality quite different from the gospel of a vindicated white manhood that many white soldiers discerned and that the commanders of the American Expeditionary Force sought to propagate. The truth that Isaac Sanders took away from war was his equality with American men of all races.

Isaac Sanders was born in Clayton, North Carolina and grew up both there and in Portsmouth, Virginia. His father, J. R. Sanders, was an African Methodist Episcopal minister.[47] With or without the consent of his father and his mother Vinnie, Isaac left home on October 27, 1917, to enlist in the Army. Sanders' early days as a soldier traced a hopeful historical arc. He trained at Camp Lee—named for Confederate General Robert E. Lee—in Virginia until March of 1918 when he was transferred to Camp Upton—named for Union Civil War General Emory Upton—in New York, and Company L of the 367th Regiment, Ninety-second Division.[48] Three months later, on June 10, 1918, Sanders and his unit left Hoboken on board the transport ship *America* and headed across the Atlantic. Looking back on this initial phase of his war service, Isaac Sanders wrote "camp life didn't agree with me very well" but noted little negative effect. All things considered, Sanders had "no kick against the service on this [the American] side of the ocean."[49]

Sanders' regiment moved into action on August 23, 1918 in the St. Mihiel sector, where they stayed through the mid-September Battle of St. Mihiel in which the A.E.F. and French Army units overwhelmed withdrawing German troops and flattened out a once troublesome salient in the Western Front. Sanders was promoted to corporal on October 6, three days before the 367th again went into action in the Marbache sector north of the eastern French town of Nancy. It was easy for Sanders to chronicle his movement to and through war, but describing the experience was a more difficult task. He called the effects of these experiences "good" but joined many other soldiers in noting that precise impressions of the fighting were "of such a nature that they can not be easily put on paper." As far as the relationship between the war and his faith was concerned, this son of a preacher noted that war "made a better Christian of me." Perhaps the catechesis of war reached Sanders in ways that his father's sermons never did.[50] In addition to these religious benefits, Sanders felt authorized by war to demand things of American society that he had not, it seems, demanded before. He wrote, "After passing through these experiences I feel that I should get a square deal before the law and everywhere that requires right and justice." With one just war for democracy won in Europe, Sanders saw clearly the righteousness of the struggle for equal participation in American civil society.

Sanders served in a regiment, the 367th Infantry, composed primarily of New-York-area African Americans and commanded by a white colonel, James A. Moss, who, like Colonel William Hayward of the 369th, believed in the martial potential of black soldiers.[51] It is possible that Sanders' awakened desire for justice and fairness had less to do with war and combat *per se*, and more to do with the environment in which he served. His unit was drawn from a generally wealthier, better educated, less oppressed African American community and took part in a training program designed by Colonel Moss to cultivate racial pride and unit morale. But Sanders pointed to a broader set of sources for his claims to "right and justice," referencing the "experiences" he had "passed through": training, transit, combat. Like many soldiers, black and white, native born and immigrant, Sanders felt that perseverance in the face of the hardships of war authorized him to obtain a "square deal." If he hadn't deserved it before, he certainly did now.[52] Those who had stood before the combat numinous and been proven true did not need to be measured *again* for their worthiness.

But many African American soldiers did not end up in the middle of the fight, surrounded by the thrilling, horrifying, sanctifying chaos. Some of these returned from their less complete encounters with the combat numinous bearing mixed feelings of worthiness. Willie Thomas of the 542nd Engineers would have welcomed the opportunity Isaac Sanders had to wield a weapon in combat and "be right in the midst of it all." During his service in the Argonne Forest, "fighting was going on all around" and the combat numinous was exerting its fascinating and terrifying push-pull, but his job was not to fight.[53] Thomas' proximity to combat affected him in two ways. The first, articulated by many who did not actually "go over the top" in combat, was a mild frustration, a restlessness to drink more deeply from the cup of war. "[W]e fellers that wasn't regular fighting boys just felt that if we was fighting, [we] could have done so much. A person feels restless when fighting is going on all around them and they not being able to take part [sic]." Real as his sacrifices were and involuntary as was his separation from the fighting, Thomas felt that his service was not quite complete, that he was not as fully authorized by war as "the boy that was fighting . . . doing all and more too than was required." He longed to take that extra, potentially fatal step.[54] Thomas also wrote that life at war invigorated his faith and drew him closer to God. "It made me trust God more and live closer to him everyday of my life."[55]

In their recollections of the affective dimension of life in the shadow of combat and in their descriptions of the positive effects of war on religious belief, Isaac Sanders and Willie Thomas support the notion that soldiers' desires to be immersed in combat, if not entirely "religious," are made more intelligible by reference to the combat numinous. Thomas and Sanders diverge, however, in their reactions to post-war America. Sanders was ready to demand justice. Thomas wrote differently. He was "glad to go to do my bit for my country and my flag," but found the post-war world "altogether different from what [he] had been made to believe [he] was to expect."[56] Thomas did not write as one girded for a direct confrontation with the forces of oppression. Rather, his experiences in and after war left him longing, wondering, and approaching the myriad troubles of the post-war era less as crises and more as disappointments. Both Isaac Sanders and Willie Thomas felt that war had made them better Christians, but the war led them to different conclusions about how best to be a Christian citizen of the United States.

RENDER UNTO PHARAOH: SERVING CHRIST AND NATION

When Julius Mitchell and Cerene Barry married on December 8, 1915, the war in Europe was, most likely, far from their thoughts. Middlesex, North Carolina and central France are an ocean apart and, like many Americans, the newlyweds had more immediate concerns than the carnage unfolding thousands of miles away. As African Americans living in the South, the Mitchell's concerns were more pressing than most. Should they "put their buckets down where they were" and work the land of the familiar South, or pack up their things and look for the Promised Land in Philadelphia, New York, or perhaps Chicago? Would local white men, their race pride enflamed by D. W. Griffith's newly released film *The Birth of a Nation*, decide to make an example of Julius, Cerene, or one of the couple's relatives? There were many thoughts, hopes, and fears to occupy the young couple; war in Europe was probably not foremost among them.[57]

If the Mitchells ever considered moving north, they opted for a modest plan. Sometime between 1916 and 1918 they settled in Norfolk, Virginia, 150 miles to the northwest of Middlesex. Julius found work in engineering there; perhaps the couple also found a Baptist church that was to their liking. But events in Europe and in Washington, D.C. would not leave them alone, and soon the war became a grim presence in their lives. On July 18, 1918, two-and-a-half years after their wedding, Julius took a new set of vows, this time betrothing him to the U.S. Army. Until the government decided otherwise, Julius would be Private Mitchell; his "family" would be Company D, 545th Engineers.[58]

Mitchell entered military training immediately and spent less than a month learning how to do the work required of him. Twenty-six days were all the military needed or could afford to turn Julius Mitchell from a civilian into a soldier, and on August 25, 1918 he began moving toward war. Jarring as this first stage of military life could be, Mitchell remembered it in mostly positive terms. He heard his country's call to duty and wanted to respond. Camp life and basic training, demeaning to some, struck Mitchell as generally beneficial. The experience, he recalled, allowed him to "think more" and made him "stronger" physically.[59]

On September 23, 1918, after moving from Virginia to New Jersey to meet a transport ship, Julius Mitchell and the 545th Engineers steamed out of Hoboken and set a course for Saint Nazaire, France. They arrived on October 6, stayed in Saint Nazaire until October 16, and then continued moving toward the front, reaching the Argonne Forest on October 27. The sheer scale of the war and its technologies of death impressed Mitchell just as it had other participants and observers. He recalled marveling at "the great things God has enabled men to do," even if those "great things" took violence to new levels. But Mitchell was not only awed by the war, he was also inspired, even revived by it. On the one hand, involvement in the war effort and exposure to combat invigorated his civic consciousness, making him "more determined to stand for the right and my colors [sic]." On the other hand, the experiences of war animated and deepened his faith, making him "[a] more devout Christian."[60]

Julius Mitchell was discharged from the Army on July 5, 1919, and returned to his wife and his work. He was unharmed, but he was changed. Mitchell felt strengthened both in his sense of civic duty—his desire to "stand for the right"—and in his commitment to Christianity. When Julius Mitchell was asked "What has been the effect of all these experiences as contrasted with your state of mind before the war?" he replied, weaving together civic and religious language, that war had made him "[a] more sober and Christ-like patriot."

What did the thirty-year-old veteran mean by this? Did he, like so many white soldiers, see a parallel between the suffering and sacrifice he had endured for nation and world and Christ's suffering on the cross? Was he, perhaps, articulating a vision of patriotism "Christ-like" in its attention to the marginal, the suffering, and the powerless? Or was Mitchell playing with words to express frustration? Did he see Christ as the paradigmatic *anti-patriot*—an example of righteous unwillingness to place ultimate hope in the state? Perhaps he was thinking darker thoughts. He could not but note that many white Americans saw African American veterans as an especially grave threat. Perhaps Julius Mitchell, war veteran and patriot, feared that the very men whose freedom he had helped ensure might try to defend their racist order by hanging him from a tree— a modern crucifixion.[61]

Booker T. Washington and W.E.B. Du Bois establish the range of meanings of Julius Mitchell's "more sober, Christ-like" patriotism. Sobriety as a practice and sobriety as an outlook were of equal importance to Washington and his cohort. They saw abstinence from alcohol as central to the intra-racial project of self-betterment and to the interracial project of maintaining a sterling image in the eyes of white America. As Isaac Fisher argued on April 24, 1915 in the *Negro Farmer*'s "Temperance Number," drunkenness among "Negroes" gravely damaged both projects. It reinforced negative stereotypes and contributed to crime and race riots; drunkenness also made Jim Crow travel an even more "cruel punishment" and it sapped strength from the race: "A Sober Race," the paper declared, "is a Powerful Race."[62] And when Fisher turned his attention to the Great War and the question of African American service, he called for a "sober"— clear-eyed—approach that recognized both racial injustice in the United States and the absolute necessity of African American service. If we withhold service out of protest, he argued, we will provide ammunition to those who stand against us. The Washingtonian understanding of *Christ-likeness*, consistently present in Fisher's writings, involved hard work, patience, endurance of suffering and an ability to keep faith with one's God through even Jobian trials. The "Christ-like patriot" would be a reformist, not a revolutionary; a faithful servant tied to the land and focused on working within the extant social structures for the benefit of self, family, race, and nation.

A Du Boisian exegesis of Mitchell's self-description is different. Regardless of one's position on temperance and prohibition, W.E.B. Du Bois would describe "sober" patriotism as affection for the United States as it *might* be *if* the persistent, vicious, institutionalized oppression of African Americans ceased and *if* all were treated equally before the law. A "sober" patriot would love the promise of the United States but would despise race hatred and would critique all caught up in its grip. The Christ-like patriot, in Du Bois' eyes, would be committed to an active struggle against injustice and would give voice to the fiery anti-establishment, anti-complacency, anti-hypocrisy message that some find in the Gospels and that all find in Du Bois himself.

The contrast among these possible readings of Mitchell's view of the war and its effects is stark and we cannot, in the end, locate Mitchell on the continuum between them. Did his experience of service straighten him up and revive his commitment to a life of self-improvement on the land? Or did his exposure to war in Europe prepare him for a different war with new travails at home? The precise contours of his thoughts are, sadly, lost to history. We can, however, note that in contrast to white soldiers, African American soldiers drew on Christ imagery less to point up the righteousness of their lives and actions, less to lay claim to heaven, and more to highlight the corruption of the Pharaoh in whose army they served and suffered. Thus when Mitchell wrote that war made him "a more sober, Christ-like patriot" he was more likely pointing to his suffering than to his virtue (and he almost certainly did not have in mind a khaki-clad, helmeted Christ with a blood-red bayonet). When Private Oliver Rogers, an African American Catholic, wrote that he "simply felt like a soldier of Christ and of the Government" he was resisting the temptation to elide the two authorities completely. The causes of Christ and of the United States could surely converge, but they were not forever one and the same. When Roscoe Jamison directed readers of *The Crisis* to look upon African American soldiers: "Stand and behold! They take the field today, / Shedding their blood like Him now held divine, / That those who mock might find a better way;" he emphasized not the divinity of martial triumph, but the divinity of bleeding. Addie Hunton, too, saw suffering as a primary characteristic of the black soldier's Christ-like nature. She "witnessed" the connection between black soldiers and Christ on May 29th, 1919, when the guns were silent and the United States was preparing to dedicate a massive new cemetery at Romagne. Hunton and Kathryn Johnson had been running a YMCA canteen for black soldiers charged with recovering and reburying the remains of the American war dead.[63] The burial work was indescribably gruesome and, according to Hunton, stretched the willingness of black soldiers to serve the U.S. government almost to the breaking point. But then Hunton and Johnson looked out the window of their YMCA kitchen and saw "what seemed to us a wonderful sight."

> Two long lines of soldiers were before us–one moving slowly over the hill and the other coming up the main road–each man bearing on his shoulder a single white cross that would rest above the grave of a fellow-hero. Quickly our mind traveled back over the centuries to Him who had borne the cross toward Golgotha, and we saw in these dark-skinned sons of America bearing those white crosses, something of the same humility and something of the same sorrow that characterized the Master, but we also beheld in them the Christ spirit grown large, beautiful and eternal with the ages.

Hunton saw the black soldiers, the white crosses, the humility and the sorrow. In these she saw Christ. Her observation, focused though it was on the procession of soldiers, also reflected fully the double nature of the African American war experience. She hoped, as Julius Mitchell,

Oliver Rogers, and Roscoe Jamison surely did as well, that these imitators of Christ were also "making an unconscious challenge to the very heart of the United States for the rights of the twelve millions of its citizens whose loyalty had thus endured the test." She hoped that as families of the fallen came to France to mourn the dead and saw the work done by the black soldiers, "a real peace, born of knowledge and gratitude, shall descend upon us, blotting out hate and its train of social and civil injustices[.]" This redemption to comity and justice would be the most meaningful recognition "of the pain and sacrifice of these dark-browned heroes of ours."[64]

Black soldiers did not match their white counterparts' levels of comfort with, and affection for Christ the warrior. In black soldiers and war workers' depictions of Christ, the emphasis is more on sacrifice and suffering than on virtue and violence. This is not to say that African American soldiers and war workers were any more or less violent in the field, more or less fond of their war experiences, or more or less inclined to resist institutionalized racism on the home front. It is, however, to argue, based on the evidence I have encountered, that black soldiers and war workers did not see this violence as imitative of Christ and Christ's saving power in history.

The absence of the righteous warrior Christ from African American reflections is important for two reasons. (One must, of course, be cautious when explaining or theorizing an absence, and I do not pretend to resolve the many questions that could attend this one.) First, it is meaningful as an instance of experience shaping theology. Few Americans knew better than African Americans the dark side of "righteous" violence waged by Christians. African American soldiers and war workers—not yet sixty years removed from slavery—were well aware of the horrors done under the guise of Christian civilization. The absence of a warrior Christ reflects, I believe, the unwillingness of African American soldiers and war workers to implicate Christ in war's inherent moral dubiousness. Second, this Christological difference says something quite profound about African American religion and African American patriotism in the Great War. The two civic natures of black soldiers and war workers—black and American—were not reconciled in a patriot Christ. Going to war for the nation was, as I have argued, an act of double importance for African American men and women. Maintaining a close relationship with God and Christ was also, for many, of great importance. These two endeavors intersected at many points, but in fighting and killing Germans, African Americans did not imagine themselves becoming more like Christ; service to country was not service to God. By maintaining this distinction, black men and women left open a wide range of "Christian" approaches to patriotism.

The Christ imagined by black soldiers and war workers offered salvation in the midst of struggle, suffering and sorrow, but unlike the Christ proclaimed by many white soldiers, did not require a sanctification of the Pharaoh nation. The struggle to reach the Promised Land could remain both *in* and *against* America. Thus, when Private Julius Mitchell of the 545th Engineers explained that war experiences had made him both a "more devout Christian" and a "more sober, Christ-like patriot," he was speaking for many African Americans, disappointed but not disillusioned by war, still drawn to the country that had called them to service and then treated them so shabbily; determined to "stand for the right and my colors [sic]" even if the consequences continued to be violent and the gains largely indiscernible.

The theologies of black soldiers and war workers accommodated the suffering and the promise of war, and found God in both.

CHAPTER FIVE

Ideal Women in an Ideal War

> There's a rose that grows in No Man's Land
> And it's wonderful to see,
> Though it's sprayed with tears, it will live for years,
> In my garden of memory.
> It's the one red rose the soldier knows,
> It's the work of the Master's hand;
> 'Mid the war's great curse stands the Red Cross Nurse,
> She's the rose of No Man's Land
> —"The Rose of No Man's Land," popular World War I song

LADY RANDOLPH CHURCHILL, the American-born mother of Winston Churchill, knew something about war. Born in 1854 to Brooklyn-based financier Leonard Jerome and his wife Clarissa, Jennie Jerome lived through the tumult of the American Civil War before her mother moved her to Paris in 1867.[1] Later in life, she witnessed first-hand England's mobilization for the Great War and likely heard stories of combat from her son, then serving as the First Lord of the British Admiralty, and from countless others. In the spring of 1916, Lady Churchill sat down with a "representative of the *New York Times*" to share with an American audience her experiences and her thoughts on what the current war would mean for women. She expounded on a wide range of topics, including the women's issues at stake in the war, the implications of wartime industry work for post-war discussions of women in the workplace and the voting booth, the financial sacrifices being offered by "more fortunate" classes in England, and changes in mourning attire among English women. At the heart of Lady Churchill's observations was the belief that the war was a transforming force. War was transforming women, she said, and was transforming societies' attitudes toward women. "Women have thrown themselves into it almost as earnestly as have the men," Lady Churchill proclaimed, and could expect for their efforts either triumph and progress or defeat and "retrogression." "If the Allies win the war the women of England, and . . . even those of the United States in a degree, will advance instantly a long step beyond the stage they had reached before the war began." The war was so momentous that it had to result in either gains or losses for women.[2]

The entry of the United States into the Great War less than one year later opened a chapter in the history of American women and war that Lady Churchill and like-minded contemporaries surely saw as promising. American soldier Walter Poague, serving with the Marines in the Azores, wrote to his mother in February of 1918, "This war is freeing women from a slavery as old as man. Women are to come into their own. It is a huge, tremendous, marvelous thing for women and worth while if only for that alone. Big days are coming and it is sister's generation who shall make the change."[3] His enthusiasm was warranted. American women found available an unprecedented range of ways to serve, and by war's end women's involvement in the effort had reached levels never before seen. On the home front, women served as military clerks, nurses, and hospitality workers in and around military encampments. They also entered the industrial workplace to replace the men who had been drafted.[4] If we follow recent scholarship on gender and the American Civil War and broaden the notion of "service" to include the contribution of goods produced in and sent from the home, the numbers of American women involved in the Great War soars.[5] On the Western Front, women were involved in clerical work and nursing, hospitality and entertainment, refugee relief and ambulance driving. More than 5,300 American women went to France to serve as nurses in the A.E.F. hospitals run by the Red Cross. At least 2,500 more served overseas in volunteer auxiliary services such as the YMCA and the Salvation Army. American women also served in the French and British armies and their volunteer auxiliaries.[6] The official report to General Pershing from E. C. Carter, Chief of the YMCA in France proclaimed, "No single factor has contributed so much to the influence of the Association upon the Army as the presence of this large company of magnificent American women. The service they have rendered is beyond praise."[7] This was, indeed, a significant development in the history of gender and warfare in America.

But though the Great War was fought by living, breathing men and women with particular histories and unique voices, these flesh-and-blood soldiers and war workers marched alongside powerful, tenacious, frequently religious character types, symbols, and myths. Mythic characters and narratives told people how to respond to war, how to act, how to conceive of morality and duty; those responding to war lived in and lived out those myths. Mythic notions of wartime gender roles shaped women's as well as men's experiences and understandings of the Great War. While American men drew on images of Christ, crusaders, and more modern American heroes, American women often turned to more general domestic ideals to frame their service. And just as many American soldiers found a circumstance in war that could validate and expand their masculinity and, in many cases, their Christianity, so too did American women find an arena for demonstrating the depth and truth of their usually domestic, broadly Christian womanhood. Like Lady Churchill, the female authors wrote of the excitement, the romance, the overpowering force of war; they were eager to "join the fray." But, as this chapter argues, they wrote from within a deeply conservative framework—a framework that demonstrates not just how "powerfully gendering" war and memories of war can be, but also how overwhelmingly gendered the American experience of the Great War was.[8]

The excellent though by no means extensive scholarship on gender and war bears the marks of a contemporary "emerging literature." It is dutifully interdisciplinary, powerfully revisionist, and properly suspicious of grand narratives and false homogenies. But examinations of gender, particularly womanhood, in wartime have had to confront the relentlessly gendered nature of the subject—the "fact" that until very recently men did the vast majority of fighting and dying while women kept "the home fires burning." Philosophers, historians, and scholars of literature and the arts trained to examine and interrogate separate spheres ideology have found this rigid gendering fascinating but also deceptive. They point to women's wishes to become men and to fight for "the cause;" they tell stories of home-front struggles and women's not-so-passive reactions to calls for increased "sacrifice." In these stories, they have found that the particularities of culture and ethnicity, the hard realities of geography, and the meaning-making power of religion condition allegedly timeless notions of "duty" and "biology."[9]

The Great War era in America offered more than its share of complexities vis-à-vis gender. While white middle class women were actively writing the final chapters in two historic political struggles—to ban alcohol from the United States and to obtain the franchise—new and recent immigrant women were pointing up the ethnic and class-based nature of "separate spheres" ideologies by working outside the home to support their families. African American women in the urban North and rural South also confronted new cultural and economic realities, and, with immigrant women, attracted the attention of white Protestant reformers bent on "civilizing" households by proselytizing domesticity.[10] The women's voices in this chapter reflect some of the complexities of the moment, but also demonstrate the attractiveness of familiar, sanctified gender roles in times of upheaval. Many of the women who wrote about their war experiences were influenced by a feminine ideal closely approximating Jean Bethke Elshtain's "Beautiful Soul."[11] On Elshtain's account, the Beautiful Soul is domestic, nurturing, innocent, and pure; she loves and waits and mourns. She does not fight, but she is a dutiful supporter of "her" "Just Warrior" if not always of "the war" or of war in general. Though most clearly present in the literature and art of war, this ideal also clearly shaped individual lives—actions, emotions, memories.[12] The Beautiful Soul ideal was particularly strong among two groups of women whom I have labeled "War Wives and Mothers," and "Sisters in Arms."[13] On the home front and the Western Front, these women served as models of domestic womanhood as they served and praised and mourned American soldiers. But war experiences are multidirectional, and some women revised and applied gender ideals in subtle, creative, personal, and public ways. In the writings of a third group, "New Woman Warriors," one finds a more ambivalent relationship to the idealized, domestic, wartime woman. "New Woman Warriors," while clearly using a "grammar of gender" influenced by the domestic feminine ideals, used that grammar to express a wider range of views of womanhood and war and to direct critiques across lines of race and class.[14] But while New Woman Warriors could be pointed in their critiques of other women, they largely "kept faith" with America's Christ-like soldiers.

War Wives and Mothers

The home front is the most obvious place to locate exemplars of domestic femininity in wartime. Historically and with few exceptions, the home front is where women have remained during war. Ruth Wolfe Fuller and Mary Dearing were two who inhabited the already consecrated domestic "sphere" and who saw their wartime service as defined, if not always contained, by their roles as War Wives and Mothers. What unites these two and connects them to other women of their age and ages past is their attention to the sacrificial aspects of their roles. As War Wives and Mothers, they reflected repeatedly on the sacrifices of self and son/husband required of them by God and nation. Both clearly struggled with their duty but found in faith and a gendered ideal orienting narratives and identities and even, it seems, a measure of solace.

Ruth Fuller's narrative, *Silver Lining: The Experiences of a War Bride*, presents as clearly and purely as any the War Wife ideal. It is the story of Fuller's response to her Just Warrior husband's preparation for, and service in, war. He trains for the fight, building up his body and acquiring lethal knowledge; she trains for his absence and keeps a stiff upper lip. She cries with his permission and then only little. She understands, unlike some she has met, that her wartime duties include surrendering her husband to the nation without protest and, for the sake of her Just Warrior, "maintain[ing] optimism and courage, keeping the lamp of inspiration trimmed."[15] While her husband wages war, Fuller serves in the capacities available to her—she keeps their house, volunteers at the Fort Devens, Massachusetts YMCA Canteen and the Red Cross; she even writes poetry.

Ruth Wolfe Fuller's poem "In Appreciation," which appeared first in the periodical *American Khakiland*, published between 1917 and 1919, demonstrates how tightly interwoven were her gender-specific understandings of service, trial, duty, and faith. She opens the poem with a reflection on the Silver Star pin that she wears over her heart to indicate that her husband is at war, and then offers a prayer to "the dear God to keep you, / My soldier, wherever you are." She continues in an explicitly religious voice, describing the divinity of the connection between her life on the home front—a living testament to him—and his life at war: "Under the emblem your image / Is written in heart-beats of mine; / It mirrors the every-day level / Of living, as wholly Divine." Fuller then looks back to the mythic loves of the chivalric age and imagines herself, castle-kept and content, intimately connected to her war-waging husband. "As Launcelot's Shield was embroidered, / A fabric for my Knight I weave. / My soul is inlaid through the pattern, / And all that I am–and believe!"[16] A man and woman in wartime are distinctively divine but also inseparably so. Her very soul forms part of his shield; all that she is and believes protects him in the violent turmoil.

Throughout her account of the war and presumably in the midst of her war experiences, Fuller understood her offering to the nation to also be an offering to God. Indeed, in explaining the difficult decision to spend the duration of the war in the home she and her husband were building together, Fuller drew from the book of Exodus, the quintessential Jewish / Christian narrative of chosenness and divine guidance in tribulation. "It would have been so comforting to be with my own people in my loneliness ... But the Pillar of Fire pointed otherwise, to my mind. It was to go back, take up life where I had so hurriedly dropped it ... and, one way or another, make good."[17] Like a faithful Israelite in the desert, she chose to follow God's guidance. Ready as she was to sacrifice company and comfort, Fuller seemed slightly less wholehearted in offering her husband. In fact, she reasoned that the strength of her love for him and her faith would convince God to let him return. "God had given me a love outshadowing my highest dreams. Why should I not trust him to guard it?"[18] The Lord had given and, she was convinced, would not take away.

Ruth Fuller acted well the part of War Wife. She offered her husband dutifully, if not cheerfully. She saw her experiences on the home front as trials of faith and sensed that they were shared in their rough outlines, if not in their poetic rendering, by thousands upon thousands of other women. Mary Hinckley Dearing occupied a slightly different space in the life of "her" soldier—her son—but her understanding of the role that she played was similar to Fuller's, down to the images and tropes she used in her account. That son, Vinton Dearing, was killed in action on July 18, 1918. Mary Dearing then took up the melancholy but noble duties of the

War Mother who has sacrificed a son. She strove to uphold the meaning-fulness of her son's death, to keep his memory alive and untainted, and to vouch for his status as a Just Warrior.

Mary Dearing's voice is preserved in both the title and the wrenching introduction to her son's collected letters, *My Galahad of the Trenches*. As the title indicates, Dearing viewed her warrior son as the embodiment of the chivalric ideal both in his approach to war and in his relationships to women, herself included. He fought the war not for thrills or revenge, but to defend "his mother and all who meant so much to him."[19] More-over, he always recognized and reverenced the beauty of "Beautiful Souls." "His knightly qualities of soul and his gentle deference and thoughtful attentions to all women placed him in the Hall of King Ar-thur's Knights—the most knightly of them all."[20] In the brief biography, Mary Dearing balances such reminiscences of her son's devotion and ten-derness with assurances that Vinton was "none the less a *real* boy, loving play, having scraps with his elder brother, throwing himself into competi-tion and sports with all his heart . . . "[21] According to his mother, Vinton Dearing, a virtuous young man fighting fairly in defense of the innocent, had distilled the Just Warrior ideal to its essence. By her account, Mary Dearing struggled more to assume the role of the War Mother than her son did to become a soldier. When war came, Dearing wrote, she was already mourning the loss of her husband and was afraid that Vinton might go to France. "I knew my boy well enough to know he would want to enlist," she wrote, "but with all my heart I rebelled. I had not as yet risen to my privilege and duty." Her "privilege" was to be a War Mother; her duty was to offer her son to the nation. Her ascent to both culminated at a "dusky, dirty" train station where she fought off tears, gave him a "last, long kiss," and bade farewell to her son "strong with the strength of ten, a glorious soldier, my Galahad, my love-child."[22]

Mary Dearing's encomium for her fallen son is also, by turns, an enco-mium for her recently dead husband and the family's irretrievable former life as Baptist missionaries in Japan. Indeed, her treatment of the two men in the introduction to Vinton's collected letters hints at an elision of husband and son in her memory. She wrote of shopping for war equip-ment with her son "like two young things buying household furniture" and spending evenings "by our glowing fire with a few friends, sometimes alone, but always gloriously happy in each other."[23] Later, writing of her husband, Dearing states that "he lived and died . . . heroically and gloriously" and "won the victor's crown as truly as did the son win his Cross on the field of honor."[24] Mary Dearing's reflections on her losses demonstrate the power of the War Wife and Mother ideal to situate fe-male and male actors in memory, if not in the moment, and to frame death and loss. In remembering her husband, she conjured martial metaphor and alluded to the salvation that, for her, death in war implied. She was most comfortable, it seems, thinking of these two departed men as fallen warriors: her husband a missionary soldier for Christ; her son a military soldier for Christ and nation. With both men gone, her duty—elegantly kept—was to mourn and remember.[25]

SISTERS IN ARMS

The American women who traveled to Europe to help wage war or simply to be near it were, at one level, crossing significant gender boundaries. By risking passage to France and working in support of an expeditionary army, Isabel Anderson, Doris Kellog, Marian Baldwin, and others were going to war as few women had gone before and they knew it. An anonymous female volunteer in the YMCA wrote to her family, "Oh! How I wish I could tell you how glad I am to be here. It's just the best thing that ever came my way; so please be happy about me. . . . "[26] One can certainly see in the fact of geographic displacement and in the excitement of those undertaking it a revision of wartime gender ideals. But the simple dichotomy suggested by such a reading—that is, those who stayed home embraced a domestic ideal, those who went to England, Belgium, and France did not—misses two important truths. First, it ignores the potential and the reality, recorded in the diaries and letters of men and women alike, for substantial and heartbreaking home-front departures from the ideal.[27] "Home" has never been a sturdy bulwark against the outside world's corruptions—many things have gone on (and come off) in the dancing light of a burning "home fire." Second, there was little to nothing about movement to, and service in, France that implied or required revision, much less abandonment, of domestic womanhood. On the contrary, many of the women who served in the war did so explicitly to act as pillars of domesticity for America's young men in France. As such, these Sisters in Arms carried out a mission remarkably similar to the home-front work of War Wives and Mothers. Their service was, however, slightly different in its symbolic orientation. In the home-like environs that Sisters in Arms maintained in Red Cross hospitals, YMCA huts, and Salvation Army canteens, they acted as reminders of womanly virtue; they engaged not in sacrifice but in the moral suasion that many saw as characteristic of Christian womanhood.

The early summer of 1918 found American men going boldly where few American men had gone before. Though the Great War was in its last half year, there were few indications on the ground that it was in anything but full and bloody bloom. German armies had staged a surprisingly successful spring offensive, crushing the British Fifth Army in the north and putting pressure on French and American troops, particularly around the village of Chateau-Thierry fifty miles to the east of Paris. German artillery shells and aerial bombs hit Paris regularly. Americans were, for the first time, dying in large numbers. "Civilization" appeared to be teetering. American eyes were focused on their relatively novice troops suffering, fighting, and dying "over there." Mythmakers found in the words of Marine Gunnery Sergeant Dan Daly a pithy statement of the American Just Warrior's spirit in war. Attempting to rally his men for a frontal assault on a German machine gun position, Daly reportedly exposed himself to the withering fire and yelled to his still-sheltered soldiers, "Come on you sons of bitches! Do you want to live forever?"

The early summer of 1918 found American *women* going and living boldly where few had gone or lived before. Stirred by a nation's need and by a desire for adventure, women of all ages traveled to France to work in YMCA canteens, Army and Red Cross field hospitals, privately funded ambulance outfits, and in numerous other religious and charitable capacities. One such Sister in Arms was Carolyn Clarke, a nurse's aide in the Red Cross. She arrived in France in the spring of 1918 with ten other women, eight nurses and two other aides. The group's first assignment was a hospital near Jouy-sur-Morin, roughly twenty-five miles south of Chateau-Thierry. Recalling the trip to Juoy via Montmirail, Clarke wrote that her group was "supperless and dusty but feeling that we were at last going to have a part in this great big war."[28] She did, in fact, "have a part." She helped establish a forward hospital that provided much needed treatment to American soldiers wounded in and around Chateau-Thierry. It is possible that men wounded responding to Gunnery Sergeant Daly's profane exhortation to mortality came under Clarke's care. One recent amputee whom she described as "a poor corporal from Kentucky who was a saloon keeper by profession" might have been one of Daly's men.

Carolyn Clarke was tending to the Kentuckian when a wounded lieutenant emerged from surgery still under the influence of ether. Clarke noted that the lieutenant, like many similarly drugged, was "swearing most unpleasantly" and using language soldiers found "irreproachable" *if* they knew that a nurse was near. The corporal from Kentucky became quite upset and nervous as the words continued to spill forth from the lieutenant's mouth, soiling Clarke's ears ever more. When she asked the saloon keeper-turned-soldier what was the matter, he replied that he "just could not stand to have me hear what the man was saying."[29] He did not calm down, Clarke recalled, until she finally left the room.

This scene looks like a snapshot of the ridiculousness of war. A soldier who had just lost a leg was upset not about the leg, but about the effect of another man's half-conscious, profane tirade on a nurse whom he did not know. The fact that this saloon keeper—who had so much else about which to be upset—focused on the defiling of Nurse Clarke's supposedly virgin ears is, however, telling. It indicates that Clarke's presence gave at least the saloon keeper (Clarke believed others as well) pause when it came to morally questionable behavior.[30] It was okay, expected, even the stuff of myth for a soldier such as Gunnery Sergeant Dan Daly to curse in the presence of fellow soldiers. When spheres collided, however, Just Warriors had to "protect" their Sisters in Arms and their "homes" from contamination. But what of Ms. Clarke and her thoughts about soldiers who sometimes cursed when wounded and drugged? In her writings, she acknowledged soldiers' minor transgressions, but always emphasized their underlying fidelity. She told the story of the cursing lieutenant not to highlight the vulgarity but to highlight the virtue *in extremis* of a wounded saloon-keeper-turned-soldier. This virtue, she believed, was deep and true and even Christ-like.[31] She gladly spoke up as a war-verified witness for the character of American men.

> We who cared for the boys lived through each battle as it was retold for us, either by a conscious patient right from the scene or by one under ether, whose descriptions were often more vivid. We lived through the war from Chateau-Thierry to the Argonne only a few hours behind the actual events, only a few miles behind the lines and we learned the spirit of our American men, kind, home-loving and unconquerable.[32]

Having "been there," Clarke could vouch—as few others could—for the wholesome morality and fighting prowess of the American fighting man. Serving men such as these was, she believed, the high point of her life: "I wouldn't give up one of those days or nights working for the soldiers for anything else this life can offer."[33]

The anonymous author of *A Red Triangle Girl in France* was also quite conscious of her ability as a Sister in Arms to shore up the moral defenses of the soldiers. She wrote of an incident in the spring of 1918 in which she engaged a lonely soldier in conversation and, thus, discouraged him from drinking. "I didn't do a thing; it was just that he was given a chance to think about 'her,' whoever she is, at home."[34] A letter that she wrote later that summer, after deciding to renew her service and stay on until the end of the war, conveyed that she sensed the value of her service—both as an individual woman and as a symbol of womanhood. "I don't see how I can stop this side of the end of the war, and ever look myself in the face again. I *know* that American women are needed here. . . . I should like to stay here for the duration. I've got my place. I know the men. . . . They are coming to me with their confidences increasingly every day, sometimes funny, but often tragic. I can not leave this service."[35] To turn from the men when they seemed most in need of her sisterhood would be to break an unspoken covenant and, it seems, to rebel against her very essence. This Sister in Arms was most interested in demonstrating the importance of the domestic sphere and her fitness to occupy it.

Another Sister in Arms, a nurse surnamed Dare, published mid-war a collection of letters titled *Mademoiselle Miss*, which could have served as a manual for the aspiring mother in war service; this in spite of the fact that the "American girl" who wrote the letters had the "rank of Lieutenant" and served "at the Front."[36] Passages in Dare's letters could mark her as a reviser of the domestic feminine ideal, one who sought to, and did, transcend a role she found constraining. She wrote on September 20, 1915, of the conversion-like effects of "hear[ing] the guns for the first time! It is a sensation so vast and lonely and crowded and cosmic all at once that one seems born into a new phase of existence where the old ways of feeling things do not answer any longer."[37] Later, she expressed again her dissatisfaction with these "old" ways of feeling and contrasted them with the awakening provided by war: "Actually, for the first time in my life I begin to feel as a normal being should, in spite of the blood and anguish in which I move I really am *useful*, that is all. . . . "[38] At the same time, however, she described herself and her patients in ways that militate against over-reading her "conversion." Her sense of newness and usefulness must be read through the role Dare imagined herself occupying when she achieved those feelings.

Throughout her letters, Ms. Dare portrayed herself as a mother and her patients as children. The first clues to her mothering role emerge in a letter dated September 28, 1915, "I do love to coddle and make comfy" and another written between November 5th and 10th, 1915, when she wrote of her patients, "my 29 children are resting after their midday soup."[39] This general sense of motherhood became more specific when an Algerian soldier named "Croya" entered her care. She wrote with more than a hint of colonialist condescension, "Perhaps Croya is the only son I shall ever have but I thank Heaven for giving me, to nurse and love, this poor wild child of the desert." Dare noted later that Croya reciprocated, referring to her as "Mama." This mother-child dynamic reached a remarkable level in a February 27, 1916 letter describing the evacuation of stable patients in anticipation of a rush of new bodies from Verdun. Among those to whom she said goodbye was a more racially apt soldier-child, "my gold-haired, pink-cheeked little sergeant Vic—the prize baby, who looked so sweet in a white chemise (I confess the weakness of reserving the best-looking one for him) and who was more afraid of being tickled than of having his fracture dressed." The wounded soldiers to whom Miss Dare administered care were, in her mind, not men waging war but innocent, wounded children, even babies. She prided herself beyond all else with creating a comfortable home for them; a home in which she was mother. Dare conveys the purity, innocence, and domestic virtue characteristic of the Sister in Arms flawlessly. She also demonstrates the extent to which her "domesticity" participated in the public racial hierarchies of the time. She would "mother" poor wild children of the desert alongside blond, pink-cheeked soldiers; she would also make clear—to her readers if not to the soldiers—who was the "prize baby."

NEW WOMAN WARRIORS

The fact that, on balance, Great War experiences did not disrupt or powerfully challenge late-Victorian notions of gender roles and ideals does not mean that moments of transgression were either absent or insignificant. The domestic ideals that many inhabited with such enthusiasm did not (and could not) contain the attitudes and experiences of all women. Female war workers sometimes used these ideals to open space for a more public presentation of their departures from, and transgressions of, gender ideals, even as they demonstrated the centrality of an ideal like the War Wife and Mother or the Sister in Arms to their wartime selves. The narratives written by Katherine Blake, Elizabeth Shepley Sergeant, and Addie Hunton, whom I have categorized as "New Woman Warriors" for their affinity with the sphere-crossing "New Woman" of the late nineteenth and early twentieth centuries, are clear and unabashed, also subtle and textured, in their critical examinations of some of the Great War's gender myths. While interested in mothering, they critique quite harshly fellow women war workers. While praising the sacrificial spirit, they question the sanctity of the altar on which those sacrifices were offered. They are engaged with, rather than resigned to, the pain, irony, and hypocrisy of the Great War.

Katherine Blake lived in Paris, was married to an Army doctor serving on the Front, and had two young children. She spent portions of the war in Paris, doing occasional relief and hospital work, and portions in the countryside when the threat from German long-range artillery and aircraft made her fear for her family's safety. She wrote of her experiences in letters to two friends, Maude Gray and Marian Wilkes. In those letters she praised the efforts of American soldiers in the tones of a War Wife, "Our troops make me proud of our country. They've done better and fought better than even the papers say. . . . It is a wonderful flame this fire of patriotism and our men are proving the *real* spirit of the United States. . . ."[40] She also chastised "old friends" inattentive to the serious business of war: "I cannot bear to know that there are people in America who can want balls and parties. It is heartless beyond belief."[41] A female soul not troubled into even a mild, empathic asceticism by war was, in Blake's eyes, an insult to true War Wives and Mothers.

Despite these traditional gestures, Blake also used her textured, passionate voice to open space for criticism of the war effort and of women's involvements in it. She scorned what she termed the "Division of American women" who had come to France, "Wives and mistresses camouflaged in the A.R.C. [American Red Cross] and the Y.M.C.A." Perhaps, she suggested, the motivations of these women were other than pure. In letters written in mid-November of 1917 and again in March of 1918, she allowed for purity of motive but argued against women in war work on strictly practical grounds. She pointed out that though "the intentions [of support service workers] are excellent, they are useless. No man and certainly no woman ought to come over here unless they have definite and necessary work to do."[42] (*The Stars and Stripes* published an editorial "Coming for the Ride" with the same message on April 26, 1918.) Further, she complicated her later encomia to A.E.F. soldiers by writing in March, albeit prematurely, "France and England have won without us. [Secretary of War] Baker's rosy interviews seem so dreadfully ludicrous. One year into the war, and only two thousand troops in the fighting line."[43] If women could be useful in slowing and stopping the decay of soldierly morals, they could also be, at least, "useless." Idealism could be grand; it could also be "ludicrous."

Elizabeth Shepley Sergeant, a reporter for *The New Republic*, lived much of her adult life well outside the literal and figurative walls of domestic womanhood. Still, in wartime she described those boundaries in sympathetic tones. Sergeant was forced across one boundary separating most women and men in the Great War when, during a battlefield tour in October of 1918, a French woman accompanying her accidentally activated a live grenade. The explosion killed the Frenchwoman instantly and sent shrapnel into Sergeant's legs and feet. While hospitalized, Sergeant used a grammar of gender with a highly traditional ring. She realized and deeply regretted that she had placed a burden on a medical system designed to help and heal those fighting the war, not those reporting it. This realization, written of in an October 21, 1918 entry, led her to feel, "desolated . . . giving so much trouble in a place where . . . women are superfluous."[44] Entering combat and sustaining injury were, in her eyes, exclusively a man's business. Three weeks later, the war came to an end, prompting her to write, "After fifteen hundred and sixty one days, the women of the world may go to bed with quiet hearts."[45] Her lack of recognition that the restless hearts of *men* might also have been quieted by war's end, or that women may have felt disappointment at the loss of a compelling source of meaning and adventure reflects again a strong affinity for idealized gender roles.

The complexity of Sergeant's relationship to the feminine ideal grew more apparent as her experience in the hospital dragged on. Having been "translated into the body of a soldier, and into the 'system' in which he lives and moves and has his being," Sergeant had both positive and negative encounters with Sisters in Arms.[46] Of the former variety were her encounters with her English nurse, "I begin to understand the New Testament when after two hours of sometimes weary waiting for her, I feel her healing touch." It is not by speech but by example–and perhaps without intent–that this nurse spreads the Gospel. Another encounter found Sergeant evaluating Sisters in Arms differently. While lying on a gurney, wrapped from head to toe in blankets, her gender thus concealed, Sergeant was approached by "two or three pretty nurse's aides of our best New York families." These women, assuming she was a wounded warrior, inquired "in tones whose imperious and patronizing ring make me squirm with indignity, who this poor dear boy is, etc."[47] In this moment, we see beneath the veneer of genuine heartfelt service. We see beneath the innocence. We find barely concealed condescension, class tension, and an overall effect that was, for Sergeant at least, not at all uplifting.[48]

Unlike the indignities that Sergeant suffered at the hands of condescending female elites, those that Addie Hunton suffered were not the result of mistaken identity in the superficial sense. They were, rather, the result of mistaken assumptions about who she was, who she could be, and where she belonged. An African American volunteer with the YMCA, Ms. Hunton was well acquainted with imperiousness and patronizing tones; she knew indignities. Until well after the war ended and in spite of a large pool of African American women ready to serve, including over 1,000 trained nurses, Hunton was one of only three African American women serving in France; the field of work for these three comprised approximately one hundred and fifty thousand African American soldiers and laborers.[49]

Addie Hunton saw herself as a traditional Sister in Arms. She styled her YMCA canteen as a domestic refuge for black soldiers and argued that more African American women were needed in France to provide "their men" with the nurture, comfort, and moral uplift that white women offered white soldiers. Hunton reflected nearly four decades of discourse on race and domesticity that, as historian Evelyn Brooks Higginbotham has argued, placed great emphasis on a black woman's ability to keep house, eventually yoking the aspirations of a race to a clean hearth and a tidy home. Cooperation between white and black women in mission work among southern black women went a long way toward convincing many members of the "female talented tenth" that the path to respectability and acceptance as fully human and fully American involved acceptance of, and strict adherence to, this model.[50] Hunton's conformity to the domestic feminine ideal is apparent too in her unfailing, frequently religiously toned praise of African American soldiers: "[T]hese colored soldiers fought as bravely as any Americans overseas, and worked with greater will; and as you saw them going to and from their long hours of labor with a song on their lips, you became convinced that the men had unconquerable souls; and the tramp, tramp, tramp of their marching feet made you feel that surely they were walking side by side with the Master, who had said unto them: Lo, I am with you always, even unto the end of the world."[51]

Addie Hunton's mere ability to inhabit a domestic ideal believed by white Americans to be most perfectly manifested in white women was potentially quite a revision of that ideal. There is, however, no evidence that this particular revision was noted by anyone outside of the African American community, or worked—in the short run at least—to upset prevailing racialist notions about the sexual depravity and generally uncivilized nature of African American women.[52] But Hunton did more than simply inhabit the ideal; she used it to lambaste white women war workers for their prejudice and hypocrisy.[53] Hunton was aware of the jarring dissonance between the stated humanitarian goals of the war and the horrors of race relations throughout America, but was nevertheless outraged by how difficult it was for black soldiers to receive attention from white Sisters in Arms, even in times of war. "[W]hite women, sometimes as many as five in a hut, gave a service that was necessarily perfunctory, because their prejudices would not permit them to spend a social hour with a homesick colored boy, or even to sew on a service stripe, were they asked to do so."[54] This cold-heartedness was widespread and institutionalized. African American soldiers, she wrote, were subject to "oppression, circumscription, intrigue, and false and wicked propaganda spread against them by their own countrymen."[55] Addie Hunton used feminine domesticity and what Higginbotham has described as "the politics of respectability"—more specifically white women's shortcomings in these overlapping discourses—to argue for the equality, even for the superiority, of black women and black soldiers.

Though revising domestic feminine ideals vis-à-vis the claims of the nation and offering nothing like Ruth Wolfe Fuller's unflinching praise of and devotion to the nation at war, Hunton remained an exemplar of the ideal vis-à-vis "the race." She offered no criticism of African American warriors and wrote of the war generally as an edifying, validating experience for black men and women. "Over the canteen in France we [women] learned to know that our young manhood was the natural and rightful guardian of our struggling race . . . we also learned to love our men better than before." It was her duty, she believed, to serve the troops and to tell of their trials and their deeds. In doing both of these, she defiantly countered the vicious negativity of white commentators on black soldiering and exposed the limits of white domesticity, while accepting and inhabiting a usually uncontroversial feminine ideal.

Domesticating War's Transgressions and Inversions

The closest thing to a well-known female voice from the Great War belongs to Shirley Millard. Her memoir, *I Saw Them Die: Diary and Recollections of Shirley Millard* was published in 1936, and has been cited in a handful of non-scholarly articles and at least one book.[56] The passage from Millard's memoir to which most modern eyes are drawn describes the gory aftermath of a springtime shell attack on the French field hospital where she was working. After hearing an explosion, Millard rushed outside to the "unforgettable sight" of a demolished barracks, its trappings of domesticity and healing thrown into gory disarray, "fragments of human bodies, arms and legs, bits of bedding, furniture, and hospital equipment" hung in the branches of a nearby tree. "For a moment," she recalled, "I could think of nothing but a Christmas tree . . . "[57] This passage is but one corner of Millard's fascinating tapestry of diary extracts and post-war reflections. She wrote compellingly and critically of war's glory and war's horror; she wrote of beauty and ugliness, camaraderie and discontent. Millard also wrote of love. More to the point, she wrote *from* love.

Shirley Millard's memoir begins with an account of how she came to write it. This bit of prologue is important given the story she tells. It is, in fact, the most important passage in the entire memoir—the lens through which all else must be read. The idea to write a book came to her, Millard wrote, while preparing to move and attempting to persuade her five-year-old son Coco to give up some of his toys. Having failed at that, she decided to empty an old trunk and there found her diary of 1918 "wrapped in a small French tricolor." Millard spent an hour reading the diary, then went to the nursery where she found "Jeanette, our beloved Scotch nana" feeding Coco his supper. Jeanette and Coco were the first to know Millard's intention to revisit her war memories. "Jeannette," she proclaimed, "I am going to write a book!"[58] This two-page narrative moment places the author and the war she writes about in familiar domestic context and allows one to see the war as a liminal experience for Millard. This frame and the war's liminality are important because the story she tells is a challenging one; it upsets categories and tells of transgression and temptation.

Millard, a volunteer nurse in a French Army hospital, left for the war well ahead of "Ted," her love interest. Her experience was an inversion of the mythic scene of the teary War Wife or War Mother bidding her resolute soldier adieu. Millard then found herself thrust headlong into service near the front, where she experienced the excitement of being at war and the pain of seeing others suffer. In the moment, Millard sensed that her war experiences had elevated her, at least temporarily, above Ted and other neophyte American soldiers. She wrote of feeling "years and

years older than Ted" and described, somewhat condescendingly, encounters with American soldiers: "They were all grinning like pleased young-
sters on the way to a picnic. . . . They don't know what they're in for, and
I do."[59] Millard had received war's revelation before many men and could
claim an authority that untested soldiers could not.

Perhaps most troubling of all, Millard wrote of romantic feelings for a
French doctor in her hospital. In a diary entry dated May 18, 1918, she
wrote of her love casually, almost dispassionately, as if it were an item of
clothing or some other manufactured object: "I wonder if Ted would
mind if I shifted to somebody else, especially a Frenchman?"[60] That
"somebody else" was the handsome "Dr. Le Brun," who eventually indicated that he had feelings for her as well. The reader never learns whether
or not Ted would have minded being replaced—though we can surmise
that he would have—since thoughts of a rendezvous with the French doctor were pushed from Millard's mind by an emotional, love-affirming four
days in Paris with Ted. On September 8, 1918, just before Ted was sent
to the front, Millard recorded the depth of her love for him.

> Just back from Paris. It has been like a dream. Did it really happen?
> Four days have changed everything. I must get it all down, for I shall
> want to read this again and again when I am old. Not that I could ever
> forget, but it is so wonderful that I don't want one moment of it to slip
> out of my mind. . . . Ted met me at the train and I knew the minute he
> put his arms around me in the dismal old Gare du Nord that he is mine
> and I am his and, war or no war, we belong together.[61]

Millard then returned to the hospital, told Dr. Le Brun that her heart
belonged to Ted, and noted, at the end of the memoir, that she and Ted
were married soon after returning from France.

Shirley Millard crossed many gender boundaries when she went to war.
One might be tempted to see these as clear moments of transgression
and milestones en route to a significant reimagining of women's roles in
wartime and post-war worlds. They are, however, something more complicated. As Millard writes at the end of her memoir, however exciting
and transgressive they were in 1917–1918, by 1936 her time at war
had become a "dark caravan that runs endlessly through the memory of
my youth." The dark caravan was safe to reveal and discuss, it seems,
because she and her readers knew that Ms. Millard was not just going
home at war's end, she was going to build a home as well. War would
test her, tempt her, and tear at her heart. It would shape her perceptions
of another conflict gathering in Europe. It would not, however, stain her
beautiful soul.

Millard's narrative and the frame that surrounds it point up the post-
war ambiguity of the war experiences of American women vis-à-vis the

political, cultural, and religious developments of the 1920s. Variations on the ideals described earlier here could indeed, in Jean Bethke Elshtain's words, "canalize" in terms of the roles they would allow women to play in American society. As the words of War Wives and Mothers, Sisters in Arms, and New Woman Warriors demonstrate, women's experiences and memories of war were so thoroughly interwoven with domestic ideals and realities that the potential public or political consequences of their service could be counterbalanced by reminders of the ways that women served. Because they had faced war within a "domestic" realm and in "traditional" roles, women's contributions could be read as a demonstration of the importance of traditional domesticity, however mobilized and however far displaced, to the battle for civilization. The WCTU's efforts on behalf of Prohibition (secured in January of 1919 while most American soldiers and war workers were still in France) seem closely related to this view of women and war service. Times arise when America needs its "Beautiful Souls" to lend their purity and beauty as such to the struggle for civilization and, when the conflict dies down, to "redeploy" to their homes and their families.

At the same time, post-war advocates of a wider public role for women in the workplace and in politics could point out that by serving in the war, women had demonstrated they could enter the public sphere at its most violent and "masculine" without becoming "like men." They could work and struggle and serve and do things thought of as less than "beautiful" but still, in the end, retain the essential qualities of the domestic woman. That this path could be trod was allowed by no less a cultural icon than Theodore Roosevelt. Writing an introduction to suffragist Harriot Stanton Blatch's 1918 pro-war, pro-woman volume *Mobilizing Woman Power*, Roosevelt proclaimed, "Most certainly I will set my face like flint against any unhealthy softening of our civilization . . . I do not mean softness in the sense of tender-heartedness; I mean the softness which extends to the head and the moral fibre."[62] To be tender, as Roosevelt surely understood ideal women to be, was not to be "soft." In fact, tenderness, made public and limned in the fire of war could be an important part of the bulwark against the decline of civilization. He continued, "I believe that the best women, when thoroughly aroused [sic], and when the right appeal is made to them, will offer our surest means of resisting this unhealthy softening . . . The doors of service now stand open and it rests with the women to say whether they will enter in!"[63] Stanton Blatch was similarly convinced. Two righteous struggles, one for woman suffrage, the other against German militarism, were tightly interwoven. She wrote, "Man power must give itself unreservedly at the front. Woman power must show not only eagerness but fitness to substitute for man power."[64] Men would go forward to fight a just war justly; women would show that they were fit to participate in public and economic life by doing the work men had done while keeping their hearts ever tender and their souls ever beautiful.

As long as women have considered following men into battle, women and men have argued over whether a war zone is a place for women. Some have observed the truth that war's flame draws too many too close and is strong enough to burn even those who do not go. Others, like Red Cross canteen manager Isabel Anderson have asked, " . . . hasn't a woman as much right to die for her country as a man?"[65] Critics and supporters have wandered in a mythic-religious world where the soldier's (last) resort to (righteous) violence is predicated on the need to protect the innocent, to defend those who cannot defend themselves; where the fighting man is inspired to heights of bravery and moral rectitude by thoughts of the domestic woman, and the "Beautiful Soul's" beauty can only be if there are those in society willing to make the ultimate sacrifice on her behalf.[66] Most American women serving at home and in France demonstrated their desire to hold and defend this sacred gendered terrain, to do their part to keep lighted the lamps of civilization, even, indeed especially, on the front lines of a most uncivil war.

CHAPTER SIX

"There Are No Dead"

> For yourself, I would have you bear in mind the immortal
> philosophy placed by Maeterlinck in the mouths of Mytyl and
> Tytyl: "Where are the dead? There are no dead." In my brief
> experience in the army no truth has been driven home to me
> so forcibly as this. Live by it.[1]
> —QUINCY SHARPE MILLS to his mother, undated

THERE WERE DEAD. One hundred and fifteen thousand American soldiers
lost to combat, injury, and illness. There were dead and there was death
enough to sicken and sadden comrades, to break hearts, to dash dreams.
And there were the living, left for a day or a lifetime to grieve, to fight on,
to reflect on what had become of the dead.

Soldiers' understandings of the afterlife are important as intellectual
artifacts of a vibrant religious culture and as evidence of the strain and
grief poured out upon young men and women by war. This strain is, perhaps, reflected in Quincy Mills' last letter to his mother. As an expression
of the physical reality of the war, the words of Belgian playwright and
Nobel laureate Maurice Maeterlinck (1862–1949) appear to be equal
parts fantasy and denial.[2] There were, of course, dead. But American soldiers who tasted combat, those who witnessed its aftermath, and those
called on to bury, disinter, and rebury corpses knew better than to accept
the historical physical sense of such a quotation. "Where are the dead?
There are no dead." Rather, the two short sentences would have been
read as they were meant, as a commentary on the reassuring *metaphysical*
reality that lay beyond the harsh physical one. The words point with a
defiant directness toward a world where the dead live on; they point to a
world so near that its existence is obvious. In this light—the intended
light—Mills' use of Maeterlinck is hopeful and comfort-giving. He asserts
individual infinity in the face of finitude horrifically manifested. Mills, by
his mother's account not a church-going Christian, wrote that all would
be right with him in death.

As important as Mills' statement of the "truth" that there are no dead
is the prescription that follows: "Live by it." Mills enjoined his mother
to live on after his death—the only condition under which she would
receive his "last letter"—in the knowledge that "there are no dead." He

did not want his mother to grieve. But how else might she configure her life given the "knowledge" that her son, though dead, lived on? What could it mean to live by the "truth" that distinctions between the dead and the living were ultimately false?

Pictures of heaven sketched by soldiers and war workers functioned, as they often have and still do, as blueprints for an ideal society. *On earth as it is in heaven.*[3] In the visions of life after death examined in this chapter, we see more than just Valhalla or a disconnected set of reflections of popular religious culture; we see instead the rough outlines of the society soldiers hoped to forge and, specifically in soldiers' and war workers' notions of the proximity of heaven to earth, the basis of surviving soldiers' justifications for their post-war efforts to bring that ideal to life in America. Though no two soldierly depictions of heaven are identical, their shared characteristics merge into an informative composite. The soldierly heaven welcomed and exulted soldiers and was defined by strong male friendship. The soldierly heaven was characterized by reunions of friends and family, and by the cessation of struggle and striving. The soldierly heaven was understood to be near to earth and porous, allowing for the continuation of relationships—sometimes even communication—between the living and the dead.[4] Soldiers did not create their heaven from whole cloth. They picked and chose among various domestic and progressive models of heaven and, in so doing, demonstrated their likes and dislikes with regard to the values expressed in those models.

The women's voices that have been interwoven with men's voices throughout this book and that formed the core of the previous chapter are noticeably few in this chapter. It is a curious and somewhat deceptive absence. Why, we might wonder, was a topic that presented itself urgently to male soldiers and war workers not taken up as frequently or in as much detail by female war workers? The most satisfying explanation is the simplest and has to do with substantial qualitative differences in the war experiences of men and women. Because the actual fighting was an exclusively male enterprise, more men were touched by death and the fear of death and, therefore, more men reflected on what would become of them if they were to be killed. Women encountered the dead and dying quite frequently, to be sure. They developed attachments to the men who entered their canteens or their wards and then found those attachments severed by death. But with a few notable exceptions, the deepest attachments among these men and women at war occurred within gender lines, and comparatively few women died or were killed in service. Perhaps the need to reflect on the contours of the afterlife was less acute absent the threat of death in combat and the stimulus of grief. It is important to note, however, that women's voices are present in less than obvious ways throughout this chapter. A large number of the soldiers who reflected on the afterlife did so in correspondence with important women in their lives: mothers, aunts, sisters, wives, fiancées, friends.[5] In a few instances, soldiers gave credit to these women for helping them develop their understandings of the afterlife, and many soldiers wrote in the apparent hope of providing comfort to mother, wife, or sister should death be their lot. Beliefs are always developed in some form of dialog, and in the case of soldiers' beliefs about the afterlife, women were participants in, and shapers of, the conversation.

HEAVENLY COMFORT, HEAVENLY PROGRESS, HOLY CONFUSION

For all the religious differences abroad in pre-war America, the *general* contours of the afterlife were not widely disputed. Many otherwise divergent voices shared the assumption that earthly memories, relationships, and institutions familiar on earth would exist in heaven. From Elizabeth Stuart Phelps and Fanny Crosby, to Dwight Moody, to William Adams Brown and Shailer Mathews, to Catholic author Francois-Rene Blot and the popular *Sacred Heart Review*, earthly and heavenly life appeared to be largely continuous. Past visions of heaven as an eternal church had mostly been discarded by many as too cold and boring for the age.[6] Clergy and popular writers, not to mention their audiences, turned instead to characterizations of the afterlife that made heaven more earthly, more familiar. The earthliness was agreed upon; the earthly ideals that would be eternally reverenced were not. To demonstrate the relationship between earthly ideals and visions of the afterlife, it is helpful to examine three divergent portrayals: the famously domestic heaven of Elizabeth Stuart Phelps; the progressive masculine heaven of William Adams Brown; and the heaven that infantry officer Vinton Dearing struggled to conceive. While the first two thinkers worked to encourage types of earthly behavior by demonstrating their heavenliness, Dearing stood in the middle of war and wondered what on earth could be in heaven.[7]

THE DOMESTIC HEAVEN

Elizabeth Stuart Phelps offered a highly detailed and intentionally comforting picture of the afterlife in three enormously popular novels published between 1868 and 1887 that were still in print and influential well into the twentieth century. In *The Gates Ajar*, *Beyond the Gates*, and *Between the Gates*, Phelps used two heroines and one hero, each on the brink of death, as heavenly tour guides. These guides worked to simultaneously describe the "true" heaven and dispel a trove of unattractive misconceptions about it. The most famous of the three guides was Aunt Winifred of *The Gates Ajar*, who presented her portrait of heaven to her grieving niece Mary. In the narrative, Mary has been incapacitated by the death of her brother Roy in the Civil War and is unable to find any comfort in the visions of heaven with which she is familiar. These visions, which are to Mary "glittering generalities, cold commonplace, vagueness, unreality," are generated in the story by male religious authorities Dr. Bland and Deacon Quirk.[8] They consist of descriptions both of heavenly stasis: "Heaven is an eternal state. Heaven is a state of holiness. Heaven is a state of happiness"—and of self-abnegating, God-magnifying quasi-activities—"We shall study the character of God. . . . We shall moreover love each other with a universal and unselfish love."[9] These visions of heaven, bland (and not at all quirky) as they are, leave Mary cold, unedified, and mired in grief.

Over and against this vision, Aunt Winifred details a heaven full of "special affections," in which the dead retain their human form and their feelings of love for the living. Activities in Aunt Winifred's heaven—the *real* heaven—do not include ceaseless study of the divine character, "What [is] more natural than that we shall spend our best energies as we spent them here–in comforting, teaching, helping, saving people whose very souls we love better than our own? In fact, it would be *un*natural if we did not."[10] Aunt Winifred also helps Mary to see that the dead are "very present with us" on earth and that her brother still cares for her and is watching over her. To Winifred, death constitutes a temporary interruption in relationships, and heaven provides the arena for their continuation and perfection. Her words to Mary capture the vision perfectly: "I mean to say that if there is such a thing as common sense, you will talk with Roy as you talked with him here,–only not as you talked with him here, because there will be no troubles nor sins, no anxieties nor cares . . . no fearful looking-for of separation."[11] Heaven is made heavenly, that is, not by an explicit proximity to God or an increase in holiness, but by human relations lived out eternally and devoid of anxiety.

Winifred's heaven—a heaven of reunion for couples and families, a heaven of continuation of earthly mission work—also elevates domesticity to a most exalted place. "A happy home is the happiest thing in the world," she tells Mary, "I do not see why it should not be in any world. . . . I expect to have my beautiful home, and my husband and [my daughter] Faith."[12] Molly, the heroine of Phelps' second novel, *Beyond the Gates*, shows us that Winifred will not be disappointed. The forty-year-old unmarried Molly gives a first-person account of her travels to and around heaven. While near death from brain fever, Molly is escorted by her deceased father first through a town filled with earth-bound spirits and then to a heaven in which lectures and concerts by deceased luminaries entertain those not engaged in mission work among the less worthy dead. The domesticity of heaven is driven home to Molly when she sees the lovely eternal home her father has built for her mother and witnesses, with a somewhat heavy heart, her parents' heavenly reunion. Her heart is buoyed, however, when she is reunited in heaven with a former love interest who wishes to be her eternal companion. Molly's vision ends and her disappointment begins when her fever subsides. She returns to earth to await her heavenly marriage and a truly heavenly home.

In all three of Phelps' accounts of heaven—*The Gates Between* is quite similar—heaven models and exalts so-called domestic virtues, particularly the love between wife and husband. Even though *The Gates Ajar* features a sister and brother separated by a war death, Aunt Winifred's own experience of heaven, which begins as the book ends, will clearly revolve around her husband. One gets the sense, too, that if Mary weds, as she ought to, her brother's spirit will necessarily play an eternal second fiddle. Indeed, the message to Molly in *Beyond the Gates* is that heaven without an eternal life partner would be a very lonely place, but that God, in His infinite domestic wisdom, provides both companions for the unmarried and new companions for the unhappily married.

THE PROGRESSIVE HEAVEN

Presbyterian theologian William Adams Brown, a member of the faculty at Union Theological Seminary from 1892–1936 and a leading voice in the American ecumenical movement, also envisioned a heaven of "earthly" activity.[13] He disagreed, however, that comfort and domesticity were the highest goods. The virtues and figures that he privileged were, in fact, of an entirely different sort. Reverend Brown described a more "masculine" progressive heaven. It was less important to Brown that the dead remain close to the living and have good seats at the heavenly Chautauqua than that they pick themselves up after their life-ending event, dust off their britches, and look for new challenges and conquests in life after death.[14] In his 1912 treatise *The Christian Hope: A Study in the Doctrine of Immortality*, Brown wrote, "much as we need comfort [in this life], there are things in life that we need more. Strength is more important, and courage, enthusiasm and loyalty, consecration and heroism."[15] The afterlife that Brown envisioned was, accordingly, not "a heaven of untroubled bliss," but rather "one of progress," in which "[t]here will still be new lessons to be learned, new battles to be fought, new experiences to be gained, new services to be rendered." Sounding every bit the minister of masculinity in a church of the Strenuous Life, he promised an eternity of challenges to those who would commit themselves to such virtues in this life. "It will not be a life of stagnation, but of activity, not of monotony but of change." As in the progressive model of society, the hearth-warming woman would have her place, but the stars of heaven would be the "battle-tested" male spirits.

> Shall we suppose that the strong men from whose heroic struggles mankind has drawn inspiration for its best living, Peter and Paul, Benedict and Francis, Luther and Cromwell, Wesley and Livingstone, have found no outlet in the new life for the missionary zeal which was the very breath of life here? To suppose this would be to cut the nerve of Christian hope, for it would make heaven less desirable than earth.[16]

Brown described heaven as an exciting place for men whose thirst for earthly adventure remained unquenched in death. For those seeking more opportunities to be heroic, heaven offered the answer.

The reasons for the divergence between Brown's and Phelps' views of the afterlife were as earthly as the heaven each described. In order to provide sanctified models for earthly social structures and personal relationships, and, in some cases, to argue obliquely for social and cultural authority, they imagined that *heaven* favored those particular institutions and personalities. One commentator on "self-indulgent, domestic, 'feminine,'" nineteenth-century consolation literature has argued that "to establish the key importance of the domestic heaven [was] to grant final victory to the passive rather than to the aggressive virtues."[17] According to this reading, the women and clergy behind the domestication of heaven were motivated by a desire to compensate for twin losses of earthly authority brought on by religious disestablishment and by the removal of women from the public sphere. Rendering heaven as home allowed those thus disempowered on earth to claim ultimate, eternal power—a "consolation prize" for lives of submission and frustration. "All the logic [of this literature] suggests to the reader: you are going to end up, if you are well-behaved and lucky, in a domestic realm of children, women, and ministers . . . so why not believe in them now?"[18] Self-consciously masculine clergymen and theologians of Progressive-Era America used this same strategy, but looked to the afterlife to demonstrate the truth and ultimate merits of their earthly vision, often explicitly countering the "feminine" understanding. Since heaven would offer adventure and conquest, it would be best on earth to pursue a life of faith that prepared one to succeed in such pursuits.

The influence of these particular visions of the afterlife in early-twentieth-century America is difficult to measure exactly. A few statistics are, however, suggestive. *The Gates Ajar* remained popular enough through the early lifetimes of most soldiers and war workers to warrant two reprints by separate publishing houses in 1910 on top of at least sixty printings between 1868 and 1899.[19] Brown's work was not nearly as popular, but many men sharing his generally progressive Christian faith occupied pulpits across the nation. What these numbers and trends don't reveal, is the potential for war to trouble seriously these heavenly waters. One indication of how the earthliness of heaven could work to unsettle and confuse rather than comfort and clarify emerges from the letters of Vinton Dearing. Dearing found it impossible to separate an increasingly tumultuous and disappointing earth from the heaven he had been raised to seek.

Heaven in Hell: The Brief Reflections of Vinton Dearing

The son of Baptist missionary parents, Vinton Dearing spent most of his youth in Yokohama, Japan. In 1916, while he was a student at Colgate University, Dearing's parents returned to the United States on furlough. His father, Dr. John Lincoln Dearing, contracted spinal meningitis while lecturing at Colgate Theological Seminary and passed away shortly thereafter.[20] President Wilson asked for a declaration of war the following April, and Dearing signed up for duty in the American Expeditionary Force in the fall of 1917. He was designated for training as an infantry officer. After completing his training and five weeks of leave with his mother, "sisters," and grandmother in Boston, Dearing departed for France as a member of the Twenty-eighth Infantry Regiment, First Division. He participated in the first major battle fought by the newly deployed American Expeditionary Force at Cantigny in May of 1918, and in the Aisne-Marne offensive, initiated July 18, 1918. For his part in the battle for Cantigny, he was awarded a Distinguished Service Cross. His part in the Aisne-Marne action was brief. Dearing was killed in the first days of the offensive, along with 60 percent of the officers in his regiment.[21]

Vinton Dearing often expressed his support for the war in the enthusiastic idiom characteristic of his fellow soldiers, but he was not fully enthralled by it. He wrote as frequently of his desire to be home sitting by the fire in conversation, as he did of the satisfaction he derived from leading his men into battle. Writing to his "sister" Peggy, likely a close female friend, Dearing attempted candor.[22] "Don't think I am discouraged, a bit cast down, perhaps, but cheero, I am at it again. I think it is because I have lost one of my best friends that I have been feeling so badly, but duty calls and it is great to obey duty, 'the stern daughter of the voice of God.'" "Duty" could not, however, cover Dearing entirely in what was, for him, a terrific emotional and theological storm. He found experiences bearing powerfully on his beliefs, almost loosing him from his moorings. "You know here one changes his mind on the important things of life. I am at sea, Peggy. I scarcely know where I stand. When you see how life is and

how quickly one can lose it you begin to think of greater things. The most
a man can do is to do his duty to the utmost."[23] Death clearly had Vinton
Dearing's attention and forced him to entertain thoughts of "greater
things" and to look for ways to get through his trials. Duty, he wrote,
was his most secure refuge.

But Dearing's confusion as to where he stood—his feeling of being "at
sea"—did not abate, and eventually touched his understanding of what
awaited him in death. Having grown up in a missionary family, Dearing
would likely have been familiar with prevailing earthly notions of heaven.
He might even have embraced a heaven of missionary activity, but writing
again to Peggy he confided he was troubled and confused.

> I sometimes wonder what heaven can possibly be like, for our concep-
> tions of it keep changing so constantly, and no two people will be satis-
> fied with the same kind of heaven, and there will always be some one
> jealous of some one else's heaven if we each have our own. But we
> don't have much time to think of heaven now. I have been in many
> cities or rather towns, where the moonlight falls through roofless walls
> and gardens, and streets are ripped up with shells . . .[24]

Dearing's ideas about the afterlife are as rich as they are brief. He presupposed individual immortality and the existence of a place called
heaven. He indicated that his ideas about heaven were in flux—moving
back and forth between at least a communal and an individual heaven.
Yet far from providing the comfort intended by Elizabeth Stuart Phelps,
the assumption that individuals survived in the afterlife, and that they
were like the individuals in his world, clouded his vision. A communal
heaven could not completely satisfy two people, let alone all of the saved.
Equally unsatisfying was an individual heaven, which Dearing was certain
would give rise to strife, like the "progressive" world around him. The
negative effects of a world at war on Dearing's view of heaven are striking
if also entirely logical. He was not among those who thought death in
war would validate an existence or purchase eternal supreme happiness—
quite the contrary. The very devaluation of life through the bloody machi-
nations of war threw Dearing, for periods, into confusion. The brief reflection that he allowed himself on heaven led him to think not of content-
ment and comfort, but of jealousy and partial satisfaction. If heaven was
to be a continuation of life on earth, Vinton Dearing was well positioned
to object. What he saw around him was hell.

Vinton Dearing's reflections on the afterlife are important to this analysis for two reasons. First and most clearly, Dearing points up a problem
with understandings of the afterlife that are tightly interwoven with a particular vision of the world. A society, however idyllic initially, will inevitably face tension, conflict, jealousy, even violence. Put in theological terms,
societies will always reflect and perhaps magnify the sinfulness of their

populations.[25] When this happens, it becomes hard if not impossible to shield the earthly heaven from similar flaws: *in heaven as it is on earth*. Second, though the content of his reflections on heaven are unique among the soldiers and war workers whose writings I have read, the dynamic that he makes explicit is quite typical. Vinton Dearing did not like the world in which he was moving at the time that he wrote to Peggy of heaven; his view of heaven reflected this dislike. The more typical American soldier, though not always and everywhere enthusiastic about his lot, was less put off by life at war than Dearing, but was no less inclined to weave his likes and dislikes, his dreams and fears, into his vision of heaven.

THE SOLDIER'S HEAVEN

Like all who have reflected on the structure and content of life after death, American soldiers and war workers described an afterlife that included some aspects of their earthly lives and excluded others. These visions of the afterlife help us understand soldiers' affections, as well as their hopes for, and critiques of, their world. The general outlines of heaven that emerge from soldierly accounts share three characteristics. First, they express no doubts that soldiers will be welcomed in heaven and, in some cases, praised for their service. Far from surprising given the implications of possible alternatives, this view of the inherent godliness of the Allied soldiers was, as we have seen, contested, and represented one side of an ongoing debate about the salvific effects of death in war. Second, soldierly visions of the afterlife did not incorporate the "thrilling" aspects of war and struggle. Instead, they featured uniformed men enjoying the camaraderie of military life—displaying the good character of the ideal soldier but not his thirst for conflict. The male relationships of army life, more than any type of action, were pleasing to God. Finally, soldiers understood heaven to be a place of reunion and repair; some went so far as to imagine reunions that involved the dead and the still living.

Three poetic examples emerging from three different war experiences treat the soldier's presence in heaven as a *fait accompli* and, in so doing, argue for divine approval of the soldierly life. Prior to his final trip to the lines in April of 1917, Edwin Abbey went to the Easter services organized by his unit's chaplain. He was so affected by a poem the chaplain distributed after the service that he sent it home to his mother and father "as an Easter memento of the firing line." The poem, Rudyard Kipling's "To Wolcott Balestier," portrays and sanctifies a familiar, if idealized, scene of male camaraderie. God appears as a commanding general; the heroic dead are his soldiers. Abbey thought it "the epitome of what one feels out here."[26]

Beyond the path of the outmost sun through utter darkness hurled –
Further than ever comet flared or vagrant star-dust swirled –
Live such as fought and sailed and ruled and loved and
    made our world.

The soldier is placed immediately in an exalted region, beyond the stars, comets, and sun, amid a pantheon of similarly valiant, presumably male, world-makers. The poem continues, making clear that this is a perfected company—a company bound to "our Father," above moralist reproach, and justified in their enjoyment of rest and comfort. "They are purged of pride because they died, they know the worth of their bays, / They sit at wine with the Maidens Nine and the Gods of the Elder Days, / It is their will to serve or be still as fitteth our Father's praise." Of course, if God asks for a task to be completed, he will find ready help among the men, but their world is not defined by such action. It involves, rather, an ongoing banquet with soldiers, sailors, rulers, and God himself. Familiarity with "the Father" does not, however, diminish respect for him.

And ofttimes cometh our wise Lord God, master of every trade,
And tells them tales of His daily toil, of Edens newly made;
And they rise to their feet as He passes by, gentlemen unafraid.

This poetic image of the afterlife resonated with Abbey and, he imagined, with others. The camaraderie of military life would continue in the afterlife. Heaven (and earth) held a special place for "gentlemen unafraid."

American soldier-poet Alan Seeger absorbed similar sentiments, and spread them through his poems. The ends served by his description of heaven are, however, more complex. Rather than painting a picture for the sake of comfort, as Abbey did in using Kipling, Seeger seemed interested in convincing fellow fighters to use the potential for comfort and camaraderie as motivation to enter battle boldly. In "Maktoob," Seeger argues that since a man has but one death to die and an interested audience of "the mighty, the elite" to please, it is best to pass through the "ebon door" as a true man should.

Guard that not bowed nor blanched with fear
You enter, but serene, erect,
As you would wish most to appear
To those you most respect.[27]

The afterlife into which soldiers would pass was far from domestic. In Seeger's eyes, "those you most respect" did not include the selfless female reform worker or the consumptive young divine, both fixtures of nineteenth-century consolation literature. But the dynamic at work was similar to the dynamic present in Phelps' "Gates" books. Seeger elevated one type of life above all others and gave true believers eternal reasons for pursuing that life on earth. Live boldly now, he proclaimed, for the bold will be your company in heaven. The brave and masculine soldier could expect to be welcomed in heaven as he had been welcomed among his comrades on earth.

A third picture in poetry comes from the experience of New York City's largely Irish "Fighting Sixty-ninth," who in March of 1918 found themselves occupying a section of the front lines near Luneville, roughly thirty miles southwest of the town of Nancy. Nationalized as the 165th Infantry and attached to the 42nd "Rainbow" Division, the unit was serving in the relatively quiet, secure Baccarat Sector and learning more of the ins and outs of trench warfare.[28] But on March 7, a German shell tore into a dugout occupied by nineteen members of the 165th Infantry's Company E, and buried them alive. Soldier-poet Joyce Kilmer took up his pen and reflected on the fate of the lost men. Not long after the tragedy, during a St. Patrick's Day "concert under the trees" for regimental personnel, Father Francis Duffy read aloud a poem written by Kilmer.[29] "Rouge Bouquet," opened with an acknowledgement of the tragedy that had occurred.

> In the woods they call Rouge Bouquet
> There is a new made grave today,
> Built by never a spade or pick,
> Yet covered by earth ten meters thick.
> There lie many fighting men,
> Dead in their youthful prime,
> Never to laugh or love again
> Or taste of the summer time."[30]

Death had claimed nineteen young men and ended forever their enjoyment of life's simple but profound pleasures. Kilmer saw and named the tragedy: The young dead would never again "laugh and love" or "taste of the summer time." But when he turned his poetic eye from the end of earthly life to the beginning of life in heaven, Kilmer saw sword-bearing angels and heroic saints welcoming men—Irish men—in uniform.

> Never fear but in the skies
> Saints and angels stand,
> Smiling with their holy eyes
> On this new-come band.
> St. Michael's sword darts through the air
> And touches the arrival on his hair,
> And sees them stand saluting there,

His stalwart sons;
And Patrick, Bridget, and Columbkill
Rejoice that in veins of warriors still
The Gael's blood runs.[31]

Saints and angels would welcome the "stalwart sons" of Ireland and
America to a heaven of swords and salutes and rejoicing over the deeds
of warriors. Kilmer did not delve deeply into the exact contours of the
afterlife; he did not make of heaven a military banquet. He was quite
explicit, however, that "this new-come band" had been welcomed in
heaven as warriors, by warriors. His fellow soldiers, he wrote, need
"never fear." Saints, angels, "the mighty, the elite" and "gentlemen unafraid" were "smiling . . . on this new come band" and would surely smile
on those who would come after them.

The presence of soldiers in heaven and the eternal recognition of their
valor seems to lean more toward Brown's heroic heaven than Phelps' domestic. Yet these visions of the afterlife were also suffused with offerings
of comfort and consolation gendered feminine by Progressive-Era theologians and modern scholars. Soldiers were concerned to find "beyond the
gates" a world familiar, cordial, and comforting to them. The heaven that
dominated and sometimes haunted soldiers' thoughts was a familiar
earthly heaven, to be sure. But the most prominent aspect of that earthliness—uniforms or no—was not progress and striving. The soldiers'
heaven was, instead, a heaven of reunion for friends and family—a comforting consequence to the deadly antecedent of war.

Through three very different war experiences, three different men held
in common, and with certainty, the belief that once dead they would be
reunited with friends and family. Vincenzo D'Aquila was an Italian American Catholic who came from a broken home.[32] He volunteered for service
in the Italian Army in 1915 and served on the Isonzo front. Hamilton
Coolidge was the son of a prominent Massachusetts family, a Protestant,
and an American aviator. Otis P. Robinson of Richmond City, Virginia
served as a private in Company B of the predominately African American
545th Engineers. D'Aquila mentioned reunion when describing the death
of his friend Frank, a fellow Italian American. After a particularly costly
attack, D'Aquila was "[a]nxious to learn how Frank fared" and, unable
to find his friend, resorted to flipping through a company roster. There
D'Aquila found Frank's name, next to which he saw the word "Disperso–
lost, dispersed–date: October 26th [1916]." He recalled the moment and
wrote, "Frank has remained 'lost' ever since, just as he was lost and bewildered all his army life, but he found the end of his trail, undoubtedly to
the happy hunting grounds. Only when we meet again, shall we hear his
story from Frank himself."[33] According to D'Aquila, the lost would be

found in the afterlife and, no matter how bewildered they had been in life, their stories would finally be told.

Fighting in the air above France, Hamilton Coolidge also lost comrades, some to accident, some to combat. When Coolidge thought of death and what waited beyond it, he too thought of enjoying his friends' company once again. In an undated letter, he wrote:

> Death is certainly not a black unmentionable thing and I feel . . . that dead people should be talked of just as if they were alive. At mess and sitting around in our quarters the boys that have been killed are spoken of all the time when any little thing reminds someone of them.[34]

He went on to describe his feelings and expectations for fallen friend and fellow pilot Quentin Roosevelt, son of the former President. "To me Quentin is just away somewhere. I know we shall see each other again and have a grand old 'hoosh,' talking over everything together. I miss him the way I miss Mother and the family, for his personality or spirit are just as real and vivid as they ever were."[35] Based on this description of activities and sentiments around the squadron, it seems that Coolidge and other pilots were slow to acknowledge that the dead had even left their company. That they would eventually be together again was, to Coolidge, obvious.

Otis P. Robinson had already endured the horrors of life in the Jim Crow South when he, like many other African American men, entered military service. The twenty-eight-year-old Robinson made it through a brief training period on American soil before embarking for France on September 23, 1918. On October 15, a mere nine days after arriving in France and twelve days short of entering the combat zone, Robinson died of influenza. Robinson's voice was not completely silenced by death. Prior to passing, he wrote or was helped to write a "last letter" to his sister Carrie G. Harris. It read, in part, "Pray for me. A pray to God in heaven is better, than, any thing else I know. May God bless you and be with you, until we meet again."[36] Ms. Harris took comfort in this letter, saved it, and reported its contents to the Virginia War History Commission along with a poem, "My Star of Hope," which described her Gold Star memorial as "A light unto my feet . . . Until we two shall meet." Otis Robinson knew that death was near when he wrote to his sister. Though he did not know whether it waited for him in the next hour, day, or week, he also knew, like Coolidge, D'Aquila, and many others, that soldiers and their loved ones could live and die, in the words of fellow American soldier Sol Segal, "confident of a reunion."[37] The war made young men familiar with loss. It gave them so keen a desire for reunion that reunion became a dominant feature of their portrayals of heaven. The afterlife was a place where there would be no separation from friends and loved ones, where struggle and strain would give way to a "grand old 'hoosh.'" Yet some soldiers, while feeling acutely the desire for reunion, felt something stronger. They felt the presence of dead friends; they wrote of their world as if it were populated by spirits of the dead; some even believed communication with the dead to be possible.

SPIRITUALISM AND THE SOLDIER

Spiritualism, or the belief that communication is possible between the living and the dead, was a widespread movement in nineteenth- and twentieth-century America. It became a public phenomenon in the 1840s when the Fox sisters reportedly heard and responded to the rappings of a ghost in their New York farmhouse, and became an important source of comfort to a nation torn by Civil War.[38] By the early twentieth century, a dizzying array of mediums and seers offered to contact the departed, and American and European intellectuals of some standing were attempting to research and verify these claims.[39] Though Christian clergymen, among others, scoffed at and condemned these "charlatans" and their tricks, they could neither deny the appeal of spiritualism nor satisfy the longings that mediums satisfied. Spiritualism remained a part of the American religious tapestry well into the twentieth century.

Experiences of war inclined American soldiers and war workers toward the belief that the dead remained a part of their world. Young men waging war did not begin attending séances *en masse*, but their writings reflect spiritualist sentiments in many places. After the death of his close friend and Yale classmate Dumaresq "Stuff" Spencer in February 1918, George Moseley wrote vividly of the loss and the enduring sense of sadness. According to Moseley, the two had been "together nearly every minute since we left home." Their companionship had bred a level of friendship and familiarity that Moseley cherished. "We got so we thought and acted the same . . . " He continued, "[S]o when God called him away I found myself absolutely alone. I took care of his body as best I could and after I had done everything I tried to forget." But Moseley's attempts to control his memories were in vain. "Stuff," or the memory of him, would allow no forgetting. "He always seems to be with me and sort of unconsciously I expect to see him everywhere I go."[40] The intensity of this and other wartime friendships made them resistant even to death.[41] Victor Chapman and Kiffin Rockwell were among the first members of the famed Franco-American Lafayette Escadrille. Rockwell recorded the Escadrille's first combat kill. Chapman was its first combat fatality.[42] Writing to Chapman's father, John Jay Chapman, Rockwell noted how widely Victor's influence was still felt.

Yet he is not dead; he lives forever in every place he has been, and in everyone who knew him, and in future generations little points of his character will be passed along. He is alive every day in this Escadrille and has a tremendous influence on our actions. Even the *mecaniciens* do their work better and more conscientiously.[43]

For many soldiers, depopulated ranks remained crowded with memories of friends—memories vivid enough to converse with, relate to, and otherwise make present.[44]

These accounts of the afterlife, important as descriptions of an imagined future, were more than just descriptions. One does not need to even scratch the surface to discover the mourning soldier struggling to come to terms with the permanence of death and, not surprisingly, coping with loss by denying loss. But there is another level of meaning to these words. As historian Drew Gilpin Faust has noticed among Civil War soldiers, there is something deeply reflexive in the way that Great War soldiers wrote about death and meaning.[45] Through descriptions of dead friends as loved, missed, and still influential, these young men modeled for their friends and loved ones the ways they hoped to be remembered, and expressed their hopes that their own deaths would bring them little more than ongoing life. It is not surprising, then, that some American soldiers wrote that death meant neither a quitting of interest in the world of the living, nor the end of communication between living and dead. There were many potential sources of such beliefs available to Great War soldiers. Some of these sources had remarkable intellectual pedigrees; some were draped in the trappings of chicanery and the low-level medium "industry." However, soldiers did not have to attend séances, adopt spiritualism, or be members in good standing of William James' American Society for Psychical Research to imagine or experience communication with the dead.[46] Acts as simple as placing a hand on a grave "to send a current of sympathy from my body," were gestures in this direction.[47] More substantial were the "last letters" soldiers often wrote to be kept by senior officers and delivered in the event of death. These letters, defiant of death's final silence, could be both prophecy and proof—when they did not foretell continued contact between the dead and the living, they constituted it.

Benjamin Lee's last letter to friend and squadron mate Charles Fuller hinted, albeit cryptically, at a Phelpsian belief that friendship would not only survive his passing but would continue to grow. "Dear Chas," he wrote, "Just a line to let you know you are not forgotten old dear–and never will be. In fact unless I am much mistaken I may have the opportunity to see how it fares with you." Not knowing where or when (if ever) Fuller might receive his letter, Lee continued, "If you are away, Tex Hawkins or Jay Schiefflein will forward this to you. If near you may come nearer. If you can use or would like any of my things–please have them. Pigskin valise, uniform? Anything at all is yours . . . "[48] Lee's self-description has much in common with Aunt Winifred's description of Mary Cabot's fallen brother Roy in *The Gates Ajar*. Lee's memory of Chas and their relationship would persist in death; he would "have the opportunity to see how it fares" with the living. Somewhat more perplexing is what Lee meant by his invitation to "come nearer." Was he referring only to the enhancement of Fuller's attachment to his memory? Was he suggesting that communications between them might be possible? Did he, like those who believed in psychometry—the ability of an object to hold and convey information about its deceased owner—believe that his relationship with Fuller might deepen if Fuller used his uniform and valise? The answers are not clear, but the ambiguities are haunting. What we can know is that in Ben Lee's last piece of correspondence with the world of the living, he looked forward, at the very least, to ongoing experiences of the world and those living in it.

Soldiers' beliefs that the dead remained close enough for conversation are understandable. Theirs was a world where death and young life intersected frequently, where it could be difficult to believe that someone was *really* gone forever, especially when letters from the dead invited the living to "come nearer." But hopes and experiences showed them that death was not the end; presence and communication continued and comfort could be found in both. Though most American soldiers were not practicing spiritualists and did not identify themselves as such, one went so far as to name his spiritualistic beliefs. He was Kenneth MacLeish: Chicagoan, Yale student, Baptist.

Before his death in aerial combat in October of 1918, Kenneth MacLeish wrote frequently of his experiences and of his growing Christian faith to his parents, his brothers, and his fiancée Priscilla Murdock. After the war, the mourning family published his edited letters to them, but his letters to Murdock remained in her keeping, unpublished, for another seventy years.[49] The details of MacLeish's pre-war views of the afterlife are lost to history. He may have found the domestic view of Elizabeth Stuart Phelps appealing. Just as he was drawn to the rhetoric of muscular Christianity, so may he have been drawn to explicitly masculine portrayals of heaven such as William Adams Brown's. In either case (or neither), MacLeish found another set of ideas compelling when preparing for war. He wrote in a February 2, 1918 letter to Priscilla:

> I think I'm going to be a spiritualist. Keep this under your hat, but did you know that Aunt Mary [Mary Robbins Hillard, headmistress of Westover School in Middlebury, Connecticut] was a rabid one? When

a woman of her education and mental ability takes it seriously, there must be something to it. She isn't inclined to kid herself.[50]

Shortly after revealing his interest in spiritualism to Priscilla, MacLeish lost his close friend, Al Sturtevant. Just what effect Aunt Mary had on his experience of this death is unclear. A letter to his mother describing his reaction to Sturtevant's death, however, bears evidence of spiritualist influence. It also sounds remarkably similar to the writings of George Moseley, Hamilton Coolidge, and Kiffin Rockwell.

MacLeish received a letter from Sturtevant after Sturtevant's fatal accident but prior to being notified of his death, and thus read the words of a dead man. He wrote to his mother after piecing the sequence of events together. "So it turned out that I got Al's letter after he was killed. I shall never forget what a shock I received, and I shall never know just what changes I underwent, but I feel perfectly sure that I shall never again experience such an awful shock." As the shock subsided, something else filled the space.

Anyway, I was sitting alone thinking how awful his death must have been and how I would miss never seeing him again, when I was impressed suddenly with the fact that Al *hadn't* gone out of my life, that he still held the same warm spot in my heart, and still had the same influence over me. I am perfectly convinced now that Al, as far as I am concerned, will always be the same fine friend that he used to be.[51]

Like so many young American men in France, MacLeish had lost but retained a friend. He would lose more. From the middle of February to the middle of March 1918, five of his friends were killed, prompting him to write to Priscilla that it was "not natural" and was apparently meant to articulate his understanding of the afterlife more fully.

On March 14, 1918, MacLeish responded to a letter from his mother describing her "point of view on the afterlife." He thanked her for breaking the ice and then wrote:

No, if I must make the supreme sacrifice I will do it gladly, and I will do it honorably and bravely, as your son should. And the life that I lay down will be my preparation for the grander, finer life that I shall take up. I shall *live!* And I shall be nearer to you than I am now, or ever have been. I shall be much happier. I firmly believe that communication is possible between a soul or spirit in this life and one in the other. I believe that this communion is finer than any on earth. You *must* not grieve![52]

MacLeish was certain that death would bring a better happier life in a fine familiar world. This he had in common with most Americans. MacLeish was equally certain that he would continue to enjoy communication and closeness with those still living. This he had in common with confessed spiritualists like his aunt, and, I believe, with many who served with him but who did not have the benefit of an aunt like Mary Hillard to help them through their experiences, questions, and emotions. MacLeish's experiences of loss and mourning, of feeling the continued presence of fallen friends, and of trying to make sense of what might wait for him beyond death were entirely ordinary. His grasp of what he called "the unseen realities," though uncommonly defined, was also no anomaly.

But MacLeish's fellow soldiers did have some access to other voices speaking in spiritualist tones. *The Stars and Stripes* inclined soldiers' ears toward the dead in observance of Memorial Day 1919. One year prior, the paper had decried the "intention of certain officers and men of the A.E.F. to celebrate Memorial Day 1918 with a program of sports and baseball." Planned levity on such a solemn day did not sit well. "Let us hark back for a moment," the 1918 piece continued, "and recall the Memorial Day in our home town years ago." Those were "days of prayer and thanksgiving–prayer for the repose of the souls who had fought for the right as God gave them to see the right, thanksgiving that those dead had not died in vain." Using a solemn tableau to evoke memories of Abraham Lincoln and the dead of America's last major conflagration, the editorialist chided fellow soldiers for being irreverent towards them in deed, if not in word. The nation, its dead, and its God were watching, he reminded them, and would not withhold judgment. Twelve months later, the war was over and troops were on their way home. Families of the dead were calling for the return of their loved ones' bodies, interrupting and redirecting a massive interment effort.[53] Not surprisingly, *The Stars and Stripes* treated Memorial Day 1919 quite differently. Gone were images of Uncle Sam and Lady Liberty. Gone was the imposing ghost of Abraham Lincoln. The call from headquarters for soldiers to "consider it a duty to assemble at the graves of their fallen comrades and there to honor to their memory" (General Order 81) appeared on page two of the paper.

The editorial board commented that Memorial Day 1919 would be marked by a different relationship between the dead and the living than had existed one year prior. "It isn't quite the same as it used to be; the dark stallions, the pale faces, the black pomp of despair of civilian days. There's a new feeling toward death, a better understanding. It is no longer strange and mysterious, it has moved among us; it has struck suddenly, mercifully, often." A new feeling toward the dead accompanied this new familiarity with death. The fallen had gone so fast, the editorialist continued, that there was no time to shake hands, no time to say good-bye, no time to reflect on the unfolding of events. Now, however, it all made sense, "loss as well as victory, death as well as discharge." Loss and death were not what they appeared to be. This was most true of the losses that hurt most: the deaths of friends and comrades. They were, in one sense, gone. But, *The Stars and Stripes* assured its readers, they remained nearby.

> So he will be with us, not in the busy rush of the life we'll take up again, but quietly at the day's end–living and real; for his going from us was unmarred by the harsh convention of civilian death, and quite cheerily, across the golden shadows, we'll answer his good night.[54]

War dead, *The Stars and Stripes* asserted, were not dead after all. They were "with us," not in the harried atmosphere of continuing physical life, but in the "golden shadows" of evening "living and real," where their good-night wishes were to be answered "cheerily." "Unmarred by the harsh convention"—the clerical and mortuary convention—"of civilian death," they remained vital and present to fellow soldiers—those who knew death best.

Where were the dead? There were no dead.

HEARING THE VOICES OF THE FALLEN

What are we to make of this composite view of the afterlife? What is the significance of a heaven characterized by comfort more than struggle, by gatherings of soldiers enjoying masculine camaraderie more than the harmony of domestic life, by promised nearness to a troubled world? Crafted by men who sought to comfort themselves as they faced death and to bring comfort to those who might mourn, these sketches of heaven offered mild critiques of the gendered heavens that informed them: the "masculine" progressive heaven (too violent, too tiring), and the feminine domestic heaven (too constraining). At the same time, they expressed soldiers' and war workers' hopes for post-war America. The soldiers appear to have had their fill of struggle and its hardships, and to have looked forward to relaxing with and enjoying their comrades and families. They appear to have expected the wages of struggle to include recognition of and respect for their service, even a position of privilege among their fellow citizens. They appear to have hoped for societal harmony, but on whose terms? The post-war actions of the American Legion—to be taken up shortly—demonstrate that veterans were more eager to claim their desired status and to force a strongly nationalist, quasi-Christian vision of societal harmony than to walk away from strife.

The matter of soldierly notions of ongoing relationships between the dead and the living is more complex. The simplest explanation of soldiers' experiences of the "presence" of fallen comrades is that grief led the living to deny the absence of the dead and that fear of death led soldiers to imagine death as a transition to a new phase of life. It would not be surprising to find among young "heroes," raised to valorize battle and the warrior, a reluctance to acknowledge the permanence of death in war. There was, however, something else at stake in hearing the voices of the fallen—something that moves beyond the personal psychologies that may have encouraged and accommodated these attitudes toward death and into the communal psychologies and politics of post-war America.

Historians Peter Brown and Ann Douglas have argued that relationships between the dead and certain groups among the living are attempts by the living to exercise authority in their society. The relationship between "knowledge" of the afterlife and earthly authority is particularly direct in spiritualism, in which the spirits of the dead counsel the living in the business of life, but is no less important to the social and cultural authority of Christianity. In both cases, the "retransfer of force from the living to the dead, from the apparently strong to the apparently weak," allows those with access to the "truth" about the afterlife to speak with certainty not only about the contours of heaven, but also about how lives on earth ought to be lived to earn praise in and access to heaven.[55] Those who can "hear" the dead can speak with authority about heaven and the qualities deemed virtuous there; they can also convey the all-important impression that the dead still care. From this perspective, soldiers' hopes for, and experiences of, ongoing relationships with the heroic dead look more like attempts to establish a cadre of uniquely qualified, authoritative interpreters of the wishes of the fallen—torchbearers of a vision verified by sacrifice. A wide swath of relationships—mothers, sisters, and nurses, as well as fellow soldiers—were initially included in this group. Quincy Mills' last letter and Kenneth MacLeish's pronouncements on spiritualism went to their mothers and, in MacLeish's case, to his fiancée as well. Former Red Cross nurse Eva Belle Babcock told the historian Lettie Galvin that the spirit of "Kramer," a sergeant who died of wounds inflicted by a German mine, contacted her every October "as strong as if he had actually written me a letter."[56] When read or felt by the survivors who received them—whether soldier or civilian—communications or injunctions to be alert could certainly serve as a reminder of a past friendship. They could remind survivors that the dead were "alive" and watching even if they were not "in touch." Not all invocations of the soldierly voice were as apolitical.

Those who directed the other-worldly voices of dead soldiers to worldly ends took their implied commission as an energizing and multidirectional call-to-arms. Some had rough outlines as to what their fallen comrades wanted them to do in the world once the war was over. But as the stated goals of the war—for the world, the nation, and the nation's subcommunities—faded into the realms of the unpopular, the impossible, or the forgotten, "spokesmen" attached the soldier-martyr's implied endorsement to a perplexing welter of organizations and plans conceived to "keep alive the spirit of the Great War." Fidelity to the "voices" of soldiers was a matter of immediate dispute. But recognized "spokesmen" for this "martyr band" narrowed over time, and so did the range of actions dead soldiers might support.

As always, the living stood ready to channel their visions through the helpless dead, claiming the martyrs' imprimatur even where it was demonstrably inappropriate. Among those interested in hearing the voices of the fallen was a group of progressive Christians charged with analyzing the soldierly religious experience and its implications for twentieth-century American Christianity. The Committee on the War and the Religious Outlook, organized by the Federal Council of Churches of Christ to observe and assess the religiousness of American soldiers in war, published its findings in the 1921 volume *Religion Among American Men*. When it came to the hold of Protestantism on the soldiers, their conclusions were mixed. But as one might expect among theological modernists, the Committee was hopeful.

The Committee gave significant space in its post-war report to soldiers' understandings of "God and immortality," emphasizing the intuitive but nonspecific knowledge that soldiers had gained of life after death. "There is almost universally a kind of belief in God and in immortality but neither conception has definitely Christian content. It is a vague notion of the general beneficence of the universe rather than faith in the God and Father of our Lord Jesus Christ....The sense of sinfulness and of need of salvation is relatively infrequent."[57] One chaplain wrote the Committee of his experiences among the soldiers in France, "Spontaneously the feeling arises as one views the broken and mangled bodies of the dead and dying and the row upon row of wooden crosses that mark the graves of the dead, 'Of course, there must be life beyond; this surely is not the end of all.'"[58] Displaying its modernist, progressive theological leanings, the Committee proclaimed, "The traditional imagery of heaven and hell has lost much of its former convincingness and with it has gone much of the sense of moral alternatives–of judgment to come;" and called for remedies that would seem more "real" and "practical" to young men.[59] Old images, doctrines, and methods of teaching had been tested and found wanting, and the Church had been exposed in its failure to stay current.

The Committee's choice of young men to represent to their readers "the instinctive confidence in a future life held by men at the front" was a "young officer, of the class of 1918 of Yale." That young man had written to his mother on March 14, 1918, "And the life that I lay down will be my preparation for the grander, finer life that I shall take up. I shall live! And I shall be nearer to you than I am now or ever have been."[60] The author was none other than self-identified spiritualist, Kenneth MacLeish. Not surprisingly, the Committee did not include in its report the spiritualist denouement—"I firmly believe that communication is possible between a soul or spirit in this life and one in the other." Why complicate an otherwise ideal authoritative testimony?

Reverend Charles W. Gilkey, pastor of Hyde Park Baptist Church in Chicago, himself vice chairman of the Committee on the War and the Religious Outlook, delivered the eulogy at Kenneth MacLeish's memorial service in February of 1919. Gilkey read the passage included in his committee's report and commented: "Most of all does this show us the real significance of his faith in immortality...a healthy-minded young man . . . facing death daily in some of its most startling forms, and keenly conscious . . . of what it meant."[61] Kenneth MacLeish, like many of his fellow soldiers, had a keen consciousness of what death meant. Thanks to the careful editing of Reverend Gilkey, MacLeish's full consciousness was lost to everyone save Priscilla Murdock, Aunt Mary Hillard, and perhaps Kenneth's mother. To craft an appropriate afterlife and to avoid pitting himself against an attractive and authoritative figure, Gilkey and the Committee on the War and the Religious Outlook cut the spiritualist heart from MacLeish's beliefs.

MacLeish was not the only soldier so treated. Before leaving for war, Quincy Mills worked under James Luby at the *New York Evening Sun.* Luby was enamored of his colleague and, upon learning of his death, compiled and edited the massive memorial volume from which I have drawn Mills' correspondence. Luby also spoke at the July 10, 1919 unveiling of a memorial plaque for Mills and two other fallen soldiers from Statesville, North Carolina. He did not have to edit down Mills' testimony, à la Gilkey on MacLeish. Instead, he poured his own progressive wine into the "heroic" and powerful, but powerless, vessel. Luby joined the overwhelming chorus of voices (Mills' voice, recall, was among them) denying that the dead were dead, and sought to provide comfort to those in attendance by describing life beyond death in progressive active terms, shunning static or domestic visions. "They are not altogether dead even in the earthly sense. They not only live in gratitude and honor but they shall live in guidance, in force, in the vitalization of good and right as active principles of life . . . I cannot think of these ardent souls as dreaming through eternity even in visions of light or orbed in clouds of glory. I will wish them effort and progress, upward struggle such as they delighted in while they were here."[62] Luby positioned himself between this world and the next and projected his wishes, the thoughts most attractive to him, onto the heaven that Mills occupied. Quincy Mills gave his mother a denial of death ("Where are the dead? There are no dead.") and enjoined her to "live by" this truth. He also published in *The Stars and Stripes* a poetic confession of longing for his adopted New York home ("But though I used to curse you / I'd pay a million fare / To hear the guard yell out tonight / 'Forty-Second Street–Times Square!'"). Luby honored Mills' complex memory by flattening it and placing a "delighted" Mills in the midst of an eternal "upward struggle."

Kenneth MacLeish's brother Archibald penned a more appropriate memorial than either Gilkey or Luby offered. In his 1919 poem, "On A Memorial Stone," the poet and future statesman memorialized fallen young men and lost youth, as he lamented the treatment he imagined they would receive.

> Now we are names that once were young
> And had our will of living weather,
> Loved dark pines and the thin moon's feather,
> Fought and endured our souls and flung
> Our laughter to the ends of earth,
> And challenged heaven with our spacious mirth.
>
> Now we are names, and men shall come
> To drone their memorable words:
> How we went out with shouting swords
> And high, devoted hearts; the drum
> Shall trouble us with stuttered roll,
> And stony latin laud the hero soul.
>
> And generations unfulfilled,
> The heirs of all we struggled for,
> Shall here recall the mythic war,
> And marvel how we stabbed and killed,
> And name us savage, brave, austere, –
> And none shall think how very young we were.[63]

Now they are, indeed, names. And the vast majority of them are forgotten. Yet, as Archibald MacLeish wrote, they truly "challenged heaven." America's clergy, popular writers, poets, and mediums had long placed themselves on the boundary between life and death, and painted elaborate, sometimes self-serving pictures of heaven. American soldiers manipulated these existing pictures of heaven, added to them, and expressed in them their hopes for status, reunion, and freedom from strife. Their voices tell a story of theological agency and creativity that contemporaries wanted to hear, as long as the plot remained predictable.

"The Same Cross in Peace": The American Legion, the Ongoing War, and American Reillusionment

> What is the use of fighting and dying, suffering and wading, cold and hungry, through the mud for the sake of democracy if we are going to sit down and let a lot of long-eared politicians, wild-eyed profiteers and mangy Bolsheviki run the country? Patriotism is the thing that we shall perpetuate. The spirit that made us fight and win the war will guide The American Legion. It is an anti-traitor alliance. The only place in the United States for the crazed agitator, the profiteer and the Bolshevik is the burying ground.[1]
>
> —CHAPLAIN JOHN INZER, American Legion

NOVEMBER 11, 1918 brought the end of the Great War. By the terms of the Armistice, the conflict among armies ended at 11 a.m. There was no dramatic, cathartic breakthrough and drive to Berlin. There was no rout. There was German fear that both were imminent, and that was sufficient. American troops on the front celebrated with their wearier French and British allies. Many soldiers in the rear areas felt cheated. Indeed, many at the front who had hoped for a more decisive victory over German militarism felt cheated as well. On the Sunday after the guns went quiet, the American Church of the Holy Trinity in Paris opened its "Military Service of Thanksgiving for Victory" with the popular hymn "Onward, Christian Soldiers."[2] The war whose end they marked had not resolved on a triumphant major chord, but it was over nonetheless.

American soldiers and war workers waged war for communal and personal redemption. They fought and died for a more democratic and, in their eyes, more Christian world order, and thus fought and died for a world and a nation that did not exist. They were neither the first nor the last. Elaine Scarry has argued more generally of war, "[I]t is to the degree that the object does not exist, or is perceived to be in danger of ceasing to exist, that ... dying and killing ... on behalf of that object ... is occasioned and necessitated."[3] Put differently, all soldiers who fight to establish or to broaden a condition—peace, freedom, democracy, Aryan hegemony, tribal autonomy—fight for a hope. If that hope remains unsatisfied when a war ends, soldiers face a choice: They can abandon the hope or they can keep fighting for it.

American soldiers of the Great War had hoped to forge in war a peaceful, unified, democratic world, but the end of war challenged those hopes. The world remained deeply troubled, violent, and undemocratic. America remained deeply troubled, violent, and undemocratic. American soldiers and war workers could have surveyed this unanticipated scene and turned from their war experiences. They could have rejected as false the promises of war and embraced the belief that the non-existent world and nation for which they fought would never exist. They could have argued quite forcefully for the meaninglessness of war in general and of the Great War in particular, and thrown up their arms in disgust. They could have become disillusioned.

No word has attached itself to the Great War as a European and American experience more completely than "disillusionment." In its classic presentation, disillusionment is the great hangover that descended upon literary, intellectual, and religious leaders, not to mention a great many soldiers, who had once been drunk on the progressive, redemptive, bloody cocktail of war.[4] This description of the war's after effects is accurate but limited; it embraces the reactions of a particularly accessible and appealing set of voices but ignores a large and arguably more important set. An early proclamation of disillusionment helps to illustrate the point.

W.E.B. Du Bois' attempt to tell the story of the African American experience of the Great War was published in the *Crisis* in June of 1919. Du Bois had been among those who supported the war and its goal of defeating tyranny in Europe; he did so because service in the war would, he believed, validate the citizenship of African Americans. However, his postwar travels in France revealed the extent of the destruction wrought by war and, more shockingly, the abysmal treatment many black soldiers received at the hands of white men and women of all ranks and stations. By June of 1919, Du Bois already knew he had been taken. He still believed that "the Negro Soldier" had been right to serve, but he was incandescent with rage.

In his "Essay Toward a History of the Black Man in the Great War," Du Bois wrote that war is a disillusioning experience for anyone—that combat loses its romance very quickly. But, he continued, the Great War had been doubly disillusioning for African American troops.

> [T]he disillusion for Negro American troops was more than this, or rather it was this and more–the flat, frank realization that however high the ideals of America or however noble her tasks, her great duty as conceived by an astonishing number of able men, brave and good, as well as of other sorts of men, is to hate "niggers." . . . Not that this

double disillusion has for a moment made black men doubt the wisdom of their wholehearted help of the Allies. . . . But these young men see today with opened eyes and strained faces the true and hateful visage of the Negro problem in America.[5]

Not only had war's violence and wastage stripped the romance of war from the black imagination—from the consciousness that African Americans shared with many white Americans—but the experience of the Great War had stripped African American soldiers of the illusion that service to the nation in a war for democracy would bring equality and the protections of the law to black soldiers and to the rest of black America. The racist duplicity of the Army and the persistence of virulent racism and racial violence in post-war America had piled a hell of broken promises atop the hell of broken bodies. Historians Arthur Barbeau and Florette Henri follow this narrative arc into post-war America and see the words of Du Bois, among others, and the race riots of 1919 as inseparable. Disillusionment, they argue, brought about the death of hope for interracial cooperation and led African Americans to struggle violently for racial equality.[6]

This argument has its legitimating points and its shortcomings. Disillusionment is clearly an apt description of Du Bois' post-war state but, as chapter 4 demonstrated, it does not describe all African American soldiers and war workers. Many men and women, black and white, entered the post-war period focused on wartime "illusions" and committed to fighting for them. The turbulent peace did not undercut their hopes for war. Instead, these veterans insisted that their wartime sacrifices had been meaningful and that their mission—their war—continued. To accept "peace" and to put the struggle aside, though not beyond them, would have been to abandon their dead and to face the exceedingly painful conclusion that the strain, suffering, disfigurement, and death had been for nothing. The thoughts and actions of American veterans in the inter-war period reveal a strong tendency toward reillusionment—the vigorous reassertion of the religiously charged ideas that framed their war experiences.

THE AMERICAN LEGION AND THE SPIRIT OF THE GREAT WAR

Almost immediately after the cessation of combat, the battle to interpret the "lessons" of the Great War began. This battle was, like the Great War itself, implicitly and explicitly religious. American veterans imagined that the forces of good were pitted against the forces of evil in an epic post-war struggle; they reflected on the forces ordering the struggle and thirsted for home-front encounters with the combat numinous. Veterans thought of the war dead and those who died struggling against "evil" on French and American soil as martyrs and imitators of Christ and invoked the power of those "sacrifices" against those who saw the world differently. With the Hun defeated in Europe, they found new enemies: communists, socialists, pacifists, and moralists—whose very existence threatened the nation. The battle lines began to form as soon as the new "peaceful" year of 1919 dawned, soldiers became veterans, and veterans began to organize.

The idea to form organizations of American Great War veterans seems to have been widespread at war's end.[7] On October 22, 1918, three weeks prior to the Armistice, Katherine Blake wrote home responding to her friends' concerns about life after the war. "Our army, and every army, stands for law, order, discipline. Our returning soldiers will not stand for any nonsense from the 'stay-at-homes' who might want to make trouble."[8] She seems to have sensed that soldiers would continue their work on the home front. She was right. Chief of Chaplains Charles Brent, supported by President Wilson and General Pershing, founded the Comrades in Service, the first A.E.F. veterans' organization, in January of 1919. Its membership, recruited by Protestant and Catholic chaplains, reached 200,000 in just three months. The Comrades sought to " '[carry] forward the all-American struggle against a common foe' and [preserve] the 'genuine comradeship and fellowship between the great historical and religious groups.' "[9] The explicitly Marxist Private Soldiers and Sailors Legion of the United States of America provided a stark contrast. Unlike the Comrades in Service who looked upon their experiences in the A.E.F. as worthy of continuation to the end of strengthening and unifying the United States, the Private Soldiers and Sailors Legion rejected "an identity of interest between officers and men, capital and labor, and government and people" and issued a "radical" call for the punishment of incompetent officers, jobs for all returning veterans, and a $500 discharge bonus.[10]

One organization, allegedly the brainchild of Theodore Roosevelt III, trumped them both.[11] Roosevelt was an immensely popular and highly decorated major in the Twenty-sixth (Yankee) Division, whose battlefield successes and lineage elevated him into General Pershing's trust. Pershing demonstrated this trust when he called upon Roosevelt to develop plans to counteract morale problems among young men waiting to go home. Roosevelt seized the mandate and used it to launch a veterans' organization that would absorb the Comrades in Service and become "one of the greatest lobbies in history."[12] After bandying about names such as "American Crusaders, The Grand Army of Civilization, and the Grand Army of the World," the first Caucus of this new veterans' group, meeting in Paris in March of 1919, arrived at a consensus. They would call themselves The American Legion.[13]

The American Legion represents the most numerically significant, unified, influential, and continuous expression of the beliefs of America's Great War soldiery in the inter-war period. While the Legion was not the only voice of American soldiers, it was, without question, the loudest on the national stage and the most popular among the soldiers themselves. By the end of its first year, 1919, from a pool of 4.5 million eligible veterans, the American Legion had a membership of over 840,000. In 1931, after a decade of fluctuation, membership topped one million. In absolute or relative terms, the Legion attracted a great many veterans.[14] The Legion was dominated by white men, but it was neither exclusively male nor exclusively white. Women who had served in the military during the war were eligible to join the Legion proper and a women's auxiliary was established for all others. The Legion left race policy to individual state Legions which led to segregated posts in many states, especially in the South. This policy did not, however, dissuade African American veterans from establishing 154 American Legion posts by 1931.[15]

The Legion was founded to "keep alive the Spirit of the Great War." In war, this spirit drew on Christian and American mythic history, beliefs about the redemptive power of strain, struggle, and war, and on a culture of masculine efficacy. Over the two decades that followed its founding, and indeed through much of the twentieth century, the Legion kept that spirit alive by describing American civilization as under attack and in urgent need of defense, by calling truly American men to confront and root out "evil," by relentlessly and effectively arguing for the privileged status of the war veteran, and by promoting a particular kind of American religious orthodoxy. The American Legion gave institutional life to a vision of America and Americanism that continues to loom large—for good and ill—in American public discourse. It is a vision of a nation with divine status, in which conflicts between duty to God and duty to nation are, simply, misunderstandings of one's duty to God. It is a vision of servicemen (and servicewomen) as saints, martyrs, and imitators of Christ, serving and dying to save the world. It is a vision of demonic enemies, internal and external, who never cease in their conspiracies to sow the nation's destruction.

An Ongoing War to End War

In the eyes of the American Legion, post-Armistice America remained locked in a battle for its very survival. This belief justified their actions and shaped much of their public rhetoric in 1919 and beyond. The power of calling the conflict between Americanist "orthodoxy" and anti-American "heresy" a war went beyond a statement of intent to do battle with these and other enemies. "War" allowed for extreme measures in confronting Bolsheviks and alien slackers. "War" made necessary the legal and extra-legal restrictions upon free speech for which the Legion called. "War" made the effeminate pacifism, frivolous moralism, and small-minded creedalism of Christian leaders pressing issues of national security and stability. "War" allowed those doing battle to envision the possibility of meaningful redemptive lives and deaths. "War" meant that opportunities to fight for "right"—opportunities that soldiers believed had been lost forever in France—could be found on American soil.

The American Legion's appeal among veterans can be attributed, at least in part, to its success in convincing former soldiers that the war was still on and that the fraternity of the combat-tested remained open. Only a month before the Legion's founding, *The Stars and Stripes* had published a poem asserting emphatically and with richly religious imagery the transformative and religious power of combat in France. The poem, "Service Chevrons," was written as a response to a War Department ruling that insignia denoting combat service could *not* be worn in the United States. The hierarchy of service established by such insignia was, from the perspective of the Department, inimical to the unity and *esprit de corps* of the entire army, and the patches themselves were too easily obtained and donned by pretenders. No matter, one soldier-poet insisted, the effects of war experiences were too profound to be hidden.

> You can strip him of his chevrons
> You can take his stripes away,
> And the badge of his division,
> Which produces your dismay;
> You can make him scrap his medals
> But no matter how you try,
> You can never, never legislate
> That glitter from his eye.

Even without adornment on his uniform, the hero would be heroic. War had changed him from the inside-out; his eyes would now be forever aglitter from the awful privilege of encountering combat.

> He has seen a summer day
> That you have never dreamed;
> He has seen flesh turn to clay,
> While affronted Heaven screamed;
> He has seen the shattered trench,
> He has seen the twisted wire,
> He has seen strong, living men
> Charred and black in molten fire;

He has seen beneath his feet
Flesh of comrades turned to clay;
As you never could have dreamed . . .
He has seen a summer day.

The anonymous poet brought to life the gruesome scenes of war: bodies and landscapes fused, flesh turned to clay, the handiwork of men shattered and twisted, Heaven screaming in horror. But his purposes were clearly more than descriptive. The poet's goal was to establish a firm boundary between those who had only imagined war and shaped the world through legislation, and those who had truly known war and shaped the world with their lives. Having divided humanity in this way, he explained the religious significance of the demarcation. The scenes of death and dismemberment had done more than shock soldiers, though they surely had done that; they had brought soldiers closer to the divine.

He has seen an autumn night
That you could never bear
With hell's flare his only light,
Pointing out hell's angel there;
He has known a single hour
When cold steel, red hail and gas
Ceased and left a holy calm
Such as come when angels pass;
He has seen his comrades stand,
Half-transfigured in release,
Knighted, spurred and panoplied
By their liege, the Prince of Peace.[16]

One who had heard the screams of "affronted Heaven," seen the approach of "hell's angel," watched the transfiguration recapitulated among soldier-saviors, and been knighted by Christ himself, had knowledge of Truth that few could approach. He needed no mere chevron to be known to himself and the world. The combination of death, destruction, and the divine would live on in him, a "glitter" in his eye, indicating membership in a brotherhood the religious and civic authority of which was unsurpassed, indeed unsurpassable. The Armistice shut the door to this fraternity. The American Legion pried it open again.

The first caucus of the American Legion decided to ignore widely made distinctions among combat-tested and non-combat-tested soldiers. They opened the organization to all men and women who had been mustered into service regardless of place and duration of service, and regardless of rank.[17] Rather than describe the war and its opportunities as gone, the

Legion offered the hope that battles of great import remained to be fought. Among the resolutions passed at the first caucus was one calling "every post of the Legion . . . to tender and volunteer [the] services of its individual members to the constituted government authorities for use in any time of public crisis to preserve law and order," and for plans to be formulated such that "the full force and power of the Legion can be swiftly mobilized and used on the side of the constitutional government and American liberty."[18] Legion leaders, themselves a mixture of those tested by combat and those not, envisioned their "force and power" being deployed against "anarchistic and un-American groups," even to the point of armed engagement.[19] Thus were men who served as cooks and military policemen in Newark offered the hope of defending America and Americanism, perhaps even to the death, alongside men who had "seen a summer day."

War veteran Amos Wilder's 1924 poem "To the American Legion," which he likely wrote while a ministry student at Yale, conveys his sense of the continued gravity of the post-war moment and the continued sense of duty to rise and fight.

> We are not our own for our lives are under bond
> To the martyr leaders who have passed beyond,
> For they still command and we cannot but respond.

> We are not our own, for we lost our liberty
> On the day they died who had longed to make men free,
> Whose compelling dream must be law for you and me.

> There are those who made no agreement with the dead,
> Who are free to laugh and to feast, but some instead
> Will be stern with thinking on those who fought and bled . . .

> For the foe remains in a thousand forms elate,
> And there is no armistice with Greed and Hate,
> And no truce with Slavery though the day grow late.

> Ay, the Foe remains who will grant us this joy more,
> The same cross in peace that our comrades found in war,
> And unite us to the heroes gone before.[20]

In Wilder's eyes, the American Legion was the American Expeditionary Force commanded by its martyred dead to a battlefield as treacherous as any seen before. The enemy on this battlefield did not wear the distinctive uniform of the German Army. She or he came, rather, in a "thousand forms" but was consistently marked by greed, hate, and slavery. Wilder was certain that war continued and argued that veterans had no choice but to fight. As grave as the situation was though, it allowed dutiful Legionnaires the possible "joy" of dying a heroic, Christ-like death—the "same cross in peace" that 115,000 young American men had "found in war."

The American Legion was, at its inception, an organization with a profoundly religious appeal and with deep religious interests. The preamble to its constitution made clear the conventionally religious dimensions of the Legion's vision by proclaiming "For God and Country we associate ourselves together . . . " Less conventional but still deeply religious was its involvement in numerous efforts to defend the righteousness of the Great War.

COMBATING THE PROBLEMS OF PEACE

With the Great War still raging in the eyes of the Legion, the unfulfilled promises of the war could be cast not as failures or fictions, but as works in progress. Events in post-war America required this reevaluation. New and old problems seemed to point daily to the failure of war to redeem the nation. Problems began even before the Legion's founding. Much to the chagrin of *The Stars and Stripes'* editorial board, the Eighteenth Amendment was ratified in January of 1919 making Prohibition the law of the land and granting a victory to moralists.[21] Also in January, the Industrial Workers of the World (IWW) struck in Seattle, bringing the city to a standstill. In May of 1919, an anonymous mail-bomber attempted to send bombs to the homes and offices of eighteen powerful Americans—state governors, U.S. senators and representatives, businessmen, commissioners and Attorney General A. Mitchell Palmer—and May Day parades in Boston, Cleveland, and New York resulted in violence. Race riots broke out in Chicago and Washington, D.C. and in urban centers across the United States during the sweltering summer of 1919, resulting in losses of life and property, and sometimes pitting black and white veterans against each other. Lynchings in the rural South rose from 58 in 1918 to 80 in 1919 and claimed as many as ten black veterans.[22] The rate of labor unrest was also off the charts during 1919. According to one historian, "[a]lmost four and a half million [American workers], a number equal to 22.5 percent of the labor force" went on strike in 1919. This was three times the national average for the period 1916–1922.[23]

Returning from France with the hope that the world and the nation had been redeemed, American soldiers were met with a powerfully dissonant reality. They found fellow Americans in violent disagreement over ideals and their application. One Legionnaire described his frustration with the situation using the IWW as his target: "Friends," he wrote, "do you wonder that the American Legionnaire hates a [W]obbly after having served under that glorious old flag of red, white, and blue, after . . . facing that living hell of gas and burning fire and every torture invented by the enemy, leaving many a comrade in a grave or foreign soil . . . [W]e came home joyously anticipating a deserved peace, to be met by a '[W]obbly' who stayed home safe from the agony of war, and hear him boast about pulling down the Stars and Stripes and hoisting up a red flag."[24] The American Legion offered an antidote to the chaos. It organized American veterans to reassert the validity of their wartime vision and fight for that vision in America as they had fought for it in France.

Legionnaires framed the ongoing war in America with language and imagery drawn directly from their war experiences. The fight was, again, against "evil" and for a properly unified, properly Christian, properly American nation. Robert Simmons, an early historian of the American Legion in Nebraska, wrote tellingly in the inter-war period of the Legion's dedication to "God and Country." The two intersected in ways familiar to the American soldier of the Great War. The "God" of whom Simmons wrote was, "[t]he same God to whom Washington knelt in the snow at Valley Forge and prayed. The same God to whom Lincoln turned to consolation and strength during the trying hours of the Civil War. And the same God in whom the American people have always had an abiding faith." The memory of the service rendered by these legendary men to God and country was sacred. Those who followed in their footsteps could, likewise, claim sacred status. The Legion, Simmons continued, was perfecting the type. Its members were "[d]edicated, too, to that country conceived from a vision in the minds of God-fearing, free-thinking men; born in the struggles of the Revolutionary War, united by fratricidal strife in the days of the Rebellion, and purged of all unworthiness and selfishness by final action in the war against Germany."[25] Simmons claimed the authority of sacred American history for the Legion while asserting the sacred status of the recently completed war. Just as veterans had been willing to die in the Great War, Simmons continued, so were they now willing to make "every sacrifice of blood and treasure," that the "instrument and the principles and doctrines that are founded upon [the Constitution]" be preserved.[26] This new war, like the Great War and the great wars gone before, would demonstrate the depth of individual commitments to God and country.

The Legion fought tenaciously on the new battlefield of the United States to achieve "victory" as they understood it. The most frequently named enemies of America and, in Legion-speak, "One hundred-percent Americanism," were the Bolshevik and the alien slacker. The Bolshevik, a modern Judas, was ready to betray America in favor of unjust new laws and a dark new order; the alien slacker, a modern Peter, had denied the nation (*not* a modern forgiving Christ) in its time of need and had thus revealed himself to be, according to the Legion, unworthy of citizenship. These were true enemies against whom all "true" Americans were called to organize and do battle.

Two covers of *The American Legion Weekly* from the summer of 1919 convey the Legion's view of the American battlefield and their place on it. The first, published on July 11, 1919, depicts a crazed-looking man, filthy and stooped, preparing to throw a bomb at "American Institutions." Striding forward from the back of the picture is a clean-cut and chiseled man with his sleeves rolled up and his eyes focused on the threatening beast-like man. He has thrown his uniform with its war-service chevrons to the ground revealing an undershirt that reads "American Legion." (See figure 7.1.) The second cover, published on August 15, 1919 and titled "Her Big Brother" shows another serviceman, this one a giant, with one hand on the shoulder of the Statue of Liberty, another formed into a fist. His foot is drawn back, prepared to kick or stomp on a group of small men and rats. The vermin group includes a "Bolshevist," an "IWW," a "Propagandist," and an "Alien Slacker." (See figure 7.2.) Both of these pictures convey quite clearly the Legion's self-understanding as a defender of America and its ideals. Vigilant, muscular, battle-tested men of action would patrol the borders of a covenanted nation and force out all who would not confess Americanism.[27]

But the Legion did not just imagine directing violence against the IWW and similar threatening groups. One year to the day after the guns of the Western Front had fallen silent, on Armistice Day 1919, a planned parade in Centralia, Washington dissolved into deadly conflict between Legionnaires and IWW members at the IWW union hall. The exact sequence of events, William Pencak notes, "are in dispute" even today. The Legion maintains that IWW members fired on marching Legionnaires without provocation. Others declare that Legion members, working hand-in-glove with logging interests, had planned to run the IWW out of town, and were fired upon when they tried to force their way into the union hall.[28] All agree, however, that gunshots fired by IWW members killed four Legionnaires—Warren Grimm, Arthur McElfresh, Ben Casagranda and Dale Hubbard—and led to the detention of a number of Wobblies, including John Lamb, Eugene Barnett, O.C. Bland, Ray Becker, Britt Smith, James McInerney, Bert Bland and Hiram Wesley Everest.[29] All agree, also, that on the evening of November 11, 1919, power was temporarily cut to the town of Centralia and that when power was restored, Wesley Everest, a former serviceman with a history of radicalism, was missing from the jail. Everest had been removed by a crowd, which exacted revenge by torturing and castrating him, and then hanging him twice—they cut him down once before he died—from a railroad bridge.[30]

Figure 7.1. Image courtesy of the American Legion.

Figure 7.2. Image courtesy of the American Legion.

Everest's corpse was then returned to the jail for his fellow unionists—"Mental Defectives" in the Legion's estimation—to ponder.[31]

The American Legion Weekly covered the clash and the Everest lynching at length and saw nothing but anti-American perfidy heroically encountered and, for the most part, thoroughly routed. Their account of events told of a peaceful unarmed parade of Great War veterans that, when passing the union hall, met an ambush set by conniving Bolshevik cowards. They told of Legionnaires demonstrating the kind of heroism and gentlemanly restraint that marks the mythic American fighting man, and of trying, with great success, to keep order in the town. The fallen former soldiers—Grimm, McElfresh, Casagranda, and Hubbard—were, on the Legion's account, martyrs whose deaths were akin to the "supreme sacrifice" made by so many American soldiers in France. The event was no mere riot; it was, as *The American Legion Weekly* contributor Jerrold Owen wrote, a momentous battle in the "Inevitable Clash between Americanism and Anti-Americanism." And anyone who doubted the significance of this clash was directed to think of a pivotal battle in the recently concluded war in Europe. "Overnight, the name 'Centralia' became as familiar to America as 'Chateau Thierry.' It was there that defiance of government, long shouted and threatened by the sworn enemies of constituted authority, the Industrial Workers of the World, took concrete form. It was the inevitable attack of the lawless upon The American Legion." War was not over. It had only just begun.[32]

The American Legion's commitment to the intimidation and marginalization of those who questioned the America for which they had fought was unflagging. They worked in close coordination with the FBI—whose budget and power they lobbied to increase—to root out all types of "subversives." They regularly sought to deprive suspected Communist and Socialist speakers and their sympathizers of public venues, and sometimes resorted to shouting them down. Legion lobbying led to the creation, in 1938, of the Dies Committee, later the House Un-American Activities Committee, the purpose of which was, under the mantle of the law, to make the lives of "subversives" miserable. Those who would move the nation away from or openly critique its form of government, and those who questioned either the virtues of capitalism or the importance of a strong "prepared" military, demonstrated by their very words their lack of commitment to America.[33]

Why did the Legion pursue Communists and Socialists with such fervor? The threat was real, to be sure. The success of Lenin's revolution in Russia, and the labor disruptions of 1919 demonstrated as much. But the challenge posed by the very *existence* of Communist and Socialist sympathizers was at least as important. According to Legion leaders, dissent of this sort threatened to render meaningless all for which they had fought, suffered, and died. When President Warren G. Harding proposed to pardon Eugene V. Debs, jailed for an anti-war speech delivered in the summer of 1918. Legion leaders made very clear the stakes of the fight against communism.[34] "[A]ny sign of mercy would betray those who sacrificed their lives and health in the common cause. [It would be] the most un-American act since the days of Benedict Arnold . . . [and a] rank injustice to not only the boys who were in the army in 1917, but to the parents and friends who suffered the loss of them."[35] Drawing on sacred history new and old, Legion leaders strove to paint "mercy" for Debs as the ultimate insult. Hanford MacNider, National Commander of the Legion, put an equally fine point on the pardon in a telegram to President Harding.

> . . . if pardon is granted to Debs or others fairly and justly convicted of treason or sedition during a time when the nation's very life was at stake, the lives of those American boys who lie on the fields of France and those who lie broken in the hospitals and homes of this country have been uselessly sacrificed and our blood has been given in vain.[36]

Whether or not the "very life" of the nation had been at stake—most would say not—MacNider treated Debs' dissent and the timing thereof as a kind of toxin that would threaten the health of the nation if released. More specifically, to let Debs rejoin the covenanted community of Americans was to forever poison memories of the Great War, to render soldiers' sufferings a waste. The waste was tied not to the failure of an international program for peace and world governance, but to the shattering of the illusion that war had unified the nation. This strategy of tying policy decisions and individual beliefs about the merits of capitalism to the "memories of the war dead" was an unsubtle but effective cooptation of the religio-civic authority of the soldier-martyr. By invoking the names of those who had given their lives for the nation and by claiming to speak on their behalf, the Legion cast opposition to its programs, policies, and views not simply as disagreement but as blasphemy and heresy.

A CREED OF CITIZENSHIP: RELIGION IN THE LEGION'S AMERICA

Scholars recall the post-war era in the United States as a time of religious conflict and suspicion about the corrosive effects of religious difference.[37] The 1920s were, after all, the decade during which the Fundamentalist-Modernist controversy was at its most heated, the Ku Klux Klan found new life on an anti-Jewish, anti-Catholic platform, and the presidential campaign of Al Smith, governor of New York and a Catholic, conjured the malignant spirits of nativism. But the 1920s were also years of interdenominational cooperation and of attempts to embrace religious difference as characteristic of American life.[38] The American Legion walked both paths. They demonstrated their ecumenism by embracing people of many faiths on the condition that they subordinate religious differences to the "more important" task of strengthening and defending the nation. They also showed their combative temper by working to push moralists and pacifists—those who questioned the near divinity of the War and the soldier—to the margins of society.

The marginalization of religious dissenters, exemplified by Legion attacks on the liberal Protestant clergyman and YMCA leader Sherwood Eddy, was a genuine and lamentable extension of the "spirit of the Great War."[39] In 1917, Sherwood Eddy published *With Our Soldiers in France.* The work was based on his observations of Allied soldiers, mostly British, with whom he came into contact as a YMCA worker. Eddy was no glorifier of war, but in his descriptions one can detect a number of assumptions about war that he shared with his more militant contemporaries. He wrote of the power of war to reveal the true man: "It has shown us the real stuff of which men are made. It is like the X-ray photographs now constantly used in all the military hospitals. . . . " Having seen British and Scottish chaplains working among soldiers, he argued that such service would benefit American clergy: "We would covet this opportunity for every young minister or Christian worker in America."[40] Yet Eddy was concerned to differentiate between service to God and service to nation, and concluded his chapter "Religion at the Front" by lamenting, "If Christians would but follow Christ, war, as an unbelievably brutal and barbarous anachronism, like its former savage contemporaries of slavery, the burning of witches, and the torture of the Inquisition, would be forever done away."[41]

After the war, Sherwood Eddy joined many other liberal Protestant leaders in embracing pacifism. He had seen the Great War and considered its relationship to Christianity. Based on his experiences and his reflection on them, he penned a scathing indictment. Eddy, then General Secretary of the YMCA, wrote in 1924 expressing feelings shared at the time by then-Detroit-based pastor Reinhold Niebuhr, *Christian Century* editor Charles Clayton Morrison, Social Gospeler Vida Scudder, and the members of the Fellowship of Reconciliation "[the war] had settled nothing, made nothing safe, [and] achieved no lasting good commensurate with the awful sacrifices of the whole world."[42] Such words marked him (and surely the others), in Legion eyes, as undeniably un-American and improperly Christian. There was no place for men like Eddy (or women like Scudder) in a nation of men who worshipped the God before whom "Washington knelt in the snow at Valley Forge and prayed." In early 1928, Eddy planned a speaking tour.[43] Edward Spafford, the National Commander of the American Legion, quite predictably saw Eddy and his views as a threat to the nation and to the Legion's ideals. Spafford took action. With a copy of Eddy's itinerary in hand, he "sent letters to department and local commanders urging that they try 'to prevent his speaking, and failing in that, to see that he is followed up with a good speaker who will instill a little radical nationalism.' "[44] Eddy became aware of the Legion's plan, published one of Spafford's letters in *The Christian Century*, and then watched as all of his speaking engagements in Kentucky and half of them in North Carolina were canceled.[45] In defending his actions, Spafford was quick to portray Eddy's speaking tour as an attack on the memory of the war dead and an attack on the nation for which they died. He said of Eddy, "a man who would preach such a doctrine [pacifism] is unworthy of the nation for which we gave our best efforts and for which our brave dead are sleeping under white crosses in France."[46] Spafford also characteristically elided peace and war to justify his efforts to silence Eddy. He told fellow Legionnaire, John Pipkin, commander of the Arkansas Legion, "all I tried to do was to discourage people from listening to the words of a man which, if said in time of war, would place that man against a wall before a firing squad." There was no doubt in Spafford's mind that Eddy and men like him were in league with the enemy.[47]

But not all clergymen were as lost as Eddy. Reverend Earl Blackman was an exemplary preacher of the Legion's nationalist faith. Blackman had become temporarily famous among readers of *The Stars and Stripes* when, in February of 1919, he offered to fight any other chaplain in the American Expeditionary Force. His planned bout with Reverend Charles Rexrode, touted in the pages of *The Stars and Stripes*, was canceled, but not before it provided wonderful fodder for contributors to the paper's sports page.[48] Blackman returned from service with the 130th Field Artillery to his pulpit in Chanute, Kansas and continued to preach and live according to the Gospel of the soldier. He kept himself in fighting shape and was a founding member of the Kansas division of the American Legion. Blackman even had a run-in with local moralists. Shortly after returning from war, he attended a local dance and drew criticism from "a small group in his congregation." Blackman responded by submitting his resignation and leaving for a two-week fishing trip. *The American Legion Weekly* reported, however, that upon his return "he found that the congregation, by a large majority, had refused to accept his resignation." Blackman then got down to the business of overhauling his church and making it more popular with the community. He installed a gymnasium in the church basement and "gave the boys in Sunday School classes lessons in boxing;" he "pounded hard at the bigotry of the church;" and did everything he could to "put religion over."[49]

In 1921, the American Legion elected Reverend Earl Blackman their National Chaplain and published an article profiling him in *The American Legion Weekly.* The paper described him as "at all times a man's man [who] represents the liberal spirit that pervades the [Legion]." Here was a man who wore the cloth at home as he had in war, who remained eager to move religion beyond its "superstitions of the past," who set himself apart from "some of his fellow ministers" by refusing to see dances as sinful, who spoke out against Sunday Blue Laws and held liberal views of Sabbath observance. Most importantly, as his own life demonstrated, Earl Blackman was a fighter who taught others to fight.[50]

Though it is tempting to see the Legion's actions against Eddy and its embrace of Blackman as militarist bullying on the one hand and affection for a choir preacher on the other, something deeper was at issue. The Legion's approach to religious leaders and to religion more generally demonstrated a deep appreciation for religion's divisive (and unitive) potential. During the war, the American Expeditionary Force and *The Stars and Stripes,* not to mention the soldiers and war workers, had worked to put religious differences aside in the name of providing the most unified fighting force possible. During the peace, the Legion continued this effort both by defining overly divisive types of faith as "un-American" and by attempting to forge a faith that all "true" Americans could embrace. The Legionnaires' vision of religion's proper place in the American public square was equal parts inclusion and coercion, respect for difference, and an emphatic insistence that differences be limited.

When it came to religious divisiveness, the Legion was an equal opportunity persecutor. They turned their artillery upon Christian pacifists, but also stood firm against the anti-Catholic, anti-Jewish Ku Klux Klan. At its 1923 national convention in San Francisco, the Legion debated three separate resolutions condemning religious bigotry and vigilante justice— both characteristic of the Klan—including one that named and explicitly condemned the Klan. Delegates finally passed a resolution that read:

> Whereas the fundamental law of our country guarantees to all peoples equal rights and equal opportunities and the right to worship God as they see fit . . . be it Resolved . . . this 17th day of October, 1923, that we consider any individual, group of individuals, or organizations, which creates, or fosters racial, religious or class strife among our people, or which takes into their own hands the enforcement of law, determination of guilt, or infliction of punishment, to be un-American, a menace to our liberties, and destructive to our fundamental law.[51]

The Legion clearly had its eyes on the Klan and on other groups that predicated American citizenship on Protestant faith. Such associations flew in the face of the soldiers' and war workers' experiences in France

and were anathema to the Legion. Religious differences had been minimized during combat in France and, if the war against America's many
foes was to be a success, religious differences had to be minimized in peace
as well.

As much as their stance against divisive religion says about the Legion's
vision of religion in post-Armistice America, the kind of religion they
embraced and tried to shape says even more. The American Legion hoped
to unify America. Religion presented at least two obstacles to unity. First,
to the extent that men and women felt God's calling to be higher than or
different from the call of the nation—as Christian pacifists did—the
tightly-knit commonwealth envisioned by many Legionnaires would always be in jeopardy. Second, Americans embraced a wide variety of gods
and revelations. In order to forge a more perfect union, differences among
American denominations and faiths had to be met and minimized. The
Legion publicly embraced Catholics and Jews during a time of deep-
running anti-Catholic, anti-Jewish sentiment. In 1928, the Legion elected
Rabbi Herman Beck their National Chaplain and replaced him with
Rabbi Lee Levinger in 1929. In 1928, National Commander Edward
Spafford raised the eyebrows of some Legionnaires when he publicly defended presidential candidate Al Smith of New York, a Catholic, against
attacks from Alabama Senator Thomas Heflin.[52] This comparative open-
ness sprang from the realization, still pending in the 1920s among large
swaths of the population, that Catholics and Jews were in the United
States to stay and could be—indeed already were—committed patriots.

Legion leaders were not satisfied, however, with keeping their own religious house open and in order. As a matter of national health, they wanted
to order the houses of America's mainline churches as well. On June 26th,
1923, Legion leaders convened a small conference of "Religious and Fraternal Organizations" at its offices in Washington, D.C. National Commander Alvin Owlsey of Texas addressed the meeting, but National Adju-
tant Lemuel Bolles and National Chaplain Father William O'Connor did
most of the talking. Those in attendance included representatives from
the Federal Council of Churches of Christ, the Salvation Army, the
YMCA, the Knights of Columbus, the National Catholic Welfare Council, the American Red Cross, the Noble Order of the Mystic Shrine, and
six chaplains of American Legion posts.[53] When Father O'Connor rose to
welcome attendees and to explain the purpose of the meeting to all those
invited, he emphasized the importance of unity and vigorous patriotism.
He suggested that attendees should "take counsel together as God-fearing
Americans to the end that from our deliberations come a rededication
of Americans–of all creeds and beliefs–to the fundamental doctrines of
patriotism, strengthened by mutual confidence and respect between those

who join in such service."⁵⁴ The men and women were gathered, in other words, to covenant among themselves and with the nation; to say before the Legion leadership and their God that they would not let religious differences interfere with the duties of citizenship.

In advance of the meeting, Lemuel Bolles had prepared a Creed of Citizenship that he hoped those in attendance could endorse. This creed was intended not to create a unity of faith, but to develop a unified willingness to subordinate faith in one's God to faith in the nation. It was intended to render irrelevant for "civic life" the many religious differences that existed among Americans.

> We . . . do solemnly affirm our faith in the government and established institutions of the United States of America. . . . We feel that unity of sentiment for a better America must be developed among all classes of citizens and that difference of opinions on subjects which cannot be decided by the finite mind must be subordinated to love of our fellow man and for the country in which we live.⁵⁵

This creed can be read in two ways, both of which are correct. The first reading, the one forwarded by the Legion, focuses on the tolerance of religious difference and diversity as part of the American experience and emphasizes especially the stand against religious prejudice manifested in the Legion's anti-Klan position. On this reading, the Creed of Citizenship encourages men and women of different faiths to work together for a healthy, stable nation. An alternate reading would see the creed as an attempt to establish a *new* religion with a new god, new rituals, new scriptures, new modes of catechesis, and a new priesthood, as well as new heresies and new taboos. This religion, based ostensibly on things the "finite mind" could decide, would allow religious differences to exist in private and would endorse a pantheon of vassal deities so long as ultimate sovereignty belonged to the nation.

It is unclear whether the men and women in attendance that June day in 1923 approved the Creed unanimously—the Legion prepared a press release in advance announcing approval. It is clear, however, that through much of the twentieth century and often with the tacit approval of America's religious leaders, the Legion worked to spread and defend a religion of the nation; a religion that embraced the symbols, texts, and saints of American history, preached the gospel of one-hundred-percent Americanism, and saw efforts to "protect" the ideas and institutions of the nation as obviously divinely sanctioned. When Protestants, Catholics, and Jews made room for this religion in their religions, they drew the praise and support of the Legion. When they did not, they drew its ire.

A TALE OF TRANSFORMATION

So much of what constituted the "spirit of the Great War" lived on in the American Legion through the inter-war period that one is hard-pressed to identify exactly what, if anything, died. At least one eulogy is appropriate. In wartime France, an army-wide campaign to "adopt" French children orphaned by the war was second only to the war itself in the coverage it received from *The Stars and Stripes'* reporters. Beginning on March 29, 1918 and running through Christmas of that year, the paper encouraged soldiers to "Take As Your Mascot A French War Orphan." Soldiers could do this by sending five hundred francs to the paper's offices. The paper, in turn, forwarded donations to the Red Cross, which selected an orphan, provided the donor with a biography, and sent periodic updates on the improving life of the child. After the campaign was launched, *The Stars and Stripes* tracked its progress in every issue (usually on the front page) and made it the subject of editorial pieces and cartoons. Reportage and editorials underscored the difference between the American soldier and his German foe. Germans made orphans; Americans made them whole. An April 12, 1918 cartoon depicted the Kaiser reading about the orphan campaign and proclaiming, "Fools! They destroy all my pleasure in this war!"[56]

Participation in the campaign was widespread and enthusiastic. Units on the front lines, units in the service areas, aviation units, and individual soldiers far exceeded donation goals. The drive even became something of a sensation on the home front. One Portland ship builder raised the equivalent of 10,000 francs to "adopt" twenty orphans.[57] By Christmas of 1918, sponsors had donated nearly two million francs to support 3,444 orphans. The brainchild of Private Harold Ross, an editor of *The Stars and Stripes* and future founder and editor of *The New Yorker*, this campaign was successful, in part, because it crystallized popular notions of the war's meaning and the significance of American participation. As they gathered funds and sent them in, soldiers made clear to themselves and to others the righteousness of America's war effort and the heinous brutality of the German adversary. The drive also succeeded because soldiers understood the pain inflicted by war. They felt it in its many manifestations and wanted to be a part of the solution.

The American Legion carried the spirit of the orphan campaign forward into post-Armistice America. Legion posts enthusiastically supported youth baseball leagues, the Boy Scouts, and numerous programs aimed more explicitly at the civic education of young Americans. They expressed concern for American families shattered by war through lobbying efforts in support of benefits for veterans' families. American children living in the midst of a war against un-American ideologies had to be cared for and cultivated. With proper attention, proper education, and proper religious development, they could be saved. The same could not be said of all children.

In 1939, Germany was again at war in Europe. German actions in the 1930s and '40s, of course, went far beyond the characterizations of Germans common between 1914 and 1918. The advances of the German army and the genocidal policies of the National Socialists generated tragic numbers of orphans and displaced children, when the children weren't killed outright. In 1939 and 1940, while the Legion was railing against communism and marking the twentieth anniversary of the "massacre" of "martyrs" at Centralia by proclaiming in an editorial, "They Did Not Die in Vain,"[58] a bill came before Congress that "offered to admit 20,000 refugee children, mostly Jews, from Hitler's Germany." Barely two decades removed from the orphan campaign, the American Legion stood firmly against the bill and "launched a special fight" to prevent the children from becoming "an opening wedge that would permit people to 'circulate throughout America propagating un-American doctrines.' " The legislation went down to defeat. The Legion was not alone in its opposition, but neither did it revise its position when the extent of Hitler's atrocities came to light.[59]

How did the doughboys who had once been enthusiastic participants in the orphan campaign become equally enthusiastic opponents of an effort to aid distressed children? Was it, as the words of Theodore Roosevelt III suggest, due to "disillusionment . . . so bitter that we tend to forget and discredit the ideals with which our country was then aflame." Had the intervening years voided the conviction "not merely that our cause was righteous but that by winning the victory we were going to bring new and better days to the world [?]"[60] It is, I believe, more appropriate to attribute the Legion's actions in the 1920s and '30s, including their insistence that Jewish children seeking refuge from the Nazis were a potential enemy, to reillusionment. For far from being discredited or vanishing, many of the ideals to which Roosevelt referred, and which I have described, thrived in the inter-war period. The Legion defended these ideals with such tenacity that they became and remain regular features of the national conversation in America. Veterans argued for the divinity of the nation, idealized the active, strenuous, potentially violent man, and thought of their dead as heroes, martyrs, and imitators of Christ. They continued to glorify war and to question the masculinity and impugn the patriotism of their critics. They even continued to theorize—with embarrassing and sometimes tragic results—about conspiratorial connections among the forces at work in their cosmos. This reillusionment was so complete, its participants so convinced of the enduring truth of their wartime framework, that they looked upon suffering children and saw not suffering children but a looming enemy to be defeated. So convinced were they of the persistence of a domestic war, that these men whom Chaplain Thomas Coakley had hailed as "Heroes in the Cause of God" could not say, as they had in 1918, "let the children come."

Conclusion

IN THE COURSE of ninety years, the events and figures of the Great War have been almost completely wiped from American memory. By the time this book is published, the last living veteran of the American Expeditionary Force will likely be dead. There will be precious few men and women alive who remember wishing a Doughboy well, waiting for letters from France, and either rejoicing at a soldier's return or mourning his death, and facing life without a husband, a brother, a father, a friend. In cruel defiance of bold proclamations from soldiers, *The Stars and Stripes*, and from the military, political, and religious leaders of the day, the names of battlefields and of heroes have been forgotten, and the Great War itself has been relegated to the status of a baffling prequel to the truly "great" war waged by America's "Greatest Generation" from 1941–1945.

Vestiges of the war remain, to be sure. Men and women so destroyed by war that they can no longer be properly identified, a significant problem in the Great War and subsequent overseas conflicts, are still memorialized and mourned at the Tomb of the Unknowns, constructed in the wake of the war and dedicated in a moving and elaborate funeral on Armistice Day, 1921. All American veterans, living and dead, are remembered and honored on November 11, the day on which, in 1918, the Great War came to an end. But the day's connection to the Great War, maintained for nearly four decades by the name "Armistice Day," is now obscured by the more generally applicable and palatable Veterans Day. The thought-world of the trench warrior is invoked, however unintentionally, when someone describes an act as "over the top," a place as "No Man's Land," or an effort as "eleventh hour." The origins of these commemorations and turns of phrase in the Great War are not, however, commonly known. Military historians and trivia buffs are familiar with the connections, but they are lost on the vast majority of Americans.

The editors of *The Stars and Stripes* sensed in June of 1919 that with the Great War's passage from event to memory, the battle to interpret and remember it would turn against them. The veterans were too few, the war tourists, dilettantes, and other uninitiated interpreters were too many. "Many will come to Belleau Wood, people who have read all about the Great War . . . Those people will see twisted trees. But they won't see the sprawling forms beneath them . . . Here and there they may pick up an empty shell. But the fingerless hand protruding from the rotting khaki blouse has been graciously buried beneath a neat white cross."[1] In the paper's final issue, the editors pleaded with their readership to justify the horror by telling the truth about war and by stymieing profiteers and aggrandizers. Only soldiers, they continued, can know the ugly face behind the mythic mask.

> Upon them rests a solemn duty. They must go home and choke the coward jingo who masks himself behind a false and blatant patriotism, and the merchant-politician, not content with stuffing his home coffers till they burst—but anxious to barter the blood of his country's young manhood for new places in the sun![2]

While choking warmongers, soldiers were also to support an almost divine instrument of peace. "We can help build a League of Nations with such sinews and such consciences for peace that no one will dare oppose it. If we don't," the author concluded, "the blood will be on our own foolish heads. . . . " The authors thus invested the Great War's religious meaning in one institution and its ability to eradicate war. We are still sifting through the rubble of its spectacular collapse.

All history is an act of memory, but memory does not occur on a level playing field. There are certain memories that live at the heart of a culture and reveal truths imagined as essential. These memories—these myths— are difficult things from which to distance oneself while still identifying fully with a culture. In the United States, the Second World War is one such memory. The Civil War is another.[3] The Great War is not. The Doughboys have not taken their place alongside the Minutemen, Union and Confederate soldiers, even the Rough Riders. Chateau-Thierry is not "the great American shrine in Europe–the Gettysburg of the A.E.F." as *The Stars and Stripes* predicted it would always be.[4] To the Revolutionary War's "Genesis," the Civil War's narrative of sin, trial, and redemption, and the Second World War's struggle between good and evil to save the innocent, the Great War is strange and vestigial—akin to stories of Biblical patriarchs engaging in sexual indiscretions. The story is there, but it is best not to dwell on it at any length. Yet the meta-lessons of the Great War, of little concern to current cultural custodians and therefore accessible mostly to historians, remain relevant.

That Americans and American scholars have let the Great War pass from cultural memory is a tragedy that matches, if it does not surpass, the tragedy of the war itself. The scale of this tragedy of memory lies not in the loss of a significant interpretive key with which we can access the deepest truths about twentieth-century American politics, literature, culture, or religion, though greater attention to the war would certainly deepen our understanding of all four. The scale of this tragedy of memory is measured by its influence on American understandings of war. Because of the erasure of the Great War, generations of Americans have not been asked to consider whether the Great War was, in fact, the prototypical twentieth-century war; whether in its ambiguities, its inconclusive outcomes, and its violent ripple effect through the ensuing decades and the affected geographies, the Great War predicted rather accurately the course and the effects of all but one subsequent American war. Because of the erasure of the Great War, the ambiguities and failures and wastes of twentieth-century wars and military actions have been understood as anomalous, bizarre, and, above all, avoidable exceptions to the aesthetically and morally pleasing rule of the Second World War. Because of the Great War's absence and the Second World War's dominance in American cultural memory, the United States has a narrative of military triumph without an adequate cautionary tale to leaven it. This unchallenged narrative has shaped understandings of the power of war to accomplish good and, more to the point, the specific goods willed by war's authors. Americans would do well, it seems, to allow that the Great War established a rule to which Korea, Vietnam, Somalia and, so far, Afghanistan and Iraq have conformed, and to recall that there has been exactly one World War Two–style military triumph since the founding of the republic.

THE RELIGIOUSNESS OF THE GREAT WAR

Also of enduring relevance are the Great War's lessons about the place of religion in the waging of American wars. For religion was not merely a marginal or secondary concern in the American experience of the Great War. American involvement in the war began and ended with talk of redemption. There were certainly those who doubted that war could have such beneficial effects, but the most prominent voices—black and white, male and female—were those that echoed a strong cultural pulse and predicted, then proclaimed, that the world had been saved and the nation redeemed.[5] The men and women who helped wage the war did not fight always and everywhere with God on their minds and a prayer in their hearts, but religion—in most cases Christianity—was a powerful force in their culture and often in their lives. Religion informed their sense of duty, gave them the language, narratives, ideas, and symbols to frame the conflict and to understand their part in it. In so doing, religion helped soldiers make what theologian Stanley Hauerwas has called the greatest sacrifice of war: the sacrifice of one's unwillingness to kill. Religion also gave supernatural order to unnatural, apparently random death and gave transcendent meaning to acute earthly suffering. Religion directed soldiers' eyes beyond death to salvation and the afterlife, where their visions of heaven expressed their affections for each other and their longings for home. The specifics of religious interpretations of war experiences varied from soldier to soldier, war worker to war worker, and sometimes reflected divergent experiences of "American-ness" as they also reflected gender ideals peculiarly amplified in times of war. But religion served in most cases to invest the war writ large and the war as personal experience with a deep national and emotional significance. The culture of religion and violence reflected in so much of the personal and public literature of the war did not vanish when the smoke cleared and the soldiers went marching home. Instead, that culture shaped the attitudes and activities of the American Legion as its founders and members worked to forge a covenanted nation, united in its worship of "American" institutions, principles, and history. The American Legion and its representatives shaped national discourse on soldiering, service, sacrifice, and dissent, and did so in ways that gave life and strength to the religious framing of the war, the nation, and the soldier.

The Great War was not a war of religion. Ecclesiology, sacramental theology, and competing understandings of religious authority were not central to the conflict. Before, during, and after the war, one would have found a great deal of affinity between the warring European and American armies on points of religious doctrine and practice. But American experiences of the war were suffused with religion to the extent that we must at least consider the notion that without the prevalence of masculinized Christianity and the many subtler ways that Christian or Judeo-Christian ideas informed Americans' attachments to one another, the nation, and the cause, American involvement in the war would not have been possible. Framed as a question, while religion clearly shaped soldiers' and war workers' experiences of combat and sustained many in war's midst, was it religion that put them there in the first place? Though one can and should argue this question both ways. I will cast my lot with those who argue the affirmative. For at the end of eight years of thinking and writing about this war, it is hard for me to imagine the broad-based enthusiastic response to Wilson's draft call, the violence against and suspicion of internal "subversives" and "hyphenates," the adoption of such demonizing rhetoric and imagery, and soldiers' enduring enthusiasm for "scrapping," without the strong involvement of religious discourse and symbol, the powerful pull of religious emotions for the nation, and a religiously informed sense—stated eloquently and repeatedly by President Wilson—of America's responsibility to set things right. Layer these factors atop the more clearly, explicitly, institutionally religious valorization, indeed sanctification, of the masculine man willing to confront and vanquish evil, and the result is the necessity, though not the sufficiency, of religion as a cause of American involvement in the Great War.

COMPARING RELIGION AND WAR ACROSS TIME AND CULTURE

The centrality of religion to the American experience of the Great War and the many ways in which religion shaped soldiers' and war workers' actions and perceptions will and should invite comparisons to other more and less storied wars and the religious lives of the Americans who waged them. There is much to be learned about the religious culture of the United States through comparisons of soldierly faith and comparisons of post-war expressions of that faith. American soldiers and war workers fought the Great War in the receding shadow of the Civil War generation, and were reared in regional religious cultures that bore the stamp of the Civil War. But religion in the United States was different in 1918 than in 1861. Were twentieth-century soldiers differently religious than Billy Yank and Johnny Reb? What do similarities and differences between the soldiers' faiths tell us about the influences of modernity, modernism, diversity, sectionalism, urbanization, industrialization, immigration, and denominational discord? What kinds of religious thought patterns were unaffected by those forces? A religious history of the Second World War has yet to be written and the tendrils of the religious experience of that war have not yet been traced into the 1950s, '60s, and '70s, but one can imagine the comparative questions that such a study might raise. Did the sons and daughters of Great War veterans enter their global conflict with hopes for adventure and redemption or with a grim realism? Did they feel they were acting in accordance with divine mandate, that they too were crusaders? To what extent did experiences of Great War veterans shape their perceptions of the religiousness of their fight? One can ask the same questions of the soldiers sent to Korea to defeat "atheistic" Communism in its push to wipe out the great missionary success story of East Asia. And what of those who waded through the troubled religious waters of the 1960s and then through the swamps and jungles of Vietnam? The rough contours of the religious critique of—and advocacy for—the war have been described, but what of those who fought? Were religious objects, beliefs, and theologies among "the things they carried"?

The ways that religion interacted with American experiences of the Great War may also invite comparison to past and current enemies, imagined, then and now, as amoral, irrational, and fanatical. The construction of fallen soldiers as saviors and martyrs, and the belief that death in a struggle against evil will bring salvation, have of late been considered part of other cultures' ways of warring, and foreign to American experiences. While these comparisons can certainly be carried too far—religious framing of American involvement in the Great War did not lead soldiers to deliberately target civilian populations regardless of how thoroughly

demonized or "otherized" those people had been—they can also legiti-
mately call into question the narratives of American exceptionalism that
either posit American war-craft as an entirely secular enterprise or American Christianity as a non-martial faith. The value of comparing interac-
tions among religion and violence in a distant generation of American
Christians and in more proximate generations of Christians, Muslims,
Jews, Hindus, Buddhists, and quasi-religious ideologues does not turn
on the assumption of moral equivalency, much less presuppose such a
conclusion. Great War–era crackdowns on radicals, "hyphenates," and
expressions of German cultural heritage, though they generally pale in
comparison to atrocities committed in the names of gods and nations and
philosophies throughout the twentieth-century and down to this day, are
nevertheless important and dark moments in American history in which
the presence or absence of religious influence may be revealed and, in
part, explained through cross-cultural comparisons.

SOLDIERLY VOICES AND AMERICAN RELIGIOUS HISTORY

If this study has accomplished one thing in addition to focusing attention
on the Great War in America, I hope it has convinced other students of
religion in America of the value of studying the voices of soldiers and
war workers and attempting to weave those voices into the increasingly
complex tapestry of American religious history. As researchers and students, regardless of the time period on which we work, we all struggle
with an imbalance in sources and in scholarship that tilts toward learned,
often clerical voices, and away from the less learned and the lay. Many of
us have, because of this imbalance, been limited in the conclusions we
can reach about the appeal and influence of certain ideas, theologies, and
movements. Soldiers and war workers, pressed as they often are up
against their own mortality, write and reflect on religion in ways and at
lengths that can move us closer to balance in the historical record. When
Corporal Paul Hendrickson was returning from France to his home in
Danville, Illinois, he wrote to a female acquaintance, Miss Cecil Rife, that
war had put him through an emotional wringer. Having been convinced
that death was going to be his lot, he was struggling to make sense of
survival. To emerge from battle was, he wrote, "as near experiencing resurrection as anything I could describe it as being."[6] Paul Hendrickson and
the other men and women whose voices fill these pages testify to, among
other things, the power of religious ideas to order and express the torrents
of emotion that flow through men and women as they encounter war and
face death. The writings of these lay men and women, and the religious

ideas present in them, can, I believe, begin to fill the empty spaces that have for too long defined twentieth-century wars in American religious historiography. At the same time, these voices can remind us that people in the pews and in the trenches engage in theological discourses that bear their stamp, shape their world, and, especially in and around times of war, shape the nation as well.

Notes

Introduction

1. Gary Mead, *The Doughboys: America and the First World War* (New York: The Overlook Press, 2000), 69; David Kennedy, *Over Here: The First World War and American Society* (New York: Oxford University Press, 1980), 169.

2. Walter Elliott, C.S.P., "The Might of the Inward Man," *Catholic World* 95, no. 56 (June 1912): 330.

3. The major exceptions to this pattern are, for the Civil War, C. C. Goen, *Broken Churches, Broken Nation: Denominational Schisms and the Coming of the Civil War* (Macon, GA: Mercer University Press, 1985), Stephen Woodworth, *While God is Marching On: The Religious World of Civil War Soldiers* (Lawrence, KS: University Press of Kansas, 2001), and Harry Stout, *Upon the Altar of the Nation: A Moral History of the American Civil War* (New York: Viking, 2006); and, on the Great War: William Hutchison. *The Modernist Impulse in American Protestantism* (Oxford: Oxford University Press, 1976), George Marsden, *Fundamentalism and American Culture: The Shaping of American Evangelicalism* (Oxford: Oxford University Press, 1980), Grant Wacker, *Heaven Below: Early Pentecostals and American Culture* (Cambridge, MA: Harvard University Press, 2001), Diane Winston *Red Hot and Righteous: The Urban Religion of the Salvation Army* (Cambridge, MA: Harvard University Press, 1999), and Richard Budd, *Serving Two Masters: The Development of the American Military Chaplaincy* (Lincoln, NE: University of Nebraska Press, 2002). These works give space to the Great War in their narratives but do not make it a central concern

4. This historiography began, for all practical purposes, with David Kennedy, *Over Here: The First World War and American Society* (New York: Oxford University Press, 1980). Since then, Jennifer Keene, Gary Mead, and Richard Slotkin have added significant works. See Jennifer D. Keene, *Doughboys, the Great War, and the Remaking of America* (Baltimore: Johns Hopkins University Press, 2001); Gary Mead, *The Doughboys: America and the First World War* (New York: The Overlook Press, 2000); Richard Slotkin, *Lost Battalions: The Great War and the Crisis of American Nationality* (New York: Henry Holt and Company, 2005); Thomas Fleming, *The Illusion of Victory: America in World War I* (New York: Basic Books, 2003).

5. Henry F. May, *The End of American Innocence: A Study of the First Years of Our Own Times, 1912–1917* (New York: Columbia University Press, 1992), xxiv.

6. Ibid., 13.

7. T. J. Jackson Lears, *No Place of Grace: Antimodernism and the Transformation of American Culture, 1880–1920* (Chicago: University of Chicago Press, 1983), 23.

8. Wacker, entire. Pentecostals rejected modernist progressive models further by collapsing the distinction between modern and Biblical times, and viewing the future as both short and apocalyptic.

9. Jay Dolan, *The American Catholic Experience* (South Bend: Notre Dame University Press, 1992), 352–53; John Piper, *American Churches in World War I* (Athens, OH: Ohio University Press, 1985), 5.

10. Dolan, 311–19.

11. Wallace Best, *Passionately Human, No Less Divine: Religion and Culture in Black Chicago, 1915–1952* (Princeton, NJ: Princeton University Press, 2005); C. Eric Lincoln and Lawrence Mamiya, *The Black Church in the African American Experience* (Durham, NC: Duke University Press, 1990); Milton Sernett, *Bound for the Promised Land: African American Religion and the Great Migration* (Durham, NC: Duke University Press, 1997).

12. E. Anthony Rotundo, *American Manhood: Transformations in Masculinity from the Revolution to the Modern Era* (New York: Basic Books, 1993), 248–49.

13. Gail Bederman, *Manliness and Civilization: A Cultural History of Gender and Race in the United States, 1880–1917* (Chicago: University of Chicago Press, 1995), 178–79.

14. Ibid., 72–120. See also G. Stanley Hall, *Adolescence: Its Psychology and Its Relations to Physiology, Anthropology, Sociology, Sex, Crime, Religion, and Education* (New York: D. Appleton Company, 1904).

15. Rotundo, 224–25.

16. Bederman, " 'Women Have Had Charge of the Church Work Long Enough': The Men and Religion Forward Movement of 1911–1912 and the Masculinization of Middle-Class Protestantism" *American Quarterly* 41, no. 3 (Sep. 1989); Lears, chap. 3; Clifford Putney, *Muscular Christianity: Manhood and Sports in Protestant America, 1880–1920* (Cambridge, MA: Harvard University Press, 2001). Gail Bederman has traced the convergence of the masculinization movement and American Protestantism to the challenges posed by the new consumer-based economic model to the *laissez-faire*-based Victorian society. "In the context of a bureaucratic interdependent society," she writes, "the old imperatives [that gains accrue predictably to the hard-working, self-denying, up-standing man] lost meaning, leading to a pervasive sense of unreality." (p. 437.)

17. Putney, 79. Those outside of the muscular Christianity movement but looking happily in included Washington Gladden who wrote, "It was high time that something should be done to bring men and religion into closer relation. Men needed religion and religion needed men. It was getting to be quite too much the business of women." Bederman, 452.

18. Bederman, *Manliness and Civilization*, 1–44; and "Women Have Had Charge of the Church Work Long Enough," entire.

19. Ibid., 56; Charles Brent, *The Splendor of the Human Body* (New York: Longmans Green, 1908). In his 1908 volume *The Splendor of the Human Body*, future Chief of Chaplains Charles Brent wrote, "to dishonor our body is to dishonor His–to crucify Him afresh and to put Him to an open shame."

20. R. Warren Conant, *The Virility of Christ: A New View* (Chicago, n.p.: 1915), 29. As of 1915, Conant himself was no sacralizer of war, but neither did he shrink from sacralizing qualities everywhere associated with the warrior.

21. Lears, 98.

22. Putney, 119. In 1912, "roughly one out of every 181 Americans was either an active or associate . . . member" of the YMCA, where mind, body, and spirit were believed best developed in unison.

23. Lears, 98. "[F]or cultivated Americans during the late nineteenth century, concern with martial virtue did help to focus many of the particular dilemmas generated by the crisis of cultural authority. To bourgeois moralists preoccupied by the decadence and disorder of their society, the warrior's willingness to suffer and die for duty's sake pointed the way to national purification; to those who craved authentic selfhood, the warrior's life personified wholeness of purpose and intensity of experience. War promised both social and personal regeneration."

24. Putney, 85.

25. Bederman, "Women Have Had Charge of the Church Work Long Enough," 439–40.

26. Kennedy, 179; Mark Meigs, *Optimism at Armageddon: Voices of American Participants in the First World War* (New York: New York University Press, 1997), 64. "The testimony of young men from the Ivy League in America, privileged in privately published volumes of letters and memorials, has left the strongest impression of American enthusiasm for war. Enough farmers and laborers, however, volunteered to bury the more privileged statistically. The thoughts of men off farms, or out of factories, or members of immigrant and racial minorities made no such unified chorus as the better educated. These men, however, often draftees, still encountered patriotic motivations. . . . they could still find in war the materials for a positive standard of identification."

27. Kennedy, 205.

28. Ibid., 51.

29. Keene, 28, 75–78; Meigs, 5, 224. In his study of soldiers' understandings of the war, Mark Meigs argues that government agencies and official sources gave soldiers the language and the ideas they used to frame their war experiences, that the pain and confusion of combat left them grasping at these official straws, and that censorship prevented them from expressing what they really felt. The unity of voice is thus, on his account, largely the product of a highly effective propaganda campaign. Jennifer Keene also focuses on official efforts, specifically on controversial progressive-minded attempts to educate soldiers to the cause, thereby making them more willing to fight.

30. Kennedy, 60–64.

31. Ibid., 147; Keene, 8. "In retrospect, the federal government's preoccupation with the potential for dissension and draft evasion seems to have been misplaced, given how readily Americans responded to the call to arms."

32. Committee on the War and the Religious Outlook, *Religion Among American Men: As Revealed by a Study of Conditions in the Army* (New York: Association Press, 1920), iv. The membership of the Committee (hereafter CWRO) consisted of twenty-eight men and women, and included many of the leading lights of American Protestantism. Among its members were Harry Emerson Fosdick,

Henry Churchill King, Walter R. Lambuth, Shailer Mathews, John R. Mott, and Robert E. Speer; Piper, 35.

33. Ray Abrams, *Preachers Present Arms: The Role of The American Churches and Clergy in World Wars I and II, with Some Observations on the War in Vietnam* (Scottsdale, PA: Herald Press, 1969); John Piper, *The American Churches in World War I* (Athens, OH: Ohio University Press, 1985); Richard Gamble, *The War for Righteousness: Progressive Christianity, the Great War, and the Rise of the Messianic Nation* (Wilmington, DE: ISI Books, 2003).

34. Drew Gilpin Faust, *This Republic of Suffering: Death and the American Civil War* (New York: Knopf, 2008). Faust's excellent history engages many of these same issues throughout.

35. See James McPherson, *For Cause and Comrades: Why Men Fought in the Civil War* (New York: Oxford University Press, 1997) for a similar discussion related to soldiers' writings from the American Civil War.

36. See Catherine Clinton and Nina Silber, ed. *Divided Houses: Gender and the Civil War* (New York: Oxford University Press, 1992) for an excellent collection of essays on gender and the American Civil War. See also Jonathan Ebel, "The Great War, Religious Authority, and the American Fighting Man" in *Church History: Studies in Christianity and Culture* 78, no. 1 (March 2009).

37. *The Stars and Stripes*, 23 May 1919, 4.

38. McPherson, 10–11. McPherson discusses the limitations of post–Civil War sources written explicitly for publication and elevates, for good reason, the unpublished, clearly unedited letters and diaries he uses so deftly. Many of the sources I have used here come from a third category: soldiers' writings preserved and subsequently published. I have treated these sources, in the main, as copies of the originals, understanding also that the soldiers themselves and subsequent editors often withheld full names of friends and acquaintances and the exact locations of units. All soldiers were, of course, writing for an audience of some sort. I have done my best to account for that audience in my interpretation of the text.

39. Kemper F. Cowing and Courtney R. Cooper, *Dear Folks at Home: The Glorious Story of the United States Marines in France as Told by Their Letters from the Battlefield* (Boston and New York: Houghton Mifflin Company, 1919), 222–23, 250. Cowing and Cooper included a letter from Private Douglas C. Mabbott, killed in action near St. Mihiel: "Dear Friends the McKees: If I don't write pretty soon you'll be forgetting all about me or thinking I've gone west, and begun pushing up daisies. Don't you ever think of it! In the month that I've been up at the front now I've been through so much of the Heinies' shell fire that I'm convinced they can't kill me."

40. Charles Genthe, *American War Narratives, 1914–1918* (New York: D. Lewis, 1969); Craig Hamilton and Louise Corbin, *Echoes from Over There* (New York: The Soldiers' Publishing Company, 1919). A majority of my sources were published before 1921, about one-third of those by mourning families. Most soldiers' memoirs (narratives written after the war) claim to be based on materials— letters and diaries—written during the war. I have accepted these claims at more-or-less face value. The lens through which soldiers viewed their war experiences was certainly changed by the events of the 1920s and '30s. Some voices were angrier in 1939 than in 1919. My decisions to treat certain voices as "wartime"

and others as "post-war" usually coincide with the temporal reality of these distinctions, but are in some places more subjective.

41. Chad Hamilton, *Torchbearers of Democracy: The First World War and the Figure of the African American Soldier* (Doctoral Dissertation, Princeton University, 2004). Hamilton's dissertation made me aware of the existence of the Virginia War Survey. I owe him a tremendous debt.

42. Thomas Barber, *Along the Road* (New York: Dodd, Mead and Company, 1924), 27.

43. Elmer Haslett, *Luck on the Wing: Thirteen Stories of a Sky Spy* (New York: E.P. Dutton and Company, 1920), 3. Haslett served as an observer with the 12th Aero Squadron, American Observation Group, and was based at Ourches near Toul, France.

44. Amos Wilder, *Armageddon Revisited* (New Haven: Yale University Press, 1994), 7.

45. See McPherson, 12–13 for a parallel discussion of Civil War soldiers' writings.

46. Leo Jacks, *Service Record, by an Artilleryman* (New York: C. Scribner's Sons, 1928), 203. See also William A. Carter with Pascal J. Plant, *The Tale of a Devil Dog, by One of Them* (Washington D.C.: Canteen Press, 1920), 50; William L. Langer and Robert B. MacMullin, *With "E" of the First Gas* (Brooklyn, Holton Printing Co., 1919), 71; and Elmer Harden, *An American Poilu* (Boston: Little, Brown and Company, 1919), 202. A wounded Elmer Harden wrote (hauntingly for the twenty-first-century reader) of the folly that war made of language and memory. Harden attempted to recall for "Cherie" something of his aural experiences of battle. "If the city of New York should topple in the sky and fall to the ground, the crash would be like a whisper to the racket of that dawn [June 10 or July 13, 1918]. I wonder that the entire regiment didn't perish from the mere sound alone. Its fury turned Jehovah's wrath into a shepherd's piping, and ten thousand Wagners, 'ragging' ten thousand orchestras, into the murmur of a parlor seashell. But what's the use–I only amuse myself–you can't hear it. I've already forgotten myself how monstrous it was. Memory cannot hold so much noise."

47. Elaine Scarry, *The Body in Pain: The Making and Unmaking of the World* (New York: Oxford University Press, 1985), 4. This is a common feature of attempts to describe pain. Elaine Scarry has argued that as worlds are unmade by the pain of disease, torture, or war, so is language itself unmade. "Physical pain does not simply resist language but actively destroys it, bringing about an immediate reversion to a state of anterior language, to the sounds and cries a human being makes before language is learned." Pain, she writes, is thus very often wholly unknowable to those not experiencing it, regardless of their physical proximity to those suffering.

48. Dearing to Mother, 21 May 1918, in *My Galahad of the Trenches: Being a Collection of Intimate Letters of Lieutenant Vinton A. Dearing* (New York: Fleming H. Revell Co., 1918) 55. See also Emmett N. Britton, *As It Looked to Him: Intimate Letters on the War* (San Francisco: Privately printed, 1919) 21, 37.

49. Wilder, 80.

50. James Anderson Winn, *The Poetry of War* (London: Cambridge University Press, 2008).

51. Kennedy, 60–64, 213; Meigs 3–6, 27–29, 224; Slotkin, 59. Commenting on soldierly writings and their common "accents," Kennedy notes how "strangely" they ring in "the modern ear." At the same time, he finds the widespread use of "the pious and inflated pronouncements" quite logical if also largely reflexive. "If the war was to redeem Europe from barbarism, it would equally redeem individual soldiers from boredom; if the fighting in France was the 'Great Adventure,' the doughboys were the great adventurers; if [head of the Committee on Public Information George] Creel and [President] Wilson could speak of the 'Crusade,' then it followed that American troops were crusaders."

52. Victor Chapman, *Victor Chapman's Letters from France, with Memoir by John Jay Chapman* (New York: Macmillan Co., 1917), 186. Richard A. Blodgett, *Life and Letters of Richard Ashley Blodgett, First Lieutenant, United States Air Service* (Boston: Macdonald and Evans, 1920), 155. Chapman confided in his uncle "Of course I shall never come out of this alive," and Blodgett wrote to a love interest identified only as "M": "I feel pretty blue just now . . . I have just signed up with aviation and I feel as though I had signed my death warrant."

53. Alfred E. Cornbeise, *The Stars and Stripes: Doughboy Journalism in World War I* (Westport, CT: Greenwood Press, 1984), xii.; Kennedy, 208, 212; Keene, 78; Meigs, 3. *The Stars and Stripes* occupies a peculiar place in Great War historiography when it occupies any place at all. David Kennedy cites it sparingly. When he does, he treats it as reflective of soldierly opinion. Mark Meigs treats it as official propaganda, imposed on soldiers from above. Jennifer Keene's treatment of *The Stars and Stripes* and Alfred Cornbeise's *The Stars and Stripes: Doughboy Journalism and World War I*, have served as my guides for use of the paper in this study. Both are alert to the fact that the paper was both official and popular, that while established and funded by the American Expeditionary Force and involved in shaping soldierly opinion, it was also remarkably reflective of soldiers' attitudes. The official American Expeditionary Force report on *The Stars and Stripes* "The Stars and Stripes: Its Purposes, History, and Achievements" can be found on Disk Two of the CD-ROM set *The United States Army in World War I* (Fort McNair, D.C.: The United States Army Center of Military History, 1998). It is sub-section V (pp. 134–42) of the "Report of the Assistant Chief of Staff, G-2B (Intelligence). The report can also be found in volume 13 of the print predecessor to the CD-ROM, *The United States Army in the World War.*

54. *The United States Army in World War I*, volume 13, 141.

55. Ibid., 102. Keene, 78. The story of a confrontation between the paper's soldier-editor and a would-be censor indicates the degree of freedom and the end for which that freedom was maintained. According to Keene, "Only once did an Intelligence Department official consider ordering the editors to stop publishing soldiers' minor criticisms of the A.E.F. Captain Mark Watson, the editor, successfully insisted that as soon as the paper stopped printing the "humorous, harmless grouches of the soldiers, just at that time will *The Stars and Stripes* be regarded as a GHQ organization, or more serious, as a J.J.P. [John Joseph Pershing] organ, and when that time comes there is one man who will suffer and that is the commander-in-chief."

CHAPTER ONE
REDEMPTION THROUGH WAR

1. Edwin A. Abbey, *An American Soldier; Letters of Edwin Austin Abbey*, 2d. (Boston: Houghton Mifflin, 1918), 1.

2. Ibid., 12.

3. Ibid., 66.

4. Ibid., 57.

5. Ibid., 66.

6. Ibid., 86.

7. Ibid., 92.

8. Ibid., 165–66.

9. Ibid., 170–72. Major Herzberg to Mrs. Abbey, 18 July 1917.

10. Francis P. Duffy, Father Duffy's Story: *A Tale of Humor and Heroism, Of Life and Death With The Fighting Sixty-Ninth* (New York: George H. Doran Company, 1919), 13.

11. *New York Age*, 12 April 1917. Also cited in Stephen L. Harris, *Harlem's Hell Fighters: The African American 369th Infantry in World War I* (Washington, D.C.: Brassey's Inc., 2003) 82–83.

12. The *New York Times*, 4 June 1916.

13. Quincy Sharpe Mills, *Editorials, Sketches, and Stories* (New York: G.P. Putnam's Sons, 1930), 722–23.

14. James Luby, One Who Gave His Life: War Letters of Quincy Sharpe Mills: With a Sketch of His Life and Ideals–A Study in Americanism and Heredity (New York and London: G.P. Putnam's Sons, 1923), 204–7.

15. Ibid., 38; Ibid., 51–2.

16. "He's Filling His Sights" in Mills, 722.

17. "Wake Up America Day," in Mills, 733.

18. "Independence Day, 1917," in Mills, 757.

19. Luby, 4.

20. *The Stars and Stripes*, 1 November 1918, 4.

21. Jim Cullen, "I's a Man Now: Gender and African American Men," in Catherine Clinton and Nina Silber, ed. *Divided Houses: Gender and the Civil War* (New York: Oxford University Press, 1992).

22. Abbey, 3.

23. See also Lambert Wood, *His Job: Letters Written by a 22-year-old Lieutenant in the World War to His Parents and Others in Oregon* (Portland, OR: The Metropolitan Press, 1932), 39. Lambert Wood, an infantry officer in the A.E.F., bore witness to this in a letter he wrote to his parents in Oregon while German troops were launching their offensive in the spring of 1918. Wood indicated that the outcome of the war would tell whether there was a "Good out there to counter 'evil.' " "These days are more crucial than the Battle of the Marne," he wrote, "[t]he whole structure of Liberty is being battered as never before, and though if there is a Supreme Being, the drive will fail; the cost in lives is awful."

24. The *New York Times*, 4 May 1993, "Amos N. Wilder, a Bible Scholar, Literary Critic, and Educator, 97." A brief biography of Amos Wilder also appears on the web site of Andover-Harvard Theological Library, which holds his papers

from 1923–1982. Interestingly, the biography mentions nothing of his war service. http://www.hds.harvard.edu/library/bms/bms00641.html.

25. Wilder, 141–42.

26. Katherine Blake, *Some Letters Written to Maude Gray and Marian Wickes 1917–1918* (New York: Privately Printed by Scribner Press, 1920), 72.

27. Cornbeise, 12. Cornbeise states the Hawley "wrote the first few issues of the paper almost singlehandedly [sic]."

28. *The Stars and Stripes*, 15 February 1918, 5.

29. See also *The Stars and Stripes*, 8 February 1918, 3. A writer for *The Stars and Stripes* argued that women would be significant beneficiaries of an Allied victory with a story that recounted the branding of one young woman and the cataloguing of others as German government property. The piece moved from horror to hope when the "eyewitness," a British Officer, reflected on American involvement. "Thank God, America, by coming into the war, will help to stamp out this beastly 'kultur' from the world and make it a safe clean place to live in for your womenfolk and mine."

30. *The Stars and Stripes*, 22 February 1918, 2; *The Stars and Stripes*, 14 June 1918, 8.

31. Kenneth MacLeish, *Kenneth: A Collection of Letters Written By Lieutenant Kenneth MacLeish, U.S.N.R.F.C., Dating from His Enlistment and During His Services in the Aviation Corps of the United States Navy, Edited and Arranged by His Mother* (Chicago: Privately Printed, 1919), 10.

32. Cowing, 80. See also William A. Wellman, *Go Get 'em! The True Story of an American Aviator of the Lafayette Flying Corps who was the only Yankee Flyer Fighting over General Pershing's Boys of the Rainbow Division in Lorraine when they first went "over the top."* (Boston: The Page Company, 1918), 4, 20, 125, 214. In his wartime memoir, William Wellman emphasized both the inhuman nature of his German foes ("The German fighter has ceased to be a human being.") and the connection between Germany and Satan.

33. Marsden, 151.

34. Ibid.

35. *The Stars and Stripes*, 29 September 1918, 4.

36. *The Stars and Stripes*, 4 October 1918, 4. This report expresses a refined soldierly view of the religiousness of the war, while also demonstrating how the war came to be embraced by both pre- and post-millennialist Christians in the United States. Battles being waged in the Holy Land and even in Europe could fit well into either worldview: victory was both a sign that history would soon come to an end supernaturally, and evidence of human-driven progress toward the millennium. *The Stars and Stripes*, though far more sympathetic to post-millennial worldviews, did not "read" the events in one way or the other. They provided the scriptural frame and let the reader do the rest.

37. Ibid.

38. Clarence Lindner, *Private Lindner's Letters, Censored and Uncensored* (San Francisco: n.p., 1939), 22.

39. Jacks, 11, 221.

40. W.E.B. Du Bois expressed this belief as late as November of 1918 when he wrote in the *Crisis* of a speech by President Wilson on September 27, 1918. The

President had said, "Shall peoples be ruled and dominated even in their own internal affairs, by arbitrary and irresponsible force, or by their own will and choice." Du Bois responded, "Is it possible that these flaming arrows were not aimed at the Vardamans in Mississippi as well as at Huns in Europe? Is it thinkable that President Wilson did not have clearly in mind Kamerun as well as Servia? It is neither possible nor thinkable if English is English and Justice is Justice, and with this true, Mr. Wilson's speech is one of the half dozen significant utterances of human history." Isaac Fisher of *Negro Farmer*, and James Weldon Johnson of *New York Age* wrote similarly. The voices of soldiers and veterans, presented in Chapter 4, reflect these sentiments as well. See also Slotkin and Kennedy.

41. Hunton and Johnson, 11–12.

42. See Leeann Whites, "The Civil War as a Crisis in Gender" and Jim Cullen, "I's a Man Now," in Clinton and Silber.

43. Walter S. Poague, *Diary and Letters of a Marine Aviator* (Chicago: n.p., 1919), 17–18.

44. Ibid., 165.

45. Scarry, 51–59; Meigs, 224.

46. Bederman, Lears, Putney, and Rotundo all address this development throughout their works.

47. Elizabeth Banks, *The Remaking of an American* (New York: Doubleday, Doran and Company, 1928), 137.

48. Ibid., 176.

49. Ibid., 181.

50. Banks, 210–12. "In Memoriam: To The American Soldiers Dead in France." Reprinted from the *Evening News* (London) on America Day, April 20, 1917. Epigram: "I heard a voice from Heaven saying unto me, Write, From henceforth blessed are the dead . . . "

In August 1914, the agonized cry of Belgium and the appeal of invaded France reached the shores of the United States, and hundred of thousands said: "They suffer greatly over there. Let us collect money and send them food and clothing and hospital supplies . . ." There were other Americans–at first a few hundred and afterwards many thousands who, while hearing the cries of Belgium and France, heard yet more the call of humanity, of all the peoples threatened, of Liberty assailed. So piercing and so clamorous was this call that it came not only to their ears but to their souls, and, looking up, they saw the VISION. Then a hand beckoned, and, because the hand was so compelling, they followed it. . . . They were not of any one class, those American men, who first saw and followed the Vision. Young University men looked up from their books and saw the light; (211) mechanics lifted up their eyes and saw it too; preachers were enveloped by it in their pulpits; blacksmiths knew it was a different light from that which blazed from their forges; farmers in the harvest fields felt that something more brilliant than the sun was round about them; lawyers, doctors, writers, and painters beheld the light and followed after the beckoning hand . . . "From among this contingent many have fallen. Most especially wherever Canadians have given their lives, there too, have Americans damped the earth of France with their blood. To all these I offer tribute on this, America's Day. . . . How quietly, how unostentatiously, how secretly have they paid the great price, these countrymen of mine. Here in a newspaper, included in a long Roll of Honor, I read a little notice: "–Canadians, ——first reported missing, now officially reported killed.

That is all. Only those who knew the man's history, as I knew it, will be aware of his nationality. Indeed, when he died, he had, technically, no nationality, though he fought and died as a soldier of the King. I remember the break in his voice as he told me of the oath of allegiance he had taken . . .

Today, the flag of his native land and the flag under which his comrades fought, are intertwined. Now, in Old St. Paul's, British and American voices join in singing their requiem: "He has sounded forth the trumpet that shall never call retreat, / He is sifting out the hearts of men before his Judgment seat; / O be swift my soul to answer Him, be jubilant my feet! / Our God is marching on." Hark! Now the voices from the graves in France join in, and we know there is no death, but only Life, for those whose souls were so swift to answer, whose feet followed, jubilant, at the beckoning of that hand in the pathway lighted by the Vision.

51. Alan Seeger, *Poems* (New York: Charles Scribner's Sons, 1919), 163–64.

52. Winn, *The Poetry of War*. Winn offers a fascinating discussion of the transformation of understandings of honor from Homer's Achilles, for whom honor and booty were one and the same, to conceptions such as Seeger's, in which the absence of a clear material interest becomes the sine qua non of honorable war-fighting.

53. See also Abbey, 6. At first, Edwin Abbey viewed the situation more sympathetically than did Seeger. He appreciated the good in both neutrality and involvement. Writing in May of 1915, Abbey described America's situation as "impossible." "Honor demands that we enter the war, humanity that we stay out." In the fall of 1915, though, Abbey heeded what he took to be the call of honor.

54. Esther Sayles Root and Marjorie Crocker, *Over Periscope and Pond: Letters from Two American Girls in Paris, October 1916–January 1918* (Boston and New York: Houghton-Mifflin Company, 1918), 131.

55. Ibid., 213.

56. Thomas Slusser, *Letters to Her, 1917–19* (Chicago: Privately printed, 1937), 86–87.

57. Dearing, 62.

58. Kennedy, ch. 1. Kennedy offers an extended discussion of this type of hope and its pervasiveness among America's social, intellectual, and political leaders.

59. Slotkin, *Lost Battalions*, entire.

60. See "Second Inaugural Address" and "The American People Must Stand Together" in Arthur Roy Leonard, ed. *War Addresses of Woodrow Wilson* (Boston: Ginn and Company, 1918) 26–31, 66–76.

61. *The Stars and Stripes*, 1 November 1918, 4.

62. *The Stars and Stripes*, 3 May 1918, 4.

63. *The Stars and Stripes*, 10 May 1918, 4.

64. Banks, 202.

65. For a historical perspective on white discomfort with African Americans under arms, see Clinton and Silber; see also Drew Gilpin Faust, *This Republic of Suffering*. During the Civil War, Confederate soldiers were ordered to shoot all black soldiers they apprehended.

66. Albert Ettinger, *A Doughboy with the Fighting Sixty-Ninth: A Remembrance of World War I* (Shippensburg, PA: White Mane Publishing Company, 1992), 7.

67. Stephen L. Harris, Harlem's *Hell Fighters: The African-American 369th Infantry in World War I* (Washington, D.C.: Brassey's, Inc. 2003), 124–33.

68. *The Stars and Stripes*, 2 August 1918, 4; 9 August 1918, 4; 13 September 1918. Despite the potentially fractious effects, *The Stars and Stripes* frequently ran articles trumpeting America's engagements in France as equal to or surpassing the major battles of the Civil War. "Ourcq another Antietam" read an August 2, 1918 headline to an article describing an American victory over German forces. One week later, an article recalled the quintessential Civil War battle in connection with the Aisne-Marne offensive. "To all the American soldiers whom fate touched on the shoulder and summoned into the Second Battle of the Marne, every other American in France takes off his hat today. They were called into a battle as fraught as Gettysburg in its consequences to the world for weal or woe, called in numbers greater far than ever the field of Gettysburg beheld."

69. Milton Sernett, *Bound for the Promised Land* (Durham: Duke University Press, 1997).

70. Arthur Barbeau and Florette Henri, *The Unknown Soldiers: Black American Troops in World War I* (Philadelphia: Temple University Press, 1974); see also Harris, *Harlem's Hell Fighters*, and Slotkin, *Lost Battalions*.

71. *The Stars and Stripes*, 24 May 1918, 1,5. Light-skinned soldiers often applied substances to their faces as night camouflage. Emphasis added. This treatment is of a piece with the treatment given African American heavyweight boxing champion Jack Johnson in the 1910s. Gail Bederman has observed that when Johnson demonstrated his superior masculinity by thrashing the Anglo boxer Jim Jeffries in 1910 and by developing romantic relationships with white women, a campaign was launched to drive him to the margins of society and, eventually, out of the country altogether. See Bederman, *Manliness and Civilization*, 1–10.

72. Emmet J. Scott, *The American Negro in the World War* (New York: Homewood Press, 1919), 62; see also Barbeau and Henri, Slotkin, and Harris.

73. Theodore Roosevelt, "The Strenuous Life," in *The Strenuous Life: Essays and Addresses* (1901; St. Clair Shores, MI: Scholarly Press, 1970), 7, 20–21. Cited in Bederman, *Manliness and Civilization*, 193–94.

74. Richard Slotkin, *The Fatal Environment: The Myth of the Frontier in the Age of Industrialization, 1800–1890* (New York: Atheneum, 1985), ch. 5; Slotkin, *Gunfighter Nation: The Myth of the Frontier in Twentieth-Century America* (Norman, OK: University of Oklahoma Press, 1998).

75. The American-ness of such thoughts was quite real, but should not be overemphasized. The writings of British men, poet Rudyard Kipling and soldier Donald Hankey, for example, evidence many of the same thoughts. Canadian Robert W. Service was equally convinced of the benefits of strain, sacrifice, and violence.

76. Lears, 100; Putney, chs. 4–5.

77. Anonymous (Dare), "Mademoiselle Miss": Letters from an American Girl Serving with the Rank of Lieutenant in a French Army Hospital at the Front (Boston: W.A. Butterfield, 1916), 49.

78. *The Stars and Stripes*, 10 May 1918, 4.

79. Virginia War History Commission Questionnaire (VWHCQ), William Thomas. The entire database is available at http://ajax.lva.lib.va.us/F/?func=file& file_name=find-b-clas13&local_base=CLAS13.

80. Dearing, 37. See also Harden, 5. Elmer Harden, an American serving in the French Army in 1918, wrote that the Great War "that great refiner's fire, has burned away much of the dross cumbering humankind, and left us face to face with the true metal [sic] of a myriad of souls before whose naked purity and selflessness we bow in homage."

81. Sergeant, 31, 33.

82. VWHCQ, Christopher Watts.

83. Rotundo, 234–35. The men and women conveyed in their reflections on the war the very view of strenuous exercise and physical labor that drove Progressive-Era approaches to the physical and moral education of young men.

84. Hervey Allen, *Toward the Flame* (New York: George H. Doran Company, 1926), 24.

85. *The Stars and Stripes*, 1 November 1918, 4. Even in the words of those who claimed to be attracted to war for earthly glory alone, belief in war's transformative effects could emerge. Joseph Hutter, whose letter to the editor of *The Stars and Stripes* featured both his desire to reach the front and "shoot a Hun" and his enduring disappointment at being frustrated in that quest, gestured in the direction of the religious when he wrote that those in the rear areas didn't have "the advantage of becoming thoughtful men . . . "

86. Paul B. Elliott, ed., *On the Field of Honor: A Collection Of War Letters and Reminiscences of Three Harvard Undergraduates Who Gave Their Lives in the Great Cause* (Boston: Privately Printed by Merrymount Press, 1920), 61–62.

87. Isabel Anderson, *Zigzagging* (Boston: Houghton Mifflin Company/Riverside Press Cambridge, 1918), 169. Based on her encounters with American soldiers, Isabel Anderson, a senior hospital worker with the Red Cross, vouched for the redemptive power of war. She found that, as Austin suspected, "the young men of the American Expeditionary Force are better, morally and physically, than were these same young men at home."

88. VWHCQ, James Lark.

89. Julia Catherine Stimson, *Finding Themselves: The Letters of an American Army Chief Nurse in a British Hospital in France* (New York: Macmillan Company, 1918), 170.

90. Rudolf Otto, *The Idea of the Holy: An Inquiry into the Non-Rational Factor in the Idea of the Divine and Its Relation to the Rational* (London: Oxford University Press, 1958), 20.

CHAPTER TWO
CHANCE THE MAN-ANGEL AND THE COMBAT NUMINOUS

1. Otto, 31.

2. While the focus of this chapter will be soldiers' attempts to make sense of death and survival in war, a secondary concern is to draw the eyes of scholars of religion to the words and thoughts of those who, though articulate in many ways,

sometimes struggled to articulate their thoughts on the divine. Soldiers and war workers often used theological language in confusing ways, ways that might discourage scholars of religion from attempting to analyze them. My contention is that by working through the imprecision, we can learn a great deal about lay engagement with the theological challenges of modernity, and sense something of the ferment out of which post-war theologies would emerge and to which those theologies would speak.

3. Kennedy, 211. Kennedy writes that in soldiers' accounts of shelling "one occasionally finds the faintly dawning realization that modern military combat was something quite different from what the eager troops had been led to expect."

4. Keene, 49.

5. Drew Gilpin Faust, *This Republic of Suffering: Death and the American Civil War* (New York: Knopf, 2008). Faust's excellent history engages many of these same issues throughout, but does so most directly in her first chapter, "Dying."

6. Adams, 73.

7. Hamilton and Corbin, ed., 54.

8. Ibid., 185.

9. Edmund Genet, *War Letters of Edmond Genet* (New York: Scribner's Sons, 1918) xviii, 33, 43–46. In a February 1915 letter to his mother, Genet describes a church service and writes, "Mother, if I am taken in battle and you hear of it, which you will, will you have a little service or something like that and in it sing hymn 621? The choir sang it at Church Sunday and I think it is beautiful and so fitting for those in this war. I suppose the hymns all have the same numbers in the Episcopal hymnal. 621 is the hymn."

10. Ibid., 121. Original emphasis.

11. Ibid., 121, 134.

12. A. L. Bartley, *Tales of the World War* (Dallas: Clyde C. Cockrell Co., 1935), 59. As he recalled, many survivors shared his interpretation of the experience: "I found the majority of the boys had similar feelings to those I had experienced and they agreed that if hell was any worse than this they wanted to go as far in the opposite direction as would be possible." See also Cowing, 164. Writing to his brother in early July of 1918, Private Walter Lamb took note of both his good luck and the source of that luck: "We have been doing some battling the last month, as you probably have seen by the papers. But I have been pretty lucky. The good Lord has been with me." With no sense of irony, Lamb noted three sentences later the ridiculousness of the German notion that the "the good Lord" was with them. " 'Gott Mit Uns.' Imagine, the dirty cowards! God with them after the work they have done."

13. Cowing, 43.

14. Greayer Clover, *A Stop at Suzanne's, and Lower Flights* (New York: George H. Doran Company, 1919), 22. Emphasis mine. But even in his acknowledgment that all were equally subject to chance, James Crowe let another sentiment slip in. "If so good a flyer as Greayer *had* to fall," he wrote, then we all must be vulnerable. Whether through a habit of speech or a habit of mind, Crowe left room in his telos-free, chance-ruled world for the notion that Greayer Clover's death had been designed—that "Greayer had to fall."

15. John I. Kautz, *Trucking to the Trenches: Letters from France, June–November* 1917 (Boston and New York: Houghton Mifflin Company, 1918), 43.

16. Anonymous, *A Red Triangle Girl in France* (New York: George H. Doran Company, 1918), 129–30.

17. Dearing, 53.

18. Paul Tillich, *Systematic Theology*, 3 vols. (Chicago: University of Chicago Press, 1951–1963).

19. Dearing, 39.

20. Anonymous, *A Red Triangle Girl in France*, 127.

21. Hamilton Coolidge, *Letters of an American Airman* (Boston: Privately Printed, 1919), 113–14.

22. Abbey, 92.

23. Christian Blumenstein, *Whiz bang!* (Buffalo: Christian Blumenstein, 1927), 8.

24. Dearing, 53.

25. Allen, 50. See Winn, 201–2 for a discussion of Allen's post-war poetry. The here-mentioned reaction of James Crowe to the death of his friend Greayer Clover ("[I]t is all chance and what happened to him may happen to any of us, any time.") juxtaposed Clover's talents as a flyer and the laws of chance in a telling way. Whether Crowe understood chance to operate unpredictably and without telos, to behave according to certain laws, or to be a personalized demi-deity, he knew that "it" was "all chance" whether one lived or died, and that human talents were of no consequence in meriting life. The design may have been clear, hidden, or non-existent, but its implications for human actors was clear.

26. Jack Morris Wright, *A Poet of the Air: Letters of Jack Morris Wright, First Lieutenant of the American Aviation in France. April 1917–January 1918* (Boston: Houghton Mifflin Company, 1918), 147.

27. Edward F. Lukens, *Blue Ridge Memoir* (Baltimore: n.p., 1922), 92.

28. Briggs Adams, *The American Spirit: Letters of Briggs Kilburn Adams, Lieutenant of the Royal Flying Corps* (Boston: The Atlantic Monthly Press, 1918), 36.

29. Ibid., 37–38.

30. "Report of the Chief of the Air Service, A.E.F.," in *The United States Army in World War I* (Washington, D.C.: The United States Army Center of Military History, 1993), vol. 15, 265. This CD-ROM is a digitized version of the original *The United States Army in the World War, 1917–1919*, a collection of official documents from the war. For a brief narrative account of the rapid development of the American Air Service, see Byron Farwell, *Over There: The United States in the Great War, 1917–1918* (New York: W.W. Norton and Co., 1999).

31. Ibid., 53.

32. MacLeish, 16.

33. Harden, 128–29.

34. Ibid., 135–36.

35. Harden, 192. Emphasis added.

36. Ibid., 192–93.

37. Ibid.

38. Ibid.

39. Blumenstein, 17.

40. The differences among, and debates between, theological liberals, some of whom were modernists, and theological conservatives, and some of whom were Fundamentalists, has been well documented in the work of William Hutchison and George Marsden. Differing conceptions of the relationship among humanity, history, and the divine are clearly evident if one compares the writings and thoughts of Walter Rauschenbusch, Shailer Mathews, or Harry Emerson Fosdick with the work of J. Gresham Machen, the worldview expressed in the Scofield Reference Bible, and the pre-war and wartime writings of Frank Bartleman. In the former, generally speaking, God work's through and with humanity toward a kind of communal salvation and an earthly Kingdom of God. In the latter, God's plans for individuals and for humanity will unfold without significant consideration of human initiative.

41. For extended discussions of these effects, see Gamble, Hutchison, Marsden, and Marty.

42. J. Glen Gray, *The Warriors: Reflections on Men in Battle* (Lincoln, NE: University of Nebraska Press, 1998); William James, "The Moral Equivalent of War" in Staughton Lynd and Alice Lynd, eds. *Nonviolence in America: A Documentary History* (Maryknoll, NY: Orbis Books, 1995); Jean Bethke Elshtain, *Women and War* (Chicago: University of Chicago Press, 1987).

43. I do not use Otto's concept of the *numinous* to forward an argument that the non-rational holy—which Otto took to be real and irreducible—was *actually* present in the shells, gas clouds, and fatal chaos of the Western Front. Rather, I am interested in the Ottonian flavor of soldiers' perceptions of the forces present in combat and the convergence between soldierly and Ottonian language when soldiers and war workers described their encounters with those forces. This convergence is, I believe, more than coincidental. What Otto was critiquing and proposing in Germany during the Great War was also on the minds of American soldiers and war workers as they served. Many wrote that modern faith had been gutted by moralists and creedalists.

44. Otto, 6.

45. Ibid., 10–11.

46. Otto, 26.

47. Louis F. Ranlett, *Let's Go! The Story of A.S. no. 2448602253* (Boston: Houghton Mifflin Co., 1927), 253.

48. Ibid., 285–86.

49. Marian Baldwin, *Canteening Overseas* (New York: MacMillan Company, 1920), 21.

50. James Norman Hall, *Kitchener's Mob: The Adventures of an American in the British Army* (Boston: Houghton Mifflin Company, 1916), 67.

51. Charles B. Nordhoff, The Fledgling (Boston and New York: Houghton Mifflin Company, 1919), 40–41. See also, Benjamin Lee, *Benjamin Lee, 2d: A Record Gathered from Letters, Note-books, and Narratives of Friends by his Mother Mary Justice Chase* (Boston: Cornhill, 1920), 318. Fuller wrote for his deceased friend Ben Lee, and presumably himself, that "human life was an infinitesimal thing beside the fact of battle"; and Lindner, 56–57. In an August 26, 1918 letter, Lindner commented that "the soul of man is humbled before the grandeur of the scene and its awful potency."

52. Otto, 60. Direct, personal experiences of "actual 'holy' situations" or their description in scripture were the "best means" by which "this numinous basis . . . can be induced, incited, and aroused." "Little of it can usually be noticed in theory and dogma, or even in exhortation, unless it is actually heard. Indeed no element in religion needs so much as this the *viva vox . . .*"

53. Elizabeth Walker Black, *Hospital Heroes* (New York: Charles Scribner's Sons, 1919), 119, 122, 41.

54. *The Stars and Stripes*, 13 September 1918, 2. Emphasis added.

55. *The Stars and Stripes*, 15 November 1918, 4.

56. T. J. Jackson Lears provides an unsurpassed analysis of "anti-modernism" in early-twentieth-century America, placing this sense of mediation and "evasive banality" at the motive center of the movement.

CHAPTER THREE
SUFFERING, DEATH, AND SALVATION

1. Kiffin Rockwell, *War Letters of Kiffin Yates Rockwell, Foreign Legionnaire and Aviator, France 1914–1916, with Memoir and Notes by Paul Ayres Rockwell* (Garden City, NJ: The Country Life Press, 1925), 56.

2. See Genet, 33; John H. Morrow, Jr. and Earl Rogers, eds. *A Yankee Ace in the R.A.F.: The World War I Letters of Captain Bogart Rogers* (Lawrence, KS: University of Kansas Press, 1996), 43; Bogart Rogers wrote to his soon-to-be fiancée from Camp Hicks, Texas that he was not going to survive. "Honestly dear, I don't see a prayer for myself. The odds are all wrong and—unless I'm able to learn a lot more about flying than I know—curtains." See also Chapman, 186; Blodgett, 155.

3. Abbey, 64; Genet, 189–90. The desire that family be notified promptly in the event of his death was one of the reasons cited by Edmund Genet for his transfer to aviation and, eventually, the Lafayette Escadrille. He wrote to his mother in July of 1916, "You can feel sure now, Mother, that whatever may happen to me in any way that the Franco-American Flying Corps will take good care of me and notify you immediately. 'Twill be far different from my being in the Legion where you might never get any news of me at all. . . ."

4. Faust, entire.

5. Gary Laderman, *Rest in Peace: A Cultural History of Death and the Funeral Home in Twentieth-Century America* (New York: Oxford University Press, 2003), 1.

6. James Norman Hall, *Kitchener's Mob: The Adventures of an American in the British Army* (Boston: Houghton Mifflin Company, 1916), 168. Hall's memoir was recommended by Edmund Genet to his mother as an accurate picture of life on the Western Front.

7. Ranlett, 231.

8. Haniel Long, ed. *From the War Letters of Carnegie Tech Men* (Pittsburgh: Carnegie Institute of Technology, 1918), 28–29.

9. Ibid.; See also C. Earl Baker, *Doughboy's Diary* (Shippensburg, PA: Burd Street Press: 1998), 60–63. Corporal Chester Baker of the 112th Infantry Regi-

ment, Twenty-eighth Division recorded his first encounter with the dead, also as a personal marker. "Sergeant Cutshall and I went to the aid of Private Elmer Murdock of Franklin, Pennsylvania, when a shell blew him right out of the trench. We could do nothing for him except stay with him until his badly mangled body stopped twitching. This was my first experience of watching one of my buddies 'go west,' which was the doughboys' euphemism for dying, the ultimate trip home"; William H. Cunningham, ed., *The Boston High School of Commerce in the World War* (Norwood, MA: Plimpton Press, 1921), 117.

10. Carter and Plant, 55.
11. MacLeish, 60.
12. Harden, 8–9.
13. Genet, 324–25.
14. Sergeant, 156.
15. I owe much of the development of these points to discussions with Professor Kathryn Lofton of Yale University and with the students in my course on Religion, Violence, and American Culture in the Spring Semester of 2006, particularly Amy Patel.
16. Seeger, 144.
17. For Seeger and most soldiers, spring *was* the season in which major offensive operations were launched and, thus, was the season of the soldier's death. This inversion, however ironic, is an accurate description of infantry-based combat. Read in the context of his broader corpus, the images of spring in Seeger's "Rendezvous" refer at least as much to "death as rebirth" as they do to the irony of the traditional military calendar.
18. Seeger, 61.
19. Ibid., 142–43.
20. Ibid., 171.
21. Rockwell, xx.
22. Rockwell, 13–18.
23. Rockwell, 48. See also Rockwell, 88; Chapman, 156. Kiffin Rockwell also described fighting and dying to his friend and fellow Legionnaire and pilot, Victor Chapman. "There is nothing like it, you just float across the field, you drop, you rise again. The sack, the 325 extra rounds, the gun have no weight. And a ball in the head and its all over–no pain."
24. Rockwell, 51.
25. Chapman, 41.
26. Rockwell, 56, 67. Rockwell wrote to his "Dear, Good, Sweet, Second Mother" Mrs. Alice Weeks in August of 1915, after Weeks' son Kenneth, a fellow Legionnaire, had been reported missing in action, "I want to live now more than I ever did in my life, but not from the selfish standpoint. This war has taught me many things, and now I want to live to do whatever good is possible."
27. Kennedy, 180–82.
28. Henry S. Kingman, *Section Sixty-one: Selection from Letters of Henry S. Kingman, Member S.S.A.U. 61, Norton-Harjes Ambulance Corps, May to October 1917*, (Minneapolis: Privately Printed, 1917), 16.
29. Poague, 20.
30. Adams, 43.

31. Coleman Tiletson Clark and Salter Storrs Clark, Soldier Letters: Coleman Tiletson Clark and Salter Storrs Clark, Jr.: Their Stories in Extracts from their Letters and Diaries (New York: Middleditch Company, 1919), 173.

32. Geoffrey I. Rossano, ed. *The Price of Honor: The World War One Letters of Naval Aviator Kenneth MacLeish* (Annapolis, MD.: Naval Institute Press, 1991), x–xi, 5. Rossano wrote a full and concise biography of MacLeish as an introduction to his edition of MacLeish's correspondence with Priscilla Murdock.

33. MacLeish, 9.

34. For more on the French Army's crisis of morale in the summer of 1917, see John Keegan, *The First World War* (New York: Alfred A. Knopf, 1999); and Niall Ferguson, *The Pity of War: Explaining World War I* (New York: Basic Books, 1998).

35. MacLeish, 27.

36. Ibid., 37.

37. Ibid., 73.

38. Ibid., 89.

39. Robert Cortes Holliday, ed., *Joyce Kilmer: Poems, Essays and Letters*, vol. 2 (New York: Doubleday, Doran and Company, 1940), 128.

40. Ibid., 2:132.

41. Holliday, 1:108.

42. Allen, 52. See British soldier-author Donald Hankey's *Student in Arms* for an interesting comparison.

43. Harold Speakman, *From A Soldier's Heart* (New York: The Abingdon Press, 1919), 66.

44. Carolyn W. Clarke, *Evacuation 114 As Seen from Within* (Boston: Hudson Printing Company, 1919), 19.

45. Blake, 144.

46. Father Thomas Frances Coakley, 1880–1957. For more on Coakley's pre- and post-war activities, including his staunch anti-Communist stance, see Kenneth J. Heinemen, *A Catholic New Deal: Religion and Reform in Depression Pittsburgh* (State College, PA: Penn State Press, 1999), 131–32. The Catholic Truth Society was founded in 1884 for the printing and dissemination of inexpensive "devotional, educational, or controversial[ist]" tracts and pamphlets. See "Catholic Truth Society" in F. L. Cross and E. A. Livingstone, ed. *Oxford Dictionary of the Christian Church* (Oxford, UK: Oxford University Press, 1997).

47. *The Stars and Stripes*, 21 June 1918, 4.

48. *The Stars and Stripes*, 25 October 1918, 4.

49. *The Stars and Stripes*, 29 November 1918, 4.

50. See Luke 23:32–33.

51. Cornbeise, 39; Putney, 192. Putney's asserts that soldiers were uncomfortable with this framework, specifically the YMCA's tendency to "position Christ in the trenches." I have found little evidence to support this claim.

52. Ebel, "The Great War, Religious Authority, and the American Fighting Man," *Church History* 72, no. 2 (June 2009).

53. John Ellis and Michael Cox, *The World War I Databook: The Essential Facts and Figures for All the Combatants* (London: Aurum, 2001), 270; Mead, 353. Michael Howard sets the figure at 115,000. See Howard, 146.

54. Shirley Jackson Case, *The Origins of Christian Supernaturalism* (Chicago: University of Chicago Press, 1946), 1.

55. *The Stars and Stripes*, 29 March 1918, 3.

56. Ibid., 4. Emphasis added.

57. *The Stars and Stripes*, 27 September 1918, 4.

58. The story appears to have been quite popular. Three of my subjects recorded it, or some version of it, in their personal writings. See Lindner, 51; Wilder, 62; and Howard Vincent O'Brien, *Wine, Women, and War: A Diary of Disillusionment* (New York: J.H. Sears and Company, Inc., 1926), 32.

59. *The Stars and Stripes*, 27 September 1918, 4.

60. *The Stars and Stripes*, 25 October 1918, 4. Here, again, the American soldiers parallel Rudolf Otto, who cited as one of two essential elements of Christ's ministry, "the reaction against Pharisaism. . . ." See Otto, 165.

61. Ibid., 4. Emphasis added.

62. Ibid., 4. The editors published Father Thomas Coakley's poem, "The Holocaust," a mere column away from "Soul Savers."

63. Frank Alexander Holden, *War Memories* (Athens, GA: Athens Book Company, 1922), 142.

64. Lukens, 104–5.

65. Bartley, 114.

66. *The Stars and Stripes*, 22 November 1918, 4. Emphasis added.

67. Ibid., 4.

68. Genet, 324–25.

69. Coolidge, vii–viii. Emphasis added.

70. Spence Burton, S.S.J.E. ed., *Letters of Caspar Henry Burton* (Privately Printed, 1921), 372. Emphasis added. For more on Wilfred Grenfell and his medical and missionary work in Canada see: http://www.thecanadianencyclopedia .com/index.cfm?PgNm=TCE&Params=A1ARTA0003451.

71. Ibid., 379.

72. Ibid., 357.

73. Ibid., 358.

74. Ibid., 374–75.

75. Ibid.

76. Ibid., 379.

CHAPTER FOUR
CHRIST'S CAUSE, PHARAOH'S ARMY

1. *Heroes of 1918: Stories from the Lips of Black Fighters*, 4.

2. See *Crisis*, 1917–1918; *New York Age*, 1918; Slotkin, *Lost Battalions*, entire.

3. One of the more troubling accounts of martial excess that I encountered was written by either Sergeant E. A. Means or Sergeant Matthew Jenkins, both of Company G, 370th Infantry. The piece, "Capturing Hindenburg Cave," was published along with several other accounts written by soldiers of the Illinois-based 370th in a collection titled *Heroes of 1918: Stories from the Lips of Black Fighters*.

The account describes with great relish the killing of "275 Germans" who were attempting to surrender. According to the narrator, the Germans presented themselves "with hands in the air crying 'Kamerad! Kamerad!' " but the Americans "did not have time to take prisoners." He continued, "You ought to see those boys 'fix bayonets.' They began to sing, there always seemed to be a leader among them, while they were singing they were making the world safe for Democracy. Of course we thought of home, German mustard gas, German torpedoes, ruthless submarine, Belgian horrors, raped women, murdered babies, the desolation of France, atrocities in German Africa–and behind each thrust of the bayonet was the spirit of a wronged civilization. Fritz may be cunning, but like all other rats their purpose was foiled." (*Heroes of 1918: Stories from the Lips of Black Fighters*, 19). The account exhibits an enthusiasm for violence and for vengeance that likely exceeds what many soldiers felt in the moment. But the fact that the author casts the brutal encounter in such a positive light demonstrates at the very least that the memory of violence was appealing and a demonstrated capacity for violence was an important part of African American soldiers' war experiences.

4. W.E.B. Du Bois, *The Souls of Black Folk* (New York: W.W. Norton and Company, 1999), 11. Du Bois' book was first published in 1903. The edition used here was put together by Henry Louis Gates and Terry Hume Oliver in anticipation of the book's centenary.

5. Virginia War History Commission Questionnaire (VWHCQ), Arthur Davis. The entire database is available at http://ajax.lva.lib.va.us/F/?func=file&file _name=find-b-clas13&local_base=CLAS13.

6. VWHCQ, Guy Parham.

7. Hamilton, 1. Roughly 150,000 African American soldiers served in one capacity or another in France.

8. For more detailed treatments of the mobilization, organization, and internal race discrimination and politics of the African American units, see Hunton and Johnson, Barbeau and Henri, Harris, and Slotkin, *Lost Battalions*.

9. Barbeau and Henri, 40; Harris, chs. 8–9.

10. Barbeau and Henri, ch. 4. See also Hunton and Johnson.

11. Hunton and Johnson, 46.

12. In this especially sordid episode, a French liaison to the American General Headquarters, Major Linard, penned a confidential memo to the divisions of the French Army serving with African American troops conveying the A.E.F.'s wishes that they establish a Jim Crow–style environment for African Americans serving among them. The concern, he wrote, was that black soldiers would return to the United States having forgotten their place. See *Crisis*, May 1919, 10. See also Barbeau and Henri, 114.

13. Elsie Janis, *The Big Show: My Six Months with the American Expeditionary Forces* (New York: Cosmopolitan Book Corporation, 1919), 37.

14. Hunton and Johnson, 53.

15. VWHCQ, Robert Thomas.

16. Hamilton, 80–85.

17. See Cullen; Faust; Harding; McPherson; and Stout.

18. Vincent Harding, *There Is a River: The Black Struggle for Freedom in America* (San Diego: Harvest Books, 1981) 298–317.

19. Slotkin, 235.
20. *New York Age*, 19 October 1916, 12 April 1917.
21. *Negro Farmer*, 13 March 1915, 6.
22. VWHCQ, Isaac Sanders, James Crawley.
23. VWHCQ, William Thomas.

24. Any history of the African American experience of the Great War must attend to the blinding racism and the brutal violence that often characterized relations between African American soldiers and white American soldiers. But histories that focus only on the myriad racist stupidities of the American Expeditionary Force capture only one part of the story. Arthur Barbeau and Florette Henri's groundbreaking work, *The Unknown Soldiers: Black American Troops in World War I*, first published in 1974, describes the hideous, often violently racist, environment in which African American involvement in the war was imagined, the shaping influence of racism on the service of every black soldier, and the frustratingly tautological thinking of the Army and government officials who, because of the imagined inability of black soldiers to persevere in battle, failed to train or even adequately arm black troops and then saw in instances of "inefficient" black officers, soldiers, and units, proof that black soldiers could not persevere in battle. Barbeau and Henri wrote an angry history of a nation's neglect and exploitation of the black men and women who hoped to serve.

Whether or not Army officials set African American soldiers up to fail, there was little room in a white-dominated American society for the service of African American soldiers to be seen as successful, let alone valiant or heroic. A near obsession with theories of race and race-based nationalism combined with a turn to physical strength as a measure of manhood to make performance in the violent chaos of war the ultimate measure of the superiority of a race. This is the point of departure for Richard Slotkin's *Lost Battalions: The Great War and the Crisis of American Nationality*, which tells the stories of two New York–based units: the ethnically heterogeneous 77th Division and the predominately African American 369th Infantry. A large part of Slotkin's story is given over to the battlefield successes of the 369th and the subsequent duplicity of the Wilson administration, which offered a progressivist "social bargain" to the immigrants of the 77th Division and the African Americans of the 369th, and then not only failed to honor the bargain but also reverted to modes of discourse that regularly questioned the fitness of African Americans, Jews, Italians, Poles, and other "hyphenates" for participation in American democracy.

Barbeau and Henri, and Slotkin have written valuable histories of the "forest" of African American war experiences. Yet, oddly, the "unknown soldiers" in these histories remain largely unknown as individuals let alone as men and women of faith. Passing references to religion in each history barely acknowledge that religion may have been a part of soldiers' lives and do not begin to measure the interaction between religion and war in the lives of African Americans involved in the so-called crusade for democracy. As the work of Albert Raboteau, Evelyn Brooks Higginbotham, Eric Lincoln and Lawrence Mamiya, Vincent Harding and, more recently, Milton Sernett, Curtis Evans, and Wallace Best has demonstrated, an understanding of African American culture in the nineteenth and twentieth centuries requires attention to religion. Sernett, entire; Curtis Evans, "W.E.B.

Du Bois: Interpreting Religion and the Problem of the Negro Church," *Journal of the American Academy of Religion* 75, no. 2. Sernett has argued in *Bound for the Promised Land* that African American migrants drew upon and revised their faiths in light of the challenges, triumphs, and tragedies of this northward Exodus, while their religious institutions both acted and were acted upon by forces that many could not understand. While men and women moved from Southern rural settings to Northern cities, religious leaders and laity in the North and the South labored under the strains of vanishing and booming congregations, increased demand for social services, internal power struggles, and racist attitudes and attacks nationwide.

The most recent addition is Chad Williams, *Torchbearers of Democracy*, a dissertation written at Princeton University. It was through Williams' work that I became aware of the Virginia War Survey as a possible source for black soldiers' religious experiences of war.

25. *Crisis*, June 1919, 100. The NAACP monthly, *Crisis*, reported on the formation of this commission in June of 1919, and noted further that African American soldiers were to be included in the history. One Father William Hannigan of Richmond was to direct the "Central Committee of Negro Collaborators."

26. http://www.lva.lib.va.us/whatwehave/mil/wwiqabout.htm.

27. A single-page version of the questionnaire also circulated.

28. By the time the United States entered the Great War, Booker T. Washington was dead, though his vision of the African American's social, cultural, and economic place in American life lived on in the Tuskegee Institute, its journals, and its educational life. Throughout the early twentieth century, W.E.B. Du Bois was shaping black consciousness through the N.A.A.C.P. and through his influential essays and commentary in the monthly journal, *Crisis*.

29. http://www.lva.lib.va.us/whatwehave/mil/wwiqabout.htm.

30. Barbeau and Henri, and Slotkin make this point repeatedly.

31. Historians have learned a great deal about religion in the antebellum South from the WPA Slave Narratives, which were collected in ways that left open the possibility of race-based mistrust. Just as scholars have approached the WPA narratives with a hermeneutic of suspicion, so must one also approach African American responses to the Virginia Survey alert to potential problems in the narratives and aware of the widespread questioning of African American patriotism and fear of the spread of "Bolshevism" among African Americans, both of which may have influenced black veterans' responses.

32. VWHCQ, Emmanuel McCoy, Frank Nottingham, Elijah Powell.

33. VWHCQ, Herbert White.

34. VWHCQ, James Golden, Ellsworth Storrs.

35. Harris, 82–83; Slotkin, 56–57.

36. Harris, 97; Slotkin, ch. 3.

37. Harris, 115.

38. Harris, 115–33; Slotkin, 120–28. According to Barbeau and Henri (24–25), the East St. Louis Riots left "over 100 negroes . . . shot or mangled and beaten to various degrees of helplessness." In the wake of the Houston riots, which involved an African American army unit from "up north," thirteen black soldiers were hung.

39. Ettinger, 7; Harris, 110–11; Slotkin, 123–26.

40. See James P. Daughton, "Sketches of the Poilu's World: Trench Cartoons from the Great War" in Douglas Mackaman and Michael Mays, *World War I and the Cultures of Modernity* (Jackson, MS: University Press of Mississippi, 2000), 35–67. See also Slotkin and Harris.

41. VWHCQ, Vernon Smith.

42. Ibid.

43. Ibid. In Vernon Smith's survey, he lists the year of their arrival as 1918. The unit actually arrived in France in 1917.

44. Ibid.

45. Ibid.

46. Nina Mjagkij, *Light in the Darkness: African Americans and the YMCA, 1852–1946* (Lexington: University Press of Kentucky, 1994). Though she does not discuss Muscular Christianity or the intersections among religion, fitness, and manhood that characterized some YMCA programs in white communities, Mjagkij does document the existence and development of YMCA facilities and programs in African American communities. She thus documents the existence of one potential common source for this kind of understanding of religion, war, and manhood.

47. During Sanders' childhood, Portsmouth had two African Methodist churches, one A.M.E.Z. and one A.M.E. Emanuel A.M.E was founded in 1857 and received its first African American pastor, James Handy, in 1864. Brighton Rock A.M.E.Z. was founded in 1896. A third, Providence A.M.E.Z., was founded in 1916. I have been unable to determine which, if any, of these was J. R. Sanders' church.

48. Thanks are due to Harry Stout for pointing this out to me.

49. VWHCQ, Isaac Sanders.

50. Ibid.

51. For a brief description of James Moss' progressive approach to leading African American soldiers, see Slotkin, 136.

52. VWHCQ, Isaac Sanders.

53. VWHCQ, Willie Thomas.

54. Ibid.

55. Ibid.

56. Ibid. See Slotkin and Kennedy for discussions of the post-war economy.

57. VWHCQ, Julius Mitchell. Booker T. Washington's turn of phrase.

58. VWHCQ, Julius Mitchell.

59. Ibid.

60. Ibid.

61. Barbeau and Henri, 177. The authors state that at least ten African American veterans were lynched in 1919, "some of them still in uniform."

62. *Negro Farmer*, 24 April 1915, 3–5.

63. Faust, 67. Black soldiers were also assigned to burial duty during the Civil War. Though this work was often described as "heroic," in reality it was often assigned as punishment or delegated to prisoners of war.

64. Hunton and Johnson, 238.

CHAPTER FIVE
IDEAL WOMEN IN AN IDEAL WAR

1. Anne Sebba, *American Jennie: The Remarkable Life of Lady Randolph Churchill* (New York: W.W. Norton, 2007).

2. The *New York Times*, 4 June 1916. "Lady Churchill Talks of Woman and the War."

3. Poague, 165.

4. Lettie Galvin, *American Women in World War I: They Also Served* (Niwot, CO: University Press of Colorado, 1997).

5. Leann Whites, "The Civil War as a Crisis in Gender" and Drew Gilpin Faust, "Altars of Sacrifice: Confederate Women and the Narratives of War" in Clinton and Silber, *Divided Houses*. For additional discussions of the effects of the American Civil War on American women, see Stout, Chapter 11. See also Elizabeth Fox-Genovese, "The Civil War and the Religious Imagination of Women Writers" and Drew Gilpin Faust, " 'Without Pilot or Compass': Elite Women and Religion in the Civil War South," in Miller, Stout, and Wilson, eds. *Religion and the American Civil War* (Oxford: Oxford University Press, 1998).

6. Galvin, 44; Thomas Fleming estimates that by the end of the war over 25,000 American women had served in some capacity in France. Thomas Fleming, *The Illusion of Victory: America in World War I* (New York: Basic Books, 2004), 199.

7. "Report to the Commander-in-Chief of the Y.M.C.A. with the A.E.F." in *The United States in World War I*, volume 15, p. 463.

8. Faust in Clinton and Silber, eds. *Divided Houses*.

9. Clinton and Silber, *Divided Houses* (1993) and *Battle Scars: Gender and Sexuality in the American Civil War* (New York: Oxford University Press, 2006); Catherine A. Brekus, ed. *The Religious History of American Women: Reimagining the Past* (Chapel Hill: University of North Carolina Press, 2007); S. Jay Kleinberg, Eileen Boris, and Vicki L. Ruiz, eds. *The Practice of U.S. Women's History: Narratives, Intersections, and Dialogues* (New Brunswick, NJ: Rutgers University Press, 2007).

10. See Evelyn Brooks Higginbotham, *Righteous Discontent: The Women's Movement in the Black Baptist Church, 1880–1920* (Cambridge: Harvard University Press, 1993). Higginbotham describes how tightly interwoven domesticity and Christian faith were in the minds of white and some black Protestant women in Chapter 2.

11. In her work *Women and War*, Jean Bethke Elshtain provides an extended analysis of wartime gender roles. Defining two dominant types, men as "Just Warriors," women as "Beautiful Souls," she argues at length for the mutually reinforcing nature of these constraining, "canalizing," deeply rooted ideals. "[R]eal men and women–locked in a dense symbiosis, perceived as beings who have complementary needs and exemplify gender-specific virtues–take on, in cultural memory and narrative, the personas of Just Warriors and Beautiful Souls. Man construed

as violent, whether eagerly and inevitably or reluctantly and tragically; woman as non-violent, offering succor and compassion . . . ”

Men and women facing the traumas of war aspire to and inhabit these roles. The Just Warrior seeks to order the public world in accordance with his view of right; he is capable of devastating violence when called upon, but wages war with an eye toward his understanding of principle and the protection of the innocent. These roles have clearly been shaped by the Just War tradition and its understanding of “innocence,” which, Elshtain points out, has far more to do with imagined potential for violence than it has to do with, say, moral innocence or innocence of sin.

12. Joan W. Scott, “Gender: A Useful Category of Historical Analysis,” *The American Historical Review* 91, no. 5 (Dec. 1986), pp. 1053–75. Scott is particularly helpful in that she lays out a definition of gender that contains both a symbolic and a normative dimension, and acknowledges that understandings of gender are often made to appear beyond history. Her affinity with Elshtain on this point is striking.

13. Anonymous (Dare), *Mademoiselle Miss*, 11. Dare used this turn of phrase to describe her fellow nurses in a letter dated September 20, 1915.

14. My use of the phrase “New Woman Warrior” is not meant to connect this ideal directly to the “Women Warriors” who figured prominently in the discourse of Maud Booth of Salvation Army fame, though the Salvationist “Women Warriors,” as described in Winston, share some qualities. See Winston, 141. I take the phrase “grammar of gender” from Robert A. Orsi, “He Keeps Me Going: Women’s Devotion to Saint Jude Thaddeus and the Dialectics of Gender in American Catholicism, 1929–1965” in Jon Butler and Harry S. Stout, *Religion in American History: A Reader* (New York: Oxford University Press, 1998), 460.

15. Ruth Wolfe Fuller, *Silver Lining: The Experiences of a War Bride* (Boston and New York: Houghton-Mifflin, 1918), 14.

16. This connection between the Great War and mythic medieval court culture (which, as we have seen, occurred to numerous soldiers as well) asserted the justness, the divinity of the cause, and permitted no question as to the moral qualities of those fighting on its behalf.

17. Ibid., 32. Though she would not have been the first or the last, Fuller did not (to my knowledge) consider the relations with whom she would have remained during the war to be in any way Pharaoh-like. It is, however, interesting to consider the implications of the Exodus narrative in this context. The freedom toward which she was moving by following the “Pillar of Fire” was, perhaps, a freedom to follow more closely what she took to be the “laws” of God and nation.

18. Ibid., 37.

19. Dearing, 9. James Winn has demonstrated how false to the history of medieval knighthood the chivalric ideal and how “closed” to history it was as early as the Renaissance. Nevertheless, we see in Dearing—and in Fuller as well—that the power of the chivalric ideal touched women as well as men.

20. Ibid., 13.

21. Ibid., 11.

22. Ibid., 18.

23. Dearing, 17.

24. Ibid., 19.

25. Such stark gendering of war is not now, nor was it then, an exclusively American phenomenon. See James P. Daughton, "Sketches of the Poilu's World: Trench Cartoons from the Great War," and Janet Watson, "The Paradox of Working Heroines: Conflict over the Changing Social Order in Wartime Britain, 1914–1918" in Douglas Mackman and Michael Mays, eds. *World War I and the Cultures of Modernity* (Jackson, MS: University Press of Mississippi, 2000).

26. Anonymous, *A Red Triangle Girl in France*, Letter VII, 35.

27. Ibid., Letter XVII, 88. The same YMCA volunteer quoted here also wrote from France, "I know no less than seven men here who were definitely engaged when they left home and who have heard since that their girls were either engaged to someone else or married." For a discussion of sexual relations between Confederate women and male slaves during the Civil War, see Martha Hodes, "Wartime Dialogues on Illicit Sex: White Women and Black Men" in Clinton and Silber, *Divided Houses*.

28. Carolyn Clarke, 15.

29. Ibid., 24.

30. Ibid., 24, 30.

31. Ibid., 19. As noted in Chapter Three, Clarke also wrote reverently of the crosses marked in iodine on soldiers' foreheads—indications that they had received anti-tetanus serum in the field. The literal meaning of these marks aside, to her they were "symbolic of something more than a treatment."

32. Ibid., 30.

33. Ibid., 42.

34. Anonymous, *A Red Triangle Girl in France*, 129.

35. Ibid., 167.

36. I know very little about her identity beyond her surname and the fact that she was still in France in April of 1917, when Esther Root, another female war worker, wrote of meeting her at a social event. For historical context and a point of comparison and contrast, see Kristie Ross, "Arranging a Doll's House: Refined Women as Union Nurses," in Clinton and Silber, *Divided Houses*.

37. Anonymous (Dare), *Mademoiselle Miss*, 12.

38. Ibid., 18.

39. Ibid., 16, 29.

40. Blake, 52.

41. Ibid., 107–8.

42. Ibid., 8–9.

43. Ibid., 20.

44. Sergeant, 19.

45. Ibid., 50.

46. Ibid., 112.

47. Ibid.

48. This moment calls to the fore the issue of class tension that always underlies definitions of gender roles and ideals. One might well wonder about the extent to which the Beautiful Soul ideal was and remains an ideological club for beating down or reigning in unruly or uppity classes during wartime. While I have no

doubt that such an ideal has functioned in this way and while, as noted in the introductory chapter, most of the women's voices come from wealthier classes, this neither diminishes the religiousness of attraction to the ideal among those classes nor provides conclusive evidence that the Beautiful Soul was only an upper-class or upper-middle-class construct. The work of the Salvation Army and its large staff of female "Sallies" in the trenches—and the reception of that work by American servicemen—provides one argument to the contrary. The Salvation Army did not attract large numbers of wealthy women, and yet made itself famous and adored for the domestic nurturing services it provided close to the front lines. See Winston, ch. 4.

49. Galvin, 59, 139, 156.
50. Higginbotham, ch. 7.
51. Hunton and Johnson, 230–31.
52. Higginbotham, ch. 7. In her discussion of "the politics of respectability," Higginbotham discusses why such a politics was necessary and the stereotypes against which black women were working. On page 190, she presents an example from a 1904 newspaper, "Negro women evidence more nearly the popular idea of total depravity than men do. . . . When a man's mother, wife and daughters are all immoral women, there is no room in his fallen nature for the aspiration of honor and virtue . . . I cannot imagine such a creation as a virtuous black woman."
53. Hunton and Johnson, 11–12. As noted in Chapter One, Hunton revised the widely used crusade metaphor when describing the African American experience of the war: "We were crusaders on a quest for Democracy! How and where would that precious thing be found?"
54. Ibid., 38.
55. Ibid., 230.
56. Shirley Millard, *I Saw Them Die: Diary and Recollections of Shirley Millard* (New York: Harcourt, Brace and Company, 1936). Millard is mentioned in a number of online columns, including Pat Buchanan's "Wilson's War to End War," available at www.theamericancause.org/patwilsonswartoendwar.htm; Harry Browne's Journal, available at www.harrybrowne.org/journal0408.htm; Her memoir is also cited repeatedly in Thomas Fleming, *The Illusion of Victory: America in World War I* (New York: Basic Books, 2004).
57. Millard, 21.
58. Ibid., ix–x.
59. Ibid., 44.
60. Ibid., 43.
61. Ibid., 92.
62. Harriot Stanton Blatch, *Mobilizing Woman Power* (New York: Woman's Press, 1918), 6.
63. Ibid., 6, 8.
64. Ibid., 9.
65. Isabel Anderson, xi.
66. Jean Bethke Elshtain, *Women and War*, entire.

CHAPTER SIX
"THERE ARE NO DEAD"

1. Mills, 462.
2. Maeterlinck's corpus consists of many plays characterized as "mystical," "lyrical," and marked by fatalism. The play to which Mills refers, *The Blue Bird*, was enormously popular in the United States and was first performed in New York in 1910. It was a play for children and had a distinct "fairy-tale" feel to it. http://nobelprize.org/nobel_prizes/literature/laureates/1911/maeterlinck-bio.html; http://www.kirjasto.sci.fi/maeterli.htm.
3. Ann Douglas, "Heaven Our Home: Consolation Literature in the Northern United States, 1830–1880," *American Quarterly* 26, no. 5 (Dec. 1974).
4. Deborah Blum, *Ghost Hunters: William James and the Scientific Search for Proof of Life after Death* (New York: Penguin Press, 2006) is an interesting chronicle of turn-of-the-century efforts—led by renowned scientists and scholars—to investigate myriad claims in England and the United States of contacts between the living and the dead. The book shows that conversations about these topics were not confined to a marginal industry of sideshow mediums and conjurers, but instead reached into many of the most educated circles in the Western world.
5. Helen Dore Boylston, *"Sister": The Diary of a War Nurse* (New York: Ives Washburn, 1927), 32.
6. Colleen McDannell and Bernard Lang, *Heaven: A History* (New Haven: Yale University Press, 1988), 268–69, 288.
7. See Faust, ch. 6, for an account of similar issues as raised by the Civil War and as expressed by Elizabeth Stuart Phelps.
8. Elizabeth Stuart Phelps, *Three Spiritualist Novels* (Urbana: University of Illinois Press, 2000), 42.
9. Ibid., 40–41.
10. Ibid., 51. Original emphasis.
11. Ibid., 47.
12. Ibid., 79.
13. Henry Warner Bowden, *Dictionary of American Religious Biography* (Westport, CT: Greenwood Press, 1977), 71–72; Hutchison, 117–32, 227–44.
14. William Adams Brown, *The Christian Hope: A Study in the Doctrine of Immortality* (New York: Charles Scribner's Sons, 1912), 173–77, 193. See also Fosdick, *The Assurance of Immortality* (New York: The Macmillan Company, 1913), 140–41. "Death is a great adventure, but none need go unconvinced that there is an issue to it. The man of faith may face it as Columbus faced his first voyage from the shores of Spain. What lies across the sea, he cannot tell; his special expectations all may be mistaken; but his insight into the clear meanings of present facts may persuade him beyond doubt that the sea has another shore. Such confident faith . . . shall be turned to sight, when . . . the hope of the seers is rewarded by the vision of the new continent." Also see George A. Gordon, *Immortality and the New Theodicy* (Boston: The Riverside Press, 1897), 82, 86. Gordon writes, "A new humanity has arisen, in number exceeding the stars. It is too vast and noble to be consigned to perdition, unless all men are so consigned; and it is too crude for any sphere except one full of incentives to progress. It is this new human-

ity that the religious thinker of to-day must reckon with, whose semi-brutal character and amazing capacities for ethical improvement he must equally acknowledge, and whom he must cover with the everlasting mercy of God."

15. Brown, 193.

16. Ibid., 173, 160.

17. Douglas, 512, 514.

18. Ibid., 515.

19. Faust, 186. Faust notes that *The Gates Ajar* was reprinted fifty-five times between 1868 and 1888. According to the WorldCat database, in addition to U.S. printings in 1868, 1869, 1870, 1873, 1874, 1878, 1881, 1882, 1884, 1887, 1888, there were additional printings in 1889, 1894, 1895, 1896, and 1899; *Beyond the Gates*, first published in 1883, was printed twice in that year and then in 1884, 1885, 1886 (two times), 1887, 1892, 1898, and 1911. *The Gates Between* was published in 1887 and went through two printings. It was printed twice again in 1900.

20. William H. Brackney. "Dearing, John Lincoln" at http://www.anb.org/articles/08/08-00368.html. *American National Biography Online*, Feb. 2000. According to Brackney's article, John Lincoln Dearing and Shailer Mathews were roommates at Colgate College. Dearing's missionary career was launched through the Student Volunteer Movement.

21. Mead, 232, 264.

22. Dearing referred to two close female friends, Peggy and Louise, as "sisters."

23. Ibid., 64.

24. Ibid., 58.

25. Reinhold Niebuhr's famous articulation of this point, *Moral Man, Immoral Society* was not published until 1932, but one can see in his *Leaves from the Notebook of a Tamed Cynic* (1929) in reflections dating to the immediate aftermath of the war outlines of this sentiment.

26. Abbey, 163.

27. Seeger, 142.

28. Mead, 214.

29. Holliday, 1:105–7; 2:191. See also Duffy, 60–69; and Ettinger, 70. Both were present, as Kilmer was not, at the reading, and describe the emotional scene. Kilmer's poem was subsequently published in *The Stars and Stripes*, 16 August 1918.

30. Ibid., 105–7.

31. Ibid.

32. E-mail from family member, Ana, July 2002.

33. Vincenzo D'Aquila, *Bodyguard Unseen: A True Autobiography* (New York: R.R. Smith Inc., 1931), 130.

34. Coolidge, 228.

35. Ibid.

36. Virginia Survey, Otis P Robinson.

37. Cowing, 274.

38. Faust, 180–84. Faust offers an account of spiritualism and its appeal in Civil War–era America. She describes the questions spiritualism answered simi-

larly: "Spiritualism responded to a question of pressing importance to the soldier and his kin. As an 1861 article in the spiritualist newspaper *Banner of Light* posed it, 'he desires to know what will become of himself after he has lost his body. Shall he continue to exist?—and, if so, in what condition?' " (p. 183.)

39. Anne Braude, *Radical Spirits: Spiritualism and Women's Rights in Nineteenth-Century America* (Bloomington, IN: Indiana University Press, 2001). Braude's work remains definitive both in its description of the many manifestations of Spiritualism in nineteenth-century America and in its tracing of the many intersections between Spiritualism and the movements for women's rights. See also Blum.

40. George Moseley, *Extracts from the Letters of George Clark Moseley during the Period of the Great War* (Chicago: Privately Printed, 1923), 143.

41. Winn, ch. 5. Winn provides an excellent discussion of the history of wartime friendship and writes that, "One of the striking features of such poems [of comradeship] is the way that the surviving partner takes on the identity of the dead partner. Even before the second man dies, the two have become one." (p. 157.)

42. Genet, 188.

43. Rockwell, 142–43. Poet Benjamin Apthorp Gould wrote similarly of the fallen Chapman, asserting three times in his memorial poem the untruth of claims that Chapman was dead, and expanding Chapman's continuing influence beyond the squadron to the "race." "It is not true he died in France; / His spirit climbs the serried years / Victorious over empty fears / And proof of Freedom's last advance . . . / Himself still lives, and cannot die / While freemen shun the tyrant's heel, / While minds are true and hearts are leal, / And men look upward to the sky . . . / Mourn not for that devoted head; / He is the spirit of our race / Triumphant over Time and Space–/ He cannot die; he is not dead."

44. See also Hamilton and Corbin, 243. Sergeant Michael Donaldson of the 165th Infantry voiced a similar sentiment, being more militant than most, when writing of his many fallen comrades: " . . . you cannot kill a regiment; replacements come in and we still carried on, and the souls of the men who had fallen marched on with us against the foe."

45. Faust, 79.

46. See Blum for descriptions of the higher-level spiritualistic groups and their scientific investigations.

47. Will Judy, *A Soldier's Diary: A Day-to-Day Record in the World War* (Chicago, Judy Publishing Company, 1930), 122.

48. Benjamin Lee, 2nd: *A Record Gathered from Letters, Note-books, and Narratives of Friends by his Mother Mary Justice Chase* (Boston: Cornhill, 1920). Lee's correspondence and diary are almost completely devoid of religious reflection. Were it not for Fuller's care in preserving Lee's last letter, glued to the back cover of his personal copy of Lee's collected correspondence (held at the New York Public Library), no evidence would remain that Lee even considered the existence of an afterlife, let alone the notion that from death he might be able to observe his living friends.

49. Rossano, introduction.

50. Ibid., 91. Mary Hillard was not the only person of education and mental ability to take seriously the beliefs of spiritualism and to engage in spiritualistic practices. Other more famous figures included: William James, Arthur Conan Doyle, and H. G. Wells.

51. MacLeish, 54.

52. Ibid., 58.

53. Laderman, 47–53. See also Meigs, ch. 5.

54. *The Stars and Stripes*, 30 May 1919, 4.

55. Peter Brown, *The Cult of the Saints: Its Rise and Function in Latin Christianity* (Chicago: University of Chicago Press, 1981). Douglas, 503. See also Nina Baym, "Introduction," in Phelps, xx; and McDannell and Lang, 292. Spiritualist views of the afterlife did not differ dramatically from dominant Christian views. They shared, for the most part, Progressive-Era Christian notions of the "fluidity between life and afterlife, concern of the dead for the living, the ability of the soul to progress intellectually and spiritually, and the elimination of a dramatic Last Judgment." Where they differed "doctrinally" was in their belief in the possibility of communication between the living and the dead. Phelps' work demonstrates just how close the two realms could come to one another. There are no séances in her novels and there are explicitly anti-spiritualist statements (e.g., Aunt Winifred's remark that communication between the living and the dead would lead to breaches of the First Commandment). But as Nina Baym points out in the introduction to Phelps' collected "spiritualist" novels, the afterlife that Phelps constructs, and the relationships she imagines among the dead, and between the dead and the living, are full of spiritualist influence.

56. Galvin, 63. Babcock noted no impulse to act politically on Kramer's behalf, only that he was a regular presence in her life. Her testimony only confirms she had not forgotten the fallen sergeant and that she felt that Sergeant Kramer was paying attention to his former nurse.

57. CWRO, 53.

58. Ibid., 85. The report continued using the words of another observer. "[Soldiers] discovered a great natural conviction not reasoned but instinctive, the conviction of the certainty of a future life. The poor clay, about to be wrapped in its black blanket, was 'not him.' Thus the violent storms and tensions of war cleared the air and revealed to men their intuitive knowledge of immortality in the form of an intense and definite personal assurance."

59. Ibid., 86, 136–37. One interesting suggestion, made by a chaplain and confined to the footnotes of the report, was that the doctrine of purgatory be revived. This was seen as a logical step in light of the war, since it was difficult to believe that a soldier could be sent from the hell of the war into the eternal hell, while it was similarly difficult to believe he could go straight to heaven.

60. Ibid., 85–86.

61. MacLeish, 129.

62. Luby, 482.

63. MacLeish, 120. Archibald MacLeish's poem was published in the April 1919 issue of *Lyric*.

CHAPTER SEVEN
"THE SAME CROSS IN PEACE": THE AMERICAN LEGION, THE ONGOING WAR, AND
AMERICAN REILLUSIONMENT

1. *The American Legion Weekly,* 1 August 1919, 19.
2. "Military Service of Thanksgiving for Victory"; program printed by American Church of the Holy Trinity in Paris. Archives of the American Cathedral,
Avenue George V, Paris.
3. Scarry, 132. "If the democracy for which one dies existed in a world safe for
democracy, one would not be dying to make the world safe for democracy. If the
country for which one kills existed in a world in which there was an end of wars,
one would not be killing to make a war that ends all wars."
4. Kennedy, 92. "One of the casualties of the war for the American mind thus
seemed to have been the progressive soul, and the spiritual bloodletting very
nearly drained the last reserves of utopianism from American social thought. The
next reforming generation, after a decade of desuetude, would hearken not to the
buoyant optimism of John Dewey but to the sober voice of Reinhold Niebuhr,
preaching in Augustinian accents the doctrine of human imperfection and the
necessity of diminished hopes. The war had killed something precious and perhaps
irretrievable in the hearts of thinking men and women."
5. *Crisis,* June 1919, 63.
6. Barbeau and Henri, 178–89.
7. Many supporters wrote to *The American Legion Weekly* and emphasized
the ubiquity of the sentiment that "some sort of organization" should be founded
to keep the spirit of the war alive, and the spontaneity of the sentiment. Secretary
of War Newton Baker wrote, "This organization is so distinctly a spontaneous
out-growth of the mind and heart of the men who have been in the service that it
neither desires nor would be benefited by an official relationship with the War
Department . . . " *The American Legion Weekly,* 4 July 1919, 7.
8. Blake, 178.
9. William Pencak, *For God and Country: The American Legion, 1919–1941*
(Boston: Northeastern University Press, 1989), 50.
10. Ibid., 51.
11. The son of President Theodore Roosevelt is referred to both as Theodore
Roosevelt, Jr. and Theodore Roosevelt, III in contemporary sources and historiography. The president was actually the junior, but is not commonly referred to as
such.
12. Pencak, 49–50. According to Pencak, Chaplain Brent would later describe
the "sell out" of his comrades to "a designing, boozing organization" as "the
thing I have to repent most the rest of my life."
13. Ibid., 52–57. Roosevelt's launch of a veterans' organization while assigned
by Pershing to work on the morale issue represented a cooption of the General's
imprimatur, and one that the General could do little to counteract. Pershing was
sensitive to accusations that he was planning to use the Comrades to aid in a run
for the presidency and did not want to add to this perception by fighting for the
Comrades against the Legion. The organizations' membership rolls were eventually combined. The combination defused concerns about Pershing's political aspi-

rations, and immediately limited the influence that American clergy could exercise in shaping the war's legacy.

According to an article in the July 1934 issue of *The American Legion Monthly*, "That Earlier American Legion," the name "American Legion" had been adopted three years earlier by a preparedness organization founded by *Adventure* magazine editor Arthur Sullivant Hoffman. Hoffman wrote that he was delighted to give up his claim to the name. *The American Legion Monthly*, July 1934, 11–12, 42–46.

14. Ibid., 82–83. William Pencak contextualizes these numbers by looking at them relative not to the entire body of eligible members but to the percentage of that body likely to join a voluntary organization. (He cites mid-twentieth-century sociological data that place likely membership at thirty percent of Americans.) "If, therefore, we accept 30 percent of AEF veterans as the maximum [likely] membership pool, the Legion enrolled half that number at its lowest point. From 1939 to 1941 . . . 80 percent of veterans likely to join any organization belonged to the Legion."

15. E-mail from Joe Hovish, American Legion Historian, November 21, 2007. Hovish cited archived correspondence dated 2 April 1931.

16. *The Stars and Stripes*, 21 February 1919.

17. *The American Legion Weekly*, 18 July 1919. In its third issue, *The American Legion Weekly* announced that "any solider, sailor, or marine who served honorably between April 6, 1917 and November 11, 1918" as well as "[women] who were regularly enlisted or commissioned in the army, navy or marine corps" were eligible for Legion membership.

18. Pencak, 73.

19. Ibid., 65, 74.

20. "To the American Legion," Wilder, 32.

21. See *The Stars and Stripes*, 15 March 1918, 2; *The Stars and Stripes*, 24 May 1918, 1; *The Stars and Stripes*, 22 November 1918, 1; and *The Stars and Stripes* 13 December 1918, 1. An editorial cartoon published in *The Stars and Stripes* on January 24, 1919, addressed the issue of Prohibition. The cartoon, "My How She's Changed" depicted an exhausted thirsty soldier standing before once mighty Columbia, now a shrewish old lady with a turned-up nose and glasses. In her right hand she holds a wine goblet upside down; in her left hand is a sign reading, "U.S. Bone Dry." She welcomes the soldier back to an America that is, as far as the eye can see, a desert. The sand is littered with an empty beer can, a wine bottle, a keg, and, in the distance, a camel that appears to be dying of thirst.

22. Kennedy, 283; Barbeau and Henri, 171.

23. Robert H. Zieger, *America's Great War: World War I and the American Experience* (Lanham, MD: Rowman and Littlefield, 2000), 208.

24. Pencak, 2. Editorials and articles in *The American Legion Weekly* confirm that this sentiment predominated among the leadership of the Legion. Depictions of confrontations between Legionnaires and all elements believed to contribute to post-war disorder fill the periodical's first two volumes.

25. Ibid, 5.

26. Ibid.

27. *The American Legion Weekly* railed against the IWW in articles and editorials in almost every issue. See also Pencak, 149.

28. "The Centralia Massacre" and "The I.W.W. in Washington," Web-published essays by University of Washington Library (http://content.lib .washington.edu/iwwweb/readIWW.html). See also, http://freepages.genealogy .rootsweb.com/~cainhome/remmen_album/emil_guard/centralia_tragedy.htm; and John McClelland, Jr., *Wobbly War: The Centralia Story* (Tacoma, WA: Washington State Historical Society, 1987).

29. *The American Legion Weekly*, 5 December 1919. An interesting part of the coverage of this clash was *The American Legion Weekly's* reaction to the "home-grown" nature of this group of Wobblies. In a strangely backhanded compliment, one writer commented that American Wobblies were a different and more virile sort than their foreign comrades.

30. Pencak, 151; Zieger, 196–97.

31. *The American Legion Weekly*, November 1919, April 1920; "The Centralia Massacre," and "The I.W.W. in Washington," Web-published essays by University of Washington Library

32. *The American Legion Weekly*, November 1919, April 1920.

33. *The American Legion Weekly* and the minutes of the National Conventions of the American Legion offer full discussions of each of these topics. See also Pencak, entire.

34. http://www.eugenevdebs.com/pages/histry.html.

35. Pencak, 157.

36. Ibid., 158.

37. See Martin Marty, *Modern American Religion, Volume 2: The Noise of Conflict, 1919–1941*; George Marsden, *Fundamentalism and American Culture: The Shaping of Twentieth-Century Evangelicalism, 1870–1925*; and *William Hutchison, The Modernist Impulse in American Protestantism*.

38. Calvin Coolidge's address to the American Legion National Convention in 1924 is one stirring expression of this sentiment. The Federal Council of Churches of Christ was also working for at least Protestant ecumenism.

39. As early as November 28, 1919, *The American Legion Weekly* was reporting confrontations between Legionnaires and those of questionable faith. "Jefferson Post, in Louisville, Ky.," they wrote, had "won a skirmish in its fight on disloyalty in its city. The People's Church, whose pastor's utterances on the war have been subject to severe criticism, has been forced to disband because of the pressure exerted by the post." (p. 23.) My information on the confrontation between Sherwood Eddy and the American Legion and between the FCCC and the Legion comes entirely from William Pencak's history of the American Legion. My attempts to do further research on the topic at the National Headquarters of the American Legion in July of 2007 were hindered somewhat by the fact that the Legion destroyed the contents of its "Radicalism" files after the publication of Pencak's book.

40. Sherwood Eddy, *With Our Soldiers in France* (New York: Association Press, 1917). A copy of the text is available at http://www.lib.byu.edu/~rdh/wwi/ memoir/Eddy/EddyTC.htm.

41. Ibid.

42. Sherwood Eddy and Kirby Page, *The Abolition of War* (New York, 1924) 23, cited in Putney, 163. See also Marty, *Modern American Religion*, vol. 2, 230–31; Joseph Kip Kosek, *Spectacles of Conscience: Christian Non-violence and the Transformation of American Democracy, 1914–1956* (Unpublished dissertation, Yale University, 2004) and "American Liberal Pacifists and the Memory of Abolitionism, 1914–1933." This essay is available at http://www.vanderbilt.edu/rpw_center/pdfs/KOSEK.PDF.

43. Pencak, 167–68; Putney, 162.

44. Ibid.

45. Ibid.

46. Ibid., 6.

47. Ibid., 167–68. According to William Pencak, "Spafford went so far as to argue that those who did not favor strong military preparedness in fact 'advocated the murder of our next generation.' " The Federal Council of Churches, the ecumenical body that had worked to provide chaplains to soldiers during the war, was also suspected by the Legion of undermining Americanism and plotting against the United States. The FCC was not uniformly pacifist, but the body was concerned about programs that appeared to them to militarize American society unnecessarily.

48. *The Stars and Stripes*, 7 February 1919, 6.

49. *The American Legion Weekly*, 1921.

50. Ibid.

51. *Minutes of the National Convention of The American Legion*, 1923.

52. *The American Legion Monthly*, March 1929, 33; American Legion (AL) Archive, "Religion" File.

53. Federal Council of Churches of Christ (E. O. Watson and John Tichenor), the Salvation Army (John J. Allan and W. W. Banterse), the YMCA (L. W. De-Gast), the Knights of Columbus and the National Catholic Welfare Council (D. J. Callahan and Charles McMalroy), the American Red Cross (Robert Bondy), the Noble Order of the Mystic Shrine (Conrad Dykeman).

54. AL Archive, "Religion" File, Lemuel Bowles, June 1923.

55. Ibid.

56. *The Stars and Stripes*, 12 April 1918, 4.

57. Cornbeise, 126.

58. *The American Legion Weekly*, November 1939, 25.

59. Pencak., 262–63.

60. Theodore Roosevelt, Jr., foreword to Harold E. Hartney, *Up And At 'Em* (Harrisburg, PA: Stackpole Sons, 1940).

CONCLUSION

1. *The Stars and Stripes*, 13 June 1919, 4.

2. Ibid.

3. Slotkin, 16. Slotkin lists among these "the landing of the Pilgrims, the rally of the Minutemen at Lexington, the Alamo, the Last Stand, [and] Pearl Harbor."

4. *The Stars and Stripes*, 28 February 1918, 4.

5. Kennedy.

6. Paul B. Hendrickson to Cecil Rife, 23 May 1919. "I've experienced some of the most varied emotions and sensations in the past few months, I believe it possible for a human to experience in so short a time, for coming out of the battle field, after having made up my mind for the worst, is as near experiencing a resurrection as any thing I could describe it as being." Digitized copies of the letters and diary of Paul B. Hendrickson are available at http://my.inil.com/~jimvgill/wwipages/pbhstry.html.

Selected Bibliography

Abbey, Edwin Austin. *An American Soldier: Letters of Edwin Austin Abbey*, 2d. Boston: Houghton Mifflin, 1918.

Adams, Briggs Kilburn. *The American Spirit: Letters of Briggs Kilburn Adams, Lieutenant of the Royal Flying Corps*. Boston: The Atlantic Monthly Press, 1918.

Allen, Hervey. *Toward the Flame*. New York: George H. Doran Company, 1926.

Anderson, Isabel W. *Zigzagging*. Boston: Houghton Mifflin, 1918.

Anonymous. *"Mademoiselle Miss": Letters from an American Girl Serving with the Rank of Lieutenant in a French Army Hospital at the Front*. Boston: W.A. Butterfield, 1916.

Anonymous. *One Woman's War*. New York: The MacAulay Company, 1930.

Anonymous. *A Red Triangle Girl in France*. New York: George H. Doran Company, 1918.

Anonymous. *Those War Women, by one of them*. New York: Coward-McCann, 1929.

Anonymous. "Two Pike County Hoosiers in World War I." Bloomington, IN: Indiana Magazine of History, 1942; v. 38, pp. 269–306.

Archibald, Norman. *Heaven High, Hell Deep, 1917–1918*. New York: A. and C. Boni, Inc., 1935.

Baldwin, Marian. *Canteening Overseas, 1917–1919*. New York: The Macmillan Company, 1920.

Baker, C. Earl. *Doughboy's Diary*. Shippensburg, PA: Burd Street Press, 1998.

Banks, Elizabeth. *The Remaking of an American*. Garden City, NJ: Doubleday, Doran and Company, 1928.

Barber, Thomas H. *Along the Road*. New York: Dodd, Mead and Company, 1924.

Barkley, John Lewis. *No Hard Feelings!* New York: Cosmopolitan Book Corporation, 1930.

Bartley, Albert Lea. *Tales of the World War*. Dallas: Clyde C. Cockrell Co., 1935.

Beal, Howard W. *The Letters of Major Howard W. Beal, Headquarters First Division, Medical Department. Killed in Action July 18, 1918*. Paris: J.R.E. Guild, Printer, 1926.

Bernheim, Bertram Moses. *"Passed as Censored."* Philadelphia and London: J.B. Lippincott Company, 1918.

Beston, Henry . *A Volunteer Poilu, by Henry Sheehan*. Boston and New York: Houghton Mifflin Company, 1916.

Biddle, Charles John. *The Way of the Eagle*. New York: C. Scribner's Sons, 1919.

Black, Elizabeth Walker. *Hospital Heroes*. New York: C. Scribner's Sons, 1919.

Blake, Katherine Alexander. *Some Letters to Maude Gray and Marian Wickes, 1917–1918, by Katherine Blake*. New York: Privately Printed, 1920.

Blodgett, Richard Ashley. *Life and Letters of Richard Ashley Blodgett, First Lieutenant, United States Air Service*. Boston: Macdonald and Evans, 1920.

Blumenstein, Christian. *Whiz Bang!* Buffalo, NY: Christian Blumenstein, 1927.

Boylston, Helen Dore. *"Sister": The War Diary of a Nurse*. New York: I. Washburn, 1927.

Britton, Emmet Nicholson. *"As It Looked to Him": Intimate Letters on the War*. San Francisco: Private Printer, 1919.

Brooks, Alden. *Battle in 1918: Seen by an American in the French Army*. Paris: H. Jonquieres, 1919.

Broun, Heywood C. *The A.E.F.: With General Pershing and the American Forces*. New York and London: D. Appleton and Company, 1918.

Brown, Hilton U. *Hilton U. Brown, Jr., One of Three Brothers in Artillery: Letters and Verses*. Indianapolis: United Typothetae of America School of Printing, 1920.

Brownville, Charles Gordon. *With Christ in a Shell Hole*. Grand Rapids: Zondervan Publishing House, 1943.

Bruno, Henry Augustine. *The Flying Yankee*. New York: Dodd, Mead, and Company, 1918.

Bryan, Julien Hequembough *"Ambulance 464" Encore des Blesses*. New York: The Macmillan Company, 1918.

Buck, Beaumont Bonaparte. *Memories of Peace and War*. San Antonio: The Naylor Company, 1935.

Bullard, Robert L. *Personalities and Reminiscences of the War*. Garden City, NY: Doubleday, Page, and Company, 1925.

Burdick, Joel Wakeman. *Lorraine: 1918*. New Haven: Privately printed by Yale University Press, 1919.

Burton, Caspar Henry. *Letters of Caspar Henry Burton*. Edited by Spence Burton, S.S.J.E. Privately Printed, 1921.

Buswell, Leslie. *With the American Ambulance Field Service in France / Ambulance no. 10, Personal Letters from the Front*. Boston and New York: Houghton Mifflin Company, 1916.

Butters, Henry Augustus. *Harry Butters, R.F.A. "An American Citizen," Life and War Letters... The brief record of a California boy who gave his life for England*. New York: John Lane Company, 1918.

Callaway, A. B. *With Packs and Rifles: A Story of the World War*. Boston: Meador Publishing Company, 1939.

Camp, Charles Wadsworth. *War's Dark Frame*. New York: Dodd, Mead, and Company, 1917.

Campbell, Peyton Randolph. *The Diary-Letters of Sergeant Peyton Randolph Campbell*. Buffalo, NY: Pratt and Lambert, Inc., 1919.

Carnegie Institute of Technology. *The Soldier's Progress: From the War Letters of Carnegie Tech Men*. Pittsburgh: Carnegie Institute of Technology, 1918.

Carter, William A. *The Tale of a Devil Dog*. Washington: Canteen Press, 1920.

Catlin, Albertus Wright. *With the Help of God and a Few Marines*. Garden City, NY: Doubleday, Page and Company, 1919.

Chapman, Victor Emmanuel. *Victor Chapman's Letters from France, with Memoir by John Jay Chapman*. New York: Macmillan Co., 1917.

Chapple, Joseph Mitchell. *"We'll Stick to the Finish!" "C'est la guerre"*: *A Voice from the Soldiers and Sailors Overseas*. Boston: Chapple Publishing Company, Limited, 1918.

Church, James Robb. *The Doctor's Part: What Happens to the Wounded in War.* New York and London: D. Appleton and Company, 1918.

Clark, Coleman Tiletson and Salter Storrs Clark. *Soldier Letters: Coleman Tiletson Clark and Salter Storrs Clark, Jr.: Their Stories in Extracts from Their Letters and Diaries*. Printed by L. Middleditch Company, 1919.

Clarke, Carolyn. *"Evacuation 144" As Seen from Within*. Boston: Hudson Printing Company, 1919.

Clover, Greayer. *A Stop at Suzanne's, and Lower Flights*. New York: George H. Doran Company, 1919.

Cobb, Irvin Shrewsberry. *The Glory of the Coming: What Mine Eyes Have Seen of Americans in Action in This Year of Grace and Allied Endeavor*. New York: George H. Doran Company, 1918.

Codman, Charles. *Contact*. Boston: Little, Brown and Company, 1937.

Coleman, Frederic Abernathy . *With Cavalry in the Great War: The British Trooper in the Trench Line, Through the Second Battle of Ypres*. Philadelphia: G.W. Jacobs and Company, 1917.

Coolidge, Hamilton. *Letters of an American Airman*. Boston: Privately Printed, 1919.

Corning, Walter D. *The Yanks Crusade: A Book of Reminiscences*. Chicago: N.p., 1927.

Cowing, Kemper Frey . *Dear Folks at Home: The Glorious Story of the United States Marines in France as Told by Their Letters from the Battlefield Compiled by Kemper F. Cowing*. Boston and New York: Houghton Mifflin Company, 1919.

Crowe, James Richard. *Pat Crowe, Aviator. Skylark Views and Letters from France*, ed. W. D. Chase. New York: N.L. Brown, 1919.

Crump, Irving. *Conscript 2989: Experiences of a Drafted Man*. New York: Dodd, Mead and Company, 1918.

Cunningham, William H., ed. *The Boston High School of Commerce in the World War*. Norwood, MA: Plimpton Press, 1921.

Curtiss, Elmer H. *Going and Coming as a Doughboy*. Palo Alto: Press of F.A. Stuart, 1920.

D'Aquila, Vincent. *Bodyguard Unseen: A True Autobiography*. New York: R.R. Smith Inc., 1931.

Dawes, Charles Gates. *A Journal of the Great War*. Boston and New York: Houghton Mifflin Company, 1921.

Day, Kirkland Hart. *Camion Cartoons*. Boston: Mashall Jones Company, 1919.

De Varila, Osborne. *The First Shot for Liberty: The Story of an American Who Went Over with the First Expeditionary Force and Served His Country at the Front*. Philadelphia and Chicago: The John C. Winston Company, 1918.

Dearing, Vinton Adams. *My Galahad of the Trenches: Being a Collection of Intimate Letters of Lieutenant Vinton A. Dearing*. New York: Fleming H. Revell Co., 1918.

Derby, Richard. *"Wade in, Sanitary!" The Story of a Division Surgeon in France.* New York: Putnam, 1919.

Dexter, Mary. *In the Soldiers' Service: War Experiences of Mary Dexter.* Boston and New York: Houghton Mifflin Company, 1918.

Duffy, Francis Patrick . *Father Duffy's Story: A Tale of Humor and Heroism, of Life and Death with the Fighting Sixty-Ninth.* New York: George H. Doran Company, 1919.

DuPuy, Charles M. *A Machine Gunner's Notes.* Pittsburgh: Reed and Witting Company, 1920.

Ellinwood, Ralph E. *Behind the German Lines: A Narrative of the Everyday Life of an American Prisoner of War.* New York: Knickerbocker Press, 1920.

Elliott, Paul Blodgett, ed. *On the Field of Honor: A Collection of War Letters and Reminiscences of Three Harvard Undergraduates Who Gave their Lives in the Great Cause.* Boston: Printed for their friends by the Merrymount press, 1920.

Ellis, Allan B. *A Brief History of Appleton's "Old Company G" (Co. A, 150th Machine Gun Battalion) with the Rainbow Division in the Great War, compiled from letters written to his mother by Lieutenant Allan B. Ellis.* Appleton, Wis.: Meyer Press, 1919.

Ely, Dinsmore, 1894–1918. *Dinsmore Ely: One Who Served.* Chicago: A.C. McClurg and Company, 1919.

Emmett, Chris. *Give 'Way to the Right: Serving with the A.E.F. in France during the World War.* San Antonio, TX: The Naylor Company, 1934.

Empey, Arthur Guy. *"Over the Top" by an American Soldier Who Went.* New York: G.P. Putnam and Sons, 1917.

Ettinger, Albert M and A. Churchill. *A Doughboy with the Fighting Sixty-Ninth: A Remembrance of World War I.* Shippensburg, PA: White Mane Publishing Company, 1992.

Evarts, Jeremiah M. *Cantginy, A Corner of the War.* New York: Private Printers/ The Scribner Press, 1938.

Ferguson, John B. *Through the War with a Y Man.* N.p., 1919.

Finn, John J. "Stray Memories of St. Mihiel." Catholic World 113 (1921): 348–54.

Fleharty, R. C. *One Doughboy's Experience: Letters from R. C. Fleharty.* N.p., 1918.

Ford, Torrey Sylvester. *Cheer-up Letters, from a Private with Pershing.* New York: E. J. Clode, 1918.

Fox, Henry Landell. *What the "Boys" Did Over There by "Themselves."* New York: The Allied Overseas Veterans Stories Company, Inc, 1918.

Fuller, Ruth Wolfe. *Silver Lining: Experiences of a War Bride.* Boston and New York: Houghton Mifflin Company, 1918.

Gates, Robert Cady. *The Ancestry and World War I Letters of William Galbraith Stewart, Jr. (1896–1935) of Wilkinsburg, Allegheny County, Pennsylvania.* Springfield, MO: R.C. Gates, 1995.

Genet, Edmond Charles Clinton. *War Letters of Edmond Genet.* New York: Scribner's Sons, 1918.

Gibbons, Floyd Phillips. *"And They Thought We Wouldn't Fight."* New York: George H. Doran Company, 1918.

Gowenlock, Thomas Russel. *Soldiers of Darkness*. Garden City, NJ: Doubleday, Doran and Company, Inc., 1937.

Grasty, Charles Henry . *Flashes from the Front*. New York: The Century Company, 1918.

Greene, Warwick. *Letters of Warwick Greene, 1915–1928*, edited by Richard W. Hale. Boston: Houghton Mifflin, 1931.

Gulberg, Martin Gus. *A War Diary: Into this Story is Woven an Experience of Two Years' Service in the World War with the 75th Company, 6th Regiment, United States Marines*. Chicago: Drake Press, 1927.

Gutterson, Granville. *Tales and Tail Spins from a Flyer's Diary*. New York, Cincinnati: The Abingdon Press, 1919.

Hall, Bert. *"En l'air": Three Years on and above Three Fronts*. New York: The New Library, Inc., 1918.

Hall, James Norman. *Kitchener's Mob: The Adventures of an American in the British Army*. Boston: Houghton Mifflin Company, 1916.

Halyburton, Edgar. *Shoot and Be Damned*. New York: Coviel, Friede, 1932.

Hamilton, Craig and Louise Corbin, ed. *Echoes from Over There, by the Men of the Army and Marine Corps Who Fought in France*. New York: The Soldiers' Publishing Company, 1919.

Hanover National Bank of the City of New York. *Service Record of Men of the Hanover National Bank of the City of New York: Being an Account of the Experiences of the Men of the Hanover National Bank in the Great World War*. New York: Privately Printed, 1920.

Hanson, William L. *World War I, I Was There: A Memoir*. Gerald, MO: Patrice Press, 1982.

Harden, Elmer Stetson. *An American Poilu*. Boston: Little, Brown and Company, 1919.

Hardon, Anne Frances. *43BIS: War Letters of an American V.A.D.* New York: Private Printers, 1927.

Hart, Percival Gray. *History of the 135th Aero Squadron from July 25 to November 11, 1918*. Chicago, 1939.

Hartney, Harold Evans. *Up And At 'Em*. Harrisburg, PA: Stackpole Sons, 1940.

Harvey, Bartle M. *Me and Bad Eye and Slim: The Diary of a Buck Private*. Monrovia, CA: The Press of Chas. F. Davis, 1932.

Haslett, Elmer. *Luck on the Wing: Thirteen Stories of a Sky Spy*. New York: E.P. Dutton and Company, 1920.

Hays, Harold Melvin. *Cheerio!* New York: A.A. Knopf, 1919.

Herring, Ray DeWitt. *Trifling with War*. Boston: Meador Publishing Company, 1934.

Hoffman, Robert C. *I Remember the Last War*. York, PA: Strength and Health Publishing Company, 1940.

Hoggson, Noble Foster. *Just Behind the Front in France*. New York: John Lane Company, 1918.

Holden, Frank Alexander. *War Memories*. Athens, GA: Athens Book Company, 1922.

Holmes, R. Derby. *A Yankee in the Trenches*. Boston: Little, Brown and Company, 1918.

Hopkins, Nevil Monroe. *Over the Threshold of War: Personal Experiences of the Great European Conflict.* Philadelphia and London: J.B. Lippincott Company, 1948.

Howe, Mark Anthony De Wolfe, ed. *The Harvard Volunteers in Europe: Personal Records of Experiences in Military, Ambulance, and Hospital Service.* Cambridge: Harvard University Press, 1916.

Huard, Frances Wilson. *With Those Who Wait.* New York: G.H. Doran Company, 1918.

Hunton, Addie W. and Kathryn M. Johnson. *Two Colored Women in the American Expeditionary Forces.* New York: AMS Press, 1920.

Imbrie, Robert Whitney. *Behind the Wheel of a War Ambulance.* New York: R.M. McBride and Company, 1918.

Irwin, William Henry. *Men, Women, and War.* London: Constable and Company, 1915.

Jacks, Leo Vincent. *Service Record, by an Artilleryman.* New York: Charles Scribner's Sons, 1928.

Janis, Elsie. *The Big Show: My Six Months with the American Expeditionary Forces.* New York: Cosmopolitan Book Corporation, 1919.

Jenks, Chester Walton . *Our First Ten Thousand.* Boston: The Four Seas Company, 1919.

Johnson, Wesley R. *War Experiences of a University Student as a Doughboy.* University of North Dakota Quarterly Journal 10. 93–120.

Judy, Will. *A Soldier's Diary: A Day-to-Day Record in the World War.* Chicago: Judy Pub. Co., 1930.

Karch, Henry P. *To the Boys Back Home, Written and Dedicated to the Boys Back Home, February 22, 1919.* Cincinnati: H.P. Karch, 1919.

Kautz, John Iden. *Trucking to the Trenches: Letters from France, June–November 1917.* Boston and New York: Houghton Mifflin Company, 1918.

Kean, Robert Winthrop. *Dear Marraine, 1917–1919.* Livingston, NJ: 1969.

Kellogg, Doris. *Canteening Under Two Flags: Letters of Doris Kellogg.* East Aurora, NY: The Royerofters, 1920.

Kelly, Russell A. *Kelly of the Foreign Legion: Letters of Legionnaire Russel A. Kelly.* New York: M. Kennerley, 1917.

Kilham, Eleanor B. *Letters from France, 1915–1919.* Salem, MA: N.P., 1941.

Kilmer, Joyce. *Joyce Kilmer: Poems, Essays, and Letters: Edited with a Memoir by Robert Cortes Holliday.* New York: George H. Doran Company, 1918.

Kimmel, Stanley Preston. *Crucifixion.* New York: Gothic Publishing Company, 1922.

King, David Wooster. *"L.M. 8046": An Intimate Story of the Foreign Legion.* New York: Duffield and Company, 1927.

Kingman, Henry S. *Section Sixty-one: Selections from Letters of Henry S. Kingman, Member S. S. A. U. 61, Norton Harjes Ambulance Corps, May to October, 1917.* Minneapolis: Privately Printed, 1917.

Knapp, Shepherd. *On the Edge of the Storm: The Story of a Year in France.* Worcester, MA: Commonwealth Press, 1921.

Kramer, Harold Morton. *With Seeing Eyes: The Unusual Story of an Observant Thinker at the Front.* Boston: Lothrop, Lee and Shepard Company, 1919.

Lambie, Margaret. *Verdun Experiences*. Washington: The Courant Press, 1945 (First published in the Vassar Quarterly, November 1919).

Langer, William L. and Robert B. MacMullin. *With "E" of the First Gas, by Sergeant William L. Langer and Private Robert B. MacMullin*. Brooklyn: Holton Printing Co., 1919.

Lapradelle, Albert Geouffre. *War Letters from France*. New York: D. Appleton and Company, 1916.

Leach, George E. *War diary*. Roanoke, VA, 1962.

Leach, William James. *Poems and War Letters*. Peoria, IL: The Manual Arts Press, 1922.

Lee, Benjamin. *Benjamin Lee, 2d: A Record Gathered from Letters, Note-Books, and Narratives of Friends, by His Mother, Mary Justice Chase*. Boston: Cornhill, 1920.

Lee, Roger Irving. *Letters: 1917–1918*. Brookline, MA: Privately Printed, 1962.

Leland, Claude Granger. *From Shell Hole to Chateau with Company I; Personal Recollections of a Line Officer of the 107th U.S. Infantry, 27th Division, in France, 1918*. New York: Society of Ninth Company Veterans, 7th Regiment, New York National Guard, 1950.

Levinger, Lee J. *A Jewish Chaplain in France*. New York: The Macmillan Company, 1921.

Lindner, Clarence Richard. *Private Lindner's Letters, Censored and Uncensored*. San Francisco: Gladys Lindner, 1939.

Little, Arthur West. *From Harlem to the Rhine: The Story of New York's Colored Volunteers*. New York: Covici, Friede, 1936.

Lukens, Edward C. and E. McClure Rouzer. *A Blue Ridge Memoir and The Last Drive and Death of Major G. H. H. Emory*. Baltimore, 1922.

Mack, Arthur James. *Shellproof Mack: An American's Fighting Story*. Boston: Small, Maynard and Company, 1918.

MacLeish, Kenneth. *Kenneth: A Collection of Letters Written by Lieutenant Kenneth MacLeish, U.S.N.R.F.C., Dating from His Enlistment and During His Services in the Aviation Corps of the United States Navy, Edited and Arranged by His Mother*. Chicago: Privately Printed, 1919.

———. *The Price of Honor: The World War One Letters of Naval Aviator Kenneth MacLeish*. Edited by Geoffrey L. Rossano. Annapolis, MD: Naval Institute Press, 1991.

Mahon, John O. *The United States and World Peace: Letters Written by a Private in the U.S. Army*. New York: Adcraft Service Company, 1920.

McCarthy, George T. *The Greater Love*. Chicago: Extension Press, 1920.

McConnell, James R. *Flying for France with the Escadrille at Verdun*. Garden City, NY: Doubleday, Page and Company, Inc., 1917.

McGregor, Robert. *Let's Go Yank!* Boston: Meador Publishing Company, 1932.

Meeker, William Henry. *William Henry Meeker, His Book*. Privately printed, 1917.

Merrill, Wainwright. *A College Man in Khaki: Letters of an American in the British Artillery*. New York: G.H. Doran Company, 1918.

Millard, Shirley. *I Saw Them Die: Diary and Recollections of Shirley Millard*. New York: Harcourt, Brace, and Company, 1936.

Mills, Quincy Sharpe. *One Who Gave His Life: War Letters of Quincy Sharpe Mills: With a Sketch of His Life and Ideals*. Edited by James Luby. New York: G.P. Putnam's Sons, 1923.

———. *Editorials, Sketches, and Stories*. New York: G.P. Putnam's Sons, 1930.

Minder, Charles Frank. *This Man's War: The Day-By-Day Record of an American Private on the Western Front*. New York: Pevensey Press, 1931.

Mitchell, Clarence Van Schaick. *With a Military Ambulance in France, 1914–1915*. Princeton: Privately Printed at Princeton University Press, 1915.

Mitchell, William. *Memoirs of World War I*. New York: Random House, 1960.

Morlae, Edward. *A Soldier of the Legion*. Boston: Houghton Mifflin Company, 1916.

Morrow, John H. Jr. and Earl Rogers, ed. *A Yankee Ace in the RAF: The World War I Letters of Captain Bogart Rogers*. Lawrence: University Press of Kansas, 1996.

Morse, Katherine Duncan. *The Uncensored Letters of a Canteen Girl*. New York: H. Holt and Company, 1920.

Moseley, George Clark. *Extracts from the Letters of George Clark Moseley during the Period of the Great War*. Chicago, Privately Printed, 1923.

Muston, W. H. *"Over There": The Story of a Sky Pilot*. Yoakum, TX: Bankers Printing Company, 1923.

Niles, John Jacob. *Singing Soldiers*. New York: C. Scribner's Sons, 1927.

Nordhoff, Charles Bernard. *The Fledgling*. Boston and New York: Houghton Mifflin Company, 1919.

O'Brien Howard Vincent. *Wine, Women, and War: A Diary of Disillusionment*. New York: J.H. Sears and Company, Inc., 1926.

Orcutt, Philip Dana. *The White Road of Mystery: The Note-Book of an American Ambulancier*. New York: John Lane Company, 1918.

Ottosen, P. H., ed. *Trench artillery, A.E.F.: The Personal Experiences of Lieutenants and Captains of Artillery Who Served with Trench Mortars*. Boston: Lothrop, Lee and Shepard, 1931.

Palmer, Frederick. *My Second Year of the War*. New York: Dodd, Mead and Company, 1917.

———. *My Year of the Great War*. New York: Dodd, Mead and Company, 1915.

Peck, Charlotte Treat. *The Wife Who Went Along*. New York: Carlton Press, 1964.

Peixotto, Ernest. *The American Front*. New York: Charles Scribner's Sons, 1919.

Peterson, Wilbur. *I Went to War*. Marshall, MN: The Messenger Press, 1938.

Poague, Walter S. *Diary and Letters of a Marine Aviator*. Chicago, 1919.

Poling, Daniel Alfred. *Huts in Hell*. Boston: Christian Endeavor World, 1918.

Porter, William Townsend. *Shock at the Front*. Boston: The Atlantic Monthly Press, 1918.

Pottle, Frederick Albert. *Stretchers: The Story of a Hospital Unit on the Western Front*. London: Oxford University Press, 1929.

Powell, Edward Alexander. *Slanting Lines of Steel*. New York: The Macmillan Company, 1933.

Prentice, Sartell. *Padre: A Red Cross Chaplain in France*. New York: E.P. Dutton and Company, 1919.

Prince, Norman. *A Volunteer Who Died for the Cause He Loved: With Memoir by George F. Babbitt*. Boston and New York: Houghton Mifflin Company, 1917.

Ranlett, Louis Felix. *Let's Go! The Story of A.S. no. 2448602*. Boston and New York: Houghton Mifflin Company, 1927.

Reece, Robert Henry. *Night Bombing with the Bedouins, by One of the Squadron*. Boston and New York: Houghton Mifflin Company, 1919.

Rendinell, Joseph Edward with George Pattullo. *One Man's War: The Diary of a Leatherneck*. New York: J.H. Sears and Company, Inc., 1928.

Rice, Philip Sydney. *An Ambulance Driver in France, Being Experiences, Memories, and Impressions of The Western Front*. Wilkes-Barre, PA: 1918.

Richards, John Francisco. *War Diary and Letters of John Francisco Richards*. Kansas City, MO: Lechtman Printing Company, 1925.

Rickenbacker, Edward Vernon. *Fighting the Flying Circus*. New York: Frederick A. Stokes Company, 1919.

Riegelman, Harold. *War Notes of a Casual*. New York, 1931.

Riggs, Arthur Stanley. *With Three Armies and Behind the Western Front*. Indianapolis: The Bobbs-Merrill Company, 1918.

Robinson, William Joseph. *My Fourteen Months at the Front: An American Boy's Baptism of Fire*. Boston: Little, Brown and Company, 1916.

Rockwell, Kiffin Yates. *War Letters of Kiffin Yates Rockwell, Foreign Legionnaire and Aviator, France 1914–1916, with Memoir and Notes by Paul Ayres Rockwell*. Garden City, NJ: The Country Life Press, 1925.

Romeo, Giuseppe L. *Diary of Pvt. Giuseppe L. Romeo*. Tacoma, WA: T.V. Copeland and Son, 1919.

Roosevelt, Kermit. *War in the Garden of Eden*. New York: Charles Scribner's Sons, 1919.

Roosevelt, Quentin. *Quentin Roosevelt: A Sketch with Letters. Edited by Kermit Roosevelt*. New York: Charles Scribner's Sons, 1921.

Roosevelt, Theodore. *Average Americans*. New York: G.P. Putnam's Sons, 1919.

Root, Esther Sayles and Marjorie Crocker. *Over Periscope Pond: Letters from two American Girls in Paris, October 1916–January 1918*. Boston and New York: Houghton Mifflin Company, 1918.

Ross, Warner Anthony. *My Colored Battalion*. Chicago: W.A. Ross, 1920.

Russel, William Muir. *A Happy Warrior: Letters of William Muir Russel, an American Aviator in the Great War, 1917–1918: A Family Memorial*. Detroit, MI: Saturday Night Press, Inc., 1919.

Scudder, Robert Author. *My Experience in the World War*. Dover, NJ: R.A. Scudder, 1921.

Searcy, Earl Benjamin. *Looking Back*. Springfield, IL: Journal Press, 1921.

Seeger, Alan. *Letters and Diary of Alan Seeger*. New York: Charles Scribner's Sons, 1917.

———. *Poems*. New York: Charles Scribner's Sons, 1919.

Sergeant, Elizabeth Shepley. *Shadow Shapes: The Journal of a Wounded Woman, October 1918–May 1919*. Boston and New York: Houghton Mifflin Company, 1920.

Shainwald, Richard H. *Letters and Notes from France, June 30, 1917–November 6, 1918, Being the Personal Experiences and Reminiscences of the Author*. San Francisco: Privately Printed by Abbott Press, 1919.

Sharp, John E. *From Funston to Germany via the "Sherman" route. Stop-overs at St. Mihiel, Argonne, Meuse, Hades, and the Rhine*. Tulsa, OK: General Refining Company, 1919.

Sherwood, Elmer W. *Diary of a Rainbow Veteran, Written at the Front by Elmer W. Sherwood*; foreword by Gen. Charles P. Summerall, Chief of Staff, U.S. Army. Terre Haute, IN: Moore-Langen Company, 1929.

Sibley, Frank Palmer. *With the Yankee Division in France*. Boston: Little, Brown and Company, 1919.

Simonds, Frank Herbert. *They Shall Not Pass*. Garden City, NJ: Doubleday, Page and Company, 1916.

Slusser, Thomas Harry. *Letters to Her, 1917–19*. Chicago: Privately Printed, 1937.

Smith, Harry Leroy and James R. Eckman. *Memoirs of an Ambulance Company Officer*. Rochester, MN, The Doomsday Press, 1940.

Smith, Joseph Shuter. *Over There and Back in Three Uniforms: Being the Experiences of an American Boy in the Canadian, British, and American Armies at the Front and through No-Man's Land*. New York: E.P. Dutton and Company, 1918.

Speakman, Harold. *From a Soldier's Heart*. New York: The Abingdon Press, 1919.

Speakman, Maria Anna. *Memories*. Wilmington, DE: The Greenwood Bookshop, 1937.

Spitz, Leon. *The Memoirs of a Camp Rabbi*. New York: Bloch Publishing Company, 1927.

Stamas, Christ M. *The Road to St. Mihiel*. New York: Comet Press Books, 1957

Stearns, Gustav. *From Army Camps and Battle-fields: 76 Weekly Letters Written to Church of the Ascension, Scott and Reed Streets, Milwaukee, WI*. Minneapolis: Augsburg Publishing House, 1919.

Stephens, D. Owen. *With Quakers in France*. London: C.W. Daniel, Ltd., 1921.

Stevenson, William Yorke. *From "Poilu" to "Yank."* Boston and New York: Houghton Mifflin Company, 1918.

Stewart, Lawrence O. *Rainbow Bright*. Philadelphia: Dorrance, 1923.

Stidger, William Le Roy. *Soldier Silhouettes on Our Front*. New York: Charles. Scribner's Sons, 1918.

Stimson, Julia Catherine. *Finding Themselves: The Letters of an American Army Chief Nurse in a British Hospital in France*. New York: The Macmillan Company, 1918.

Stone, Ernest. *Battery B Thru the Fires of France: Being a Very Human and Intimate Sketch of a Few Men who Served to Stem a Tiny Eddy in one of the Greatest of Cataclysms–the World War*. Los Angeles: Wayside Press, 1919.

Straub, Elmer Frank. *A Sergeant's Diary in the World War: The Diary of an Enlisted Member of the 150th Field Artillery (Forty-second (Rainbow) Division) October 27, 1917–August 7, 1919*. Indianapolis, IN: Historical Commission, 1923.

Strickland, Riley. *Adventures of the A.E.F. Soldier*. Austin, TX.: Von Boeckmann-Jones, 1920.

Stringfellow, John S. *Hell! No! This and That: A Narrative of the Great War*. Boston: Meador Publishing Company, 1936.

Sutliffe, Robert Stewart. *Seventy-first New York in the World War*. New York: J.J. Little and Ives Company, 1922.

Swan, Carroll Judson. *My Company (Company D, 101st Engineers, 26th Division, USA)*. Boston and New York: Houghton Mifflin Company, 1918.

Taber, Sydney Richmond. *Arthur Richmond Taber: A Memorial Record Compiled by his Father*. Princeton: Privately Printed, 1920.

Thayer, George Burton. *Army Influence Over the Y.M.C.A. in France*. N.p., 1919.

Tippett, Edwin James. *Who Won the War? Letters and Notes of an M.P. in Dixie, England, France and Flanders*. Toledo, OH: Toledo Type-setting and Printing Company, 1920.

Townsend, Harry Everett. *War Diary of a Combat Artist*. Edited by Alfred E. Cornbeise. Niwot, CO: University Press of Colorado, 1991.

Trounce, Harry Davis. *Fighting the Boche Underground*. New York: Charles Scribner's Sons, 1918.

Trowbridge, Augustus. *War Letters of Augustus Trowbridge, August 28, 1917, to January 19, 1919*. Edited by Deoch Fulton. New York: The New York Public Library, 1940.

Trueblood, Edward Alva. *Observations of an American Soldier during his Service with the A.E.F. in France in the Flash Ranging Service*. Sacramento, CA: The News Publishing Company, 1919.

Truitt, Charles. *Wartime Letters From Italy*. New York: Sherwood Press, Inc., 1915.

Tyler, John Cowperthwaite. *Selections from the Letters of John Cowperthwaite Tyler, from August, 1917 to September, 1918*. Camden, NJ: R. Ellis at the Haddon Craftsmen, 1938. (Sixty-eight copies printed.)

Upson, William Hazlett. *Me and Henry and the Artillery*. Garden City, NY: Doubleday, Doran and Company, 1928.

Vance, James Isaac. *The Silver on the Iron Cross*. New York: F.H. Revell Company, 1919.

Walcott, Stuart. *Above the French Lines: Letters of Stuart Walcott, American Aviator, July 4, 1917–December 8, 1917*. Princeton: Princeton University Press, 1918.

Waldo, Fullerton Leonard. *America at the Front*. New York: E.P. Dutton and Company, 1918.

Washburn, Slater. *One of the YD, by Slater Washburn, corporal, C battery, 101st Field Artillery, Twenty-sixth Division, A.E.F.* Boston and New York, Houghton Mifflin Company, 1919.

Watne, Andrew L. *Diary of Corporal Andrew L. Watne, 188th Field Hospital Company, 117th Sanitary Train, Forty-second Division*. N.p., 1919.

Wellman, William Augustus. *Go Get 'em! The True Story of an American Aviator of the Lafayette Flying Corps Who Was the Only Yankee Flyer Fighting over*

General Pershing's Boys of the Rainbow Division in Lorraine When They First Went "Over the Top." Boston: The Page Company, 1918.

Westbrook, Stillman Foote. *Those Eighteen Months. October 9, 1917–April 8, 1919, From the War Letters of Stillman F. Westbrook*. Published for Private Distribution to the Men of the Machine Gun Company of the 104th infantry, Twenty-sixth Division, American Expeditionary Forces. Hartford, CT: The Press of the Case, Lockwood and Brainard Company, 1934.

Westover, Wendell. *Suicide Battalions*. New York: G.P. Putnam's Sons, 1929.

Wheeler, Curtis. *Letters from an American Soldier to his Father*. Indianapolis: The Bobbs-Merrill Company, 1918.

Whitehair, Charles W. *Out There*. New York: D. Appleton and Company, 1918.

Whitehouse, Arthur George Joseph. *The Fledgling: An Autobiography*. New York: Duell, Sloan and Pearce, 1964.

Wilder, Amos N. *Armageddon Revisited*. New Haven: Yale University Press, 1994.

———. *Battle-Retrospect and Other Poems*. New Haven: Yale University Press, 1923.

Wilder, Fred Calvin. *War Experiences of F. C. Wilder*. Belchertown, MA: Lewis H. Blackmer, 1926.

Wilgus, William John. *War Diary of William J. Wilgus, 1917–1919*. New York, 1922.

Williams, Ashby. *Experiences of the Great War: Artois, St. Mihiel, Meuse-Argonne*. Roanoke, VA: Stone Printing and Manufacturing Company, 1919.

Wilmot, M.E., ed. *Letters from Oregon Boys in the War, Including a Series of Letters from Oregon Boys in France*. Portland, OR: Glass and Prudhomme Company, 1918.

Winant, Cornelius. *A Soldier's Manuscript*. Boston: Privately Printed by Merrymount Press, 1929.

Winslow, Carroll Dana. *With the French Flying Corps*. New York: Charles Scribner's Sons, 1917.

Witwer, Harry Charles. *From Baseball to Boches*. Boston: Small, Maynard and Company, 1918.

Wolfe, Samuel Herbert. *In Service*. Washington, D.C.: Privately Printed, 1922.

Wollman, Solomon. *Diary of Solomon Wollman, September 15, 1917 to July 4, 1918*. Hartford, CT: The Case, Lockwood and Brainard Company, 1919.

Wood, Lambert A. *His Job: Letters Written by a 22-year-old Lieutenant in the World War to his Parents and Others in Oregon*. Portland, OR: The Metropolitan Press, 1932.

Woodward, Houston. *A Year for France: War Letters of Houston Woodward*. New Haven: Yale Publishing Association, 1919.

Wrentmore, Ernest L. *In Spite of Hell*. New York: Greenwich Book Publishers, 1958.

Wright, Jack Morris. *A Poet of the Air: Letters of Jack Morris Wright, First Lieutenant of the American Aviation in France. April 1917–January 1918*. Boston and New York: Houghton Mifflin Company, 1918.

York, Alvin Cullum. *Sergeant York: His Own Life Story and War Diary.* Edited by
Tom Skeyhill. Garden City, NY: Doubleday, Doran, and Company, Inc., 1928.
Young, Rush S. *Over the Top with the 80th, by a Buck Private.* N.p., 1933.
Zimmerman, Leander M., D.D. *Echoes from the Distant Battlefield.* Boston: R.G.
Badger, 1920.

Index